NUMBER 260

THE ENGLISH EXPERIENCE

ITS RECORD IN EARLY PRINTED BOOKS
PUBLISHED IN FACSIMILE

ODOARDO LOPEZ

A REPORT
OF THE KINGDOME
OF CONGO

LONDON 1597·

DA CAPO PRESS
THEATRVM ORBIS TERRARVM LTD.
AMSTERDAM 1970 NEW YORK

The publisher acknowledge their gratitude
to the Provost and Fellows of King's College, Cambridge
for their permission to reproduce
the Library's copy (Shelfmark: A.7.6.)
and to the Trustees of the British Museum
for their permission to reproduce the two maps
from their copy (Shelfmark: 279.e.36)

S.T.C.No. 16805
Collation: $\clubsuit^4$,$*^4$,$**^1$, A-Z^4, Aa-Ee^4
with two maps

Published in 1970 by
Theatrum Orbis Terrarum Ltd.,
O.Z. Voorburgwal 85, Amsterdam

&

Da Capo Press
- a division of Plenum Publishing Corporation -
227 West 17th Street, New York, 10011
Printed in the Netherlands
ISBN 90 221 0260 2

A REPORT
OF THE KING-
dome of CONGO, a Re-
gion of AFRICA.

And of the Countries that border
rounde about the same.

1. Wherein is also shewed, that the two Zones *Torrida & Frigida*, are not onely habitable, but inhabited, and very temperate, contrary to the opinion of the old Philosophers.

2. That the blacke colour which is in the skinnes of the *Ethiopians* and *Negroes* &c. proceedeth not from the Sunne.

3. And that the Riuer *Nilus* springeth not out of the mountains of the Moone, as hath beene heretofore beleeued: Together with the true cause of the rising and increasing thereof.

4. Besides the description of diuers Plants, Fishes and Beastes, that are found in those Countries.

Drawen out of the writinges and discourses of
Odoardo Lopez a Portingall, by
Philippo Pigafetta.

Translated out of Italian by ∫*Abraham Hartwell.*

LONDON
Printed by Iohn Wolfe. 1597.

To the most Gracious and Reuerende
Father in God, IOHN *by the proui-*
dence of God, Lord Archbishop of Can-
terbury, Primate and Metropolitane of
all Englande, and one of the Lordes
of her Maiesties most hono-
rable Priuie Coun-
cell.

MOst Reuerend Father,
my singular good and
gracious Lorde : In all
humble dutie I do offer
to your grace this poor
and slender present, *in auspicium nas-*
centis anni, which I doe most hartely
pray, may bee as happie and prospe-
rous both for your health and quiet
gouern-

The Epistle Dedicatory.

gouernement, as (thanks be to God)
your latter yeares haue beene. It is a
description of a certaine Region or
Kingdome in *Africa*, called *Congo*,
whose name is as yet scarce knowen
to our quarters of *Europe*, neyther is
there any great or solemne mention
of it in any bookes that haue beene
published of that Third parte of the
old *World*. And because this treatise
doeth comprehend not onely the nature and disposition of the *Moci-
Conghi*, which are the naturall inhabitantes and people of *Congo*, together with all the commodities and
trafficke of that Countrey, very fitte
and pleasaunt to be reade, but also the
religion which they professed, and
by what meanes it pleased God to
draw them from *Paganisme* to *Chri-
stianity*

ſtianity. I thought good thus to make it knowen to my countreymen of *England*, to the end it might be a preſident for ſuch valiant Engliſh, as do earneſtly thirſt and deſire to atchieue the conqueſt of rude and barbarous Nations, that they doo not attempt thoſe actions for commodity of Gold and Siluer, and for other tranſitorie or worldly reſpectes, but that they woulde firſt ſeeke the Kingdome of God, & the ſaluation of many thouſand ſoules, which the common enemie of mankinde ſtill detayneth in ignorance: and then all other thinges ſhall be put in their mouthes aboundantly, as may bee ſeene by the *Portingalles* in this narration. Written it was by one *Philippo Pigafetta*, an Italian, and a very good Mathematici-

an,

an, from the mouth of one *Lopez* a *Portingal*, together with two maps, the one particular of *Congo*, the other generall of all *Africa*, and eſpecially of the *Weſterne* Coaſt, from 34. degrees beyond the *Æquinoctial* northwardes, downe along to the *Cape* of *Good-Hope* in the *South*, and ſo vpwardes againe on the *Eaſterne* Coaſt by the great Iſland of *Madagaſcar*, otherwiſe called the *Iſle* of *S. Laurence*, til you come to the *Iſle* of *Socotora*, & then to the *Redde Sea*, and from *Ægypt* into the Inland *Southwards* to the Empire of *Presbiter-Iohn*. I beſeech your grace to accept of this my poore trauell, and I will not ceaſe to pray to Almightie God, according to my dutie, that hee will multiply many good years vpon you, vnder the happy

The Epistle Dedicatory.

py gouernment of our moſt gracious & foueraigne Lady Queene Eliza-beth: wherevnto the Church of *Eng-lande* is bound to ſay, Amen. From your Graces houſe in Lambehith, the firſt of Ianuarie. 1 5 9 7.

Your Graces moſt humble Seruant at commaundement,

Abraham Hartwell.

❧ The Tranſlator to the
Reader.

I Finde it true, that Sophocles writeth in his Whipp-bearer Aiax, πόνος πόνῳ πόνον φέρει: Labor labori laborem adfert, that is to ſay, Labour doth breede labour vpon labour. For after that the tranſlation of the Booke, contayning the Warres betweene the Turkes and Perſians written by Iohn-Thomas Minadoi was publiſhed, diuers of my friends haue earneſtly moued me to be ſtill doing ſomewhat, and to help our Engliſh Nation, that they might knowe and vnderſtand many things, which are common in other languages, but vtterly concealed from this poore Iſland. I haue aunſwered ſome of theſe my friends to their good ſatisfaction, and told them, that the weakeneſſe of my body would not ſuffer me to ſit long: that the houres of my leaſure were not many, vnleſſe I ſhould vnduetifully defraude thoſe to whome I am moſt beholden and bounden, of that duty and attendance which I owe vnto them: and laſtly, that I had no great pleaſure to learne or informe my ſelfe of the ſtate of other Nations, becauſe I do not as yet ſufficiently know the Eſtate of mine owne Countrey. Whereof (I am verily perſwaded) I may iuſtly auouch that which Vlyſſes proteſted of his Ithaca: οὐδέ ἔγωγε Ἧς γαίης δύναμαι γλυκερώτερον ἄλλο ἰδέσθαι: Then which poore Countrey can I neuer ſee any ſweeter. Among others that made
theſe

To the Reader.

these Motions *vnto me, one there was, who being a curious* M. R. Hack-
and a diligent searcher and obseruer of Forreine aduentures luyt.
and aduenturers, as by his good paines appeareth, came vnto
me to the house of a graue and learned Prelate *in* Suffolke, M. H. Castel-
where I lay in my returne out of Norffolke, *and there made* ton.
the like request vnto me, and I the like answere vnto him.
But it would not satisfie him: for he sayd it was an answere
answerelesse, and it should not serue my turne. And presently
presented me with this Portingall Pilgrime *lately come to*
him out of the Kingdome *of* Congo, *and apparrelled in an*
Italian vesture: *intreating me very earnestly, that I would*
take him with me, and make him English: *for he could re-*
port many pleasant matters that he sawe in his pilgrimage,
which are indeed vncouth and almost incredible to this part
of Europe. *When I sawe there was no remedie, I yeelded,*
and euen (as the Poet saith) ἑκὼν ἀέκοντί γε θυμῷ, *I brought* Homer.
him away with mee. But within two houres conference, I
found him nibling at two most honourable Gentlemen of
England, *whome in plaine tearmes he called* Pirates: *so*
that I had much adoo to hold my hands from renting of him
into many mo peeces, then his Cosen Lopez *the* Doctor
was quartered. Yet δδ'τεραι φροντίδες, *My second wits*
stayed me, and aduised me, that I should peruse all his Report,
before I would proceede to execution: which in deede I did.
And, because I sawe that in all the rest of his behauiour hee
conteyned himselfe very well and honestly, and that he vsed
this lewd speech, not altogether ex animo, *but rather* ex vi-
tio gentis, *of the now-inueterate hatred, which the* Span-
yard *and* Portingall *beare against our* Nation, *I was so*
bold as to pardon him, and so taught him to speake the English *toung. In which language, if you will vouchsafe to heare*
him, hee will tell you many notable obseruations of diuers
✿   Countreys

To the Reader.

Countreys *and* peoples *inhabiting in* Africa, *whose Names haue scarse been mentioned in* England. *As namely, the* Kingdome *of* Congo, *with all the* Prouinces *thereof, the* Kingdome *of* Angola, *the* Kingdome *of* Loango, *the* Kingdome *of the* Anzichi, *the* Kingdome *of* Matama, *the* Kingdome *of* Buttua, *the* Kingdome *of* Sofala, *the* Kingdome *of* Mozambiche, *the* Kingdome *of* Quiloa, *the* Kingdome *of* Mombaza, *the* Kingdome *of* Melinde, *with the three great* Empyres *of* Monomotapa, *of* Moenemugi, *and of* Prete-Gianni. *He will tell you the seuerall* Rites *and* Customes, *the* Climates *and* Temperatures, *the* Commodities *and* Traffiques, *of all these* Kingdomes. *He will tell you the sundry kinds of* Cattell, Fishes *and* Fowles, *strange* Beasts, *and* Monstrous Serpents, *that are to be found therein: For* Africa *was alwayes noted to be a fruitfull Mother of such fearefull and terrible* Creatures. *He will tell you of great* Lakes, *that deserue the name of* Seas: *and huge* Mountaynes *of diuers sorts, as for example,* Mountaines *scorched with heat,* Mountaines *of* Snow *proceeding of colde,* Mountaynes *of the* Sunne, Mountaynes *of the* Moone, Mountaynes *of* Christall, Mountaynes *of* Iron, Mountaynes *of* Siluer, *and* Mountaynes *of* Golde. *And lastly, he will tell you the* Originall Spring *of* Nilus, *and the true cause of the yerely increase thereof. In any of these poynts, if his Mouth shall happen to runne ouer (as I hope, much it doth not) you must needes beare with him, for he will challenge the priuilege of the* English *Prouerbe,* A Traueller may lye by authoritie, *and the old* Greeke Agnomination, πᾶς ἀλήτης οὐκ ἀληθὴς, Euery Pilgrime is not a Sooth-sayer.

But to leaue this long Allegorie, *which indeede is meant of this Booke, and to come seriously and briefly to certaine faults,*

To the Reader.

faults, that some Readers may peraduenture finde therein, I will do my best indeuor to satisfie them in such obiections as may be made. And first, they will except perhaps against the Methode *of the* Author, *because he keepeth no continuate* Order *in this* Report, *but leapeth from one* Matter *to another, without any coherence, like* Marots Poeme, *called* Du Coq a l' Asne: *and so maketh a* Hotchpot *of it. But herein* Pigafetta *is not greatly to be blamed, who gathering this* Report *out of the tumultuarie* Papers *of* Lopez, *and from his vnpremeditated speeches, vttered by mouth at seuerall times, could not so well reduce it into so exact a forme and* Methode, *as curious wits do require. He is rather to be commended, that hauing so rude and vndigested a* Chaos *to worke vpon, he could frame so handsome a little world of it as this is. If happily it be further vrged, that the* Translator *should haue taken paines to cast him in a new* Mould, *and to make his members hang proportionably one vpon another: I must answere, that I neither do, nor euer did like of that kinde of course. I was alwayes of this opinion (and therein I do still dwell) that* Authors *should be published in the same* Order, *in the same* Termes, & *in the same* Stile *which they themselues vsed. For how know I, what moued them to obserue this* Order *or that* Order, *and to make choyce of one word rather then of another? peraduenture the reason of their so doing might proue to be so strong, as I doubt it would not easily be ouerthrowne. And touching* Style, *some are* Style. *so scrupulous and so nice, that they cannot abide to haue old and auncient* Writers *to be published in* Latin, *vnlesse they do imitate one of the* Triumuiri *of the* Latin *toung,* Cicero, Cæsar *or* Salust. *If all men should be of that humour, we should be bereaued both of singular* Diuinitie, *and antique* Historie, *which haue been written by men of no great lear-*

✱ 2   *ning,*

To the Reader.

ning, *as* Monkes *and* Friers, *whome (though they were very simple and meane, yet) it pleased God in the times of ignorance, to vse as meanes to preserue vnto vs those* Monuments *of* Antiquitie. *And therefore I could wish, that they might be published in their owne* Style, *and (as it were) in* Puris Naturalibus, *yea though they write false* Latin, *as some of them do. On the other side, some of our* Critikes *are so* Criticall *and so* audacious, *that when they publish any of the foresayd* Triumuiri, *or any other* Classicall Author, *they will transpose, and omit, and foyst into the* Text *many words and many* conceytes, *whereof the* Author *neuer dreamed, as* Euſtathius *and* Seruius *haue done vpon* Homer *and* Virgill. *But if algates some* Enthuſiaſme *haue come vpon our* Critikes, *that hath reuealed vnto them* tanquam ex antro Trophonij, *the certaintie of the* Authors *writing and meaning, to be such as they haue confidently set downe, let me be bold to intreate them, that they would muſter their conceytes in the* Margine *(if the* Margine *will hold them: as I doubt it will not in this* Hypercriticall *world) or else that they would reiect them (as some of them haue done) to the later end of their publications, vnder the title of* Corrections, Caſtigations, Emendations, Animaduerſions, Variæ Lectiones, *or such like,* Vt suo quiſque vtatur iudicio & ſenſu abundet, *That euery man may vse his owne iudgement, and abound in his owne sense. But* Maledicta Gloſſa quæ corrumpit Textum. *Curſed be that* Gloſſe *that corrupteth the* Text. *And sory I am, that some of our later* Diuines *haue erred in this point, euen in tranſlating the* Holy Scripture.

Another exception may be taken againſt the Paradoxes *that are maintayned in this* Treatiſe, *As namely, contrary to the opinion of the old world, and of the auncient* Philoſophers,

To the Reader.

phers, That the two Zones, Torrida, and Frigida, are both habitable and inhabited. *But hereunto if the Authors reasons here alleaged do not sufficiently answere, I do referre them, that will not yeeld therein, to the excellent Treatise of* Iosephus a-Costa, *de* Natura Noui Orbis, *printed this last yeare, and composed by him in* Anno 1584. *in which* Theologicall *and* Philosophicall *worke, he doth at large both by good reasons and also by his owne experience proue this his position to be true. And therefore I protest vnto you, it was one of the chiefe* Motiues, *which moued me to translate this* Report, *to the end it might be more publikely knowen, that it was not the single fancie of one man, touching the temperature of these two* Zones, *but also of diuers others that by their owne trauell haue tryed the certayntie thereof: among whome, this* Lopez *was one, who deliuered this* Relation *in* Anno 1588, *being foure yeares after the* Treatise *made by* Iosephus-a-Costa. *And I do not doubt, but that within few yeares you shall haue it confirmed by many others that are and haue been trauellers, who haue not as yet published their knowledge and trials in this behalfe. In the meane time we do great iniurie to them that haue been alreadie so desirous to acquaint vs with their labours, and to make vs know as much as they know vpon their credites and honesties: when in stead of shewing our selues thankefull vnto them for the same, we skoffe and mocke at them, and confidently sweare that they are lyers, and opposite to all auncient* Philosophers. *But in a word, I will answere herein with an Argument, which* Aristotle *vseth,* Εἴπερ ἐστιν ἐν βροτοῖς ψευδολο- *Rhetoric,* γεῖν πιθανὸν· νομίζειν χρῆγε ᷉ τϵναντίον, Ἅπις ἀληθῆ πολλά *lib. 2.* συμβαίνειν βροτοῖς. *i.* Siquidem in vsu est hominibus, mentiri id quod credibile : existimare oportet & contrarium, Incredibilia multa hominibus, contingere

❀ 3   vera ;

To the Reader.

vera : *which for the better vnderstanding I must paraphrase in* English : *If it be an vsuall thing among men, that when a thing is reported, which is very credible and like to be true, yet afterwards it falleth out to be a starke lye: Then must we needes thinke on the contrary, That many Reports or things which are incredible, do in the end fall out to be true. In which case, as* Credulitie *leaneth a little to* Foolerie, *so* Incredulitie *smelleth somewhat of* Atheisme.

Another Paradox is, That the heate of the Sunne is not the cause of Whitenesse or Blacknesse in the Skinnes of men. *This* Position *in the* Negatiue *he may safely defend against all* Philosophers, *by vertue of the reasons that he hath vouched in this* Report, *which in deede do vtterly ouerthrow their* Affirmatiue. *But because neither any auncient Writer before this age, nor he himselfe, hath euer been able to declare the true cause of these colours in humane bodies, very honestly and modestly he leaueth it vndecided, and referreth it to some secret of Nature, which hitherto hath been knowne to God alone, and neuer as yet reuealed to man. And therefore I do wish, that some sound* Naturall Philosopher, *such as* Fernelius *that wrote* De abditis rerum causis, *or as* Leuinus Lemnius de Occultis Naturæ miraculis, *or as* Franciscus Valesius de Sacra Philosophia, *would enter into the* Closet *of* Contemplation, *to finde out the true* Naturall *cause thereof. In the meane while I hold still with my* Author *in the* Negatiue.

The third Paradoxe *touching the* Amazones *mentioned in this booke, I do not see, why it should be counted a* Paradox *to beleeue, that there is such a* Nation, *considering how many* Authors *both* Greeke *and* Latine, *both* Historiographers *and* Cosmographers, *both* Diuine *and* Prophane, *haue acknowledged that* Nation, *and the* Countrey

To the Reader.

trey *wherein it inhabited. But our new Writers fay, that a little after* King Alexanders *death it was vtterly ouer-throwne and quite extinguifhed. What ?* Vfque ad vnam *? not one of them left aliue ? Certainely that depopulation muft needes proceede, either from the peculiar vifitation of God almighties owne hand, or elfe it was the ftrangeft flaughter that euer was heard of, that of a whole* Nation, *being fo populous as that was, there fhould not remaine fome few, that efcaped. But yet fuppofe that fome* Hypfiphile, *or* Penthefilea, *or* Thaleftris, *or fome fuch other, did wifely conueigh hir felfe away,* cum Dijs Penatibus, cum Matre, & cum filia, *and being guided by fome happie* Venus, *arriued in a farre remote* Region, *and there obferued the cuftomes and fafhions of their owne* Natiue Countrey : *Might not thefe three, together with fome other women that were defirous of* Rule *and gouernment, and allured by them to be of their* Socie-tie ; *might not they (I fay) in procefſe of time, (for it is a long time fince* Alexander *died) breede a* New Nation *of* A-mazones, *although we neuer heard, in what* Climate *they remained? Yea it may be for any thing that I know, this latter generation might growe againe to be fo populous, that they could fend foorth* Colonies *from them into other places, and ſo plant themfelues in diuers* Countreys. *For I heare that there are of them about* Guiana, *and heere in this* Report *I reade that fome of them ſerue in the warres of the King of* Monomotapa. *And I hope that in good time, fome good* Guianian *will make good proofe to our* England, *that there are at this day both* Amazones, *and* Headlefſe men. *And thus much for the* Paradoxes.

The laft exception which may be made againft this booke, is the difcourfe of the Conuerfion *of the* Kingdome of Congo *to* Chriftianitie, *which is amplified, and fet out with*

※ 4   ſuch

To the Reader.

such Miracles *and* Superstitious Vanities, *as though it had been plotted of purpose for the glorie and aduancement of the* Pope *and his* Adherents : *Wherein, because it doth concerne matter of* Religion, *I will deale more warily and seriously to satisfie my* Reader. *True it is that the* Inhabitants *of* Congo *were all* Pagans *and* Heathens, *vntill they entertayned Traffike with the* Portingales : *Among whome, one* Massing Priest *became a meanes to conferre with a* Noble Man *of* Congo *concerning* Christianitie, *who taking liking thereof, as being a Man of good inclination and disposition, was very desirous to be further instructed. The* Priest *being wise, tooke oportunitie to make way for his* Countreymens *traffike, and also for planting of the* Christian Faith *in that* Region, *It may be in hope to be preferred and aduanced in a new established* Church, *as commonly our trauelling* Priests *vse to do, that wanting maintenance, or being vpon some occasion discontented at home, do leape ouer sea into forreine partes, not for the desier which they haue to gaine* Christian Soules, *or to preach the Gospell, but to procure to themselues either dignities or wealth. But I do not say that this* Priest *was such a one : for I neither haue reason nor authoritie so to say. For he sent ouer into* Portingall *for some fellowes to helpe him, who being come into* Congo, *laboured so much, that in time the* King *and his people consented to become* Christians. *Then did the* Portingall-Priests *bestirre themselues nimbly in* Baptising *the* King, *the* Queene, *the* Lordes, *and the* Commons. *They built* Churches, *they erected* Altars, *they set vp* Crosses, *and at last brought in a* Bishop. *And all this was done (I must needes confesse) with all pompe and solemnitie, after the* Romish *maner, which in deede is so plausible, as it is able to allure any simple Man or Woman, euen with the very sight thereof.*

To the Reader.

thereof. Yet will I not denie, but that these Priests *had a good intent, and for my part I do beleeue that they were in* bona fide, *because they conuerted a great part of the* People, *not to* Poperie, *but to* Christianitie, *the true foundation of all* Religion. *And this Action, which tendeth to the glory of* God, *and may be a notable example to the* World, *of doing the like, shall it be concealed and not committed to memorie, because it was performed by* Popish Priests *and* Popish meanes? *God forbid.* S. Paule *maketh mention of* Philip. 1. 18. *diuers that preached* Christ, Some of enuie and strife, and not purely, *and* Some of loue and good will. What then? Yet Christ is preached, whether it be vnder pretence, or sincerely, and therein do I ioy. *So these* Men *are not to be regarded, whether they preached* Christ *for vaineglory, and for maintenance of* Poperie, *or of a sincere minde: but certaine it is, that* Christ *was preached by them, and therein ought we to ioy. In* Marke *and in* Luke, Marke. 9. S. Iohn *saith to* Christ, Maister, we sawe one casting Luke. 9. out Deuils in thy Name, but we forbad him, because he followeth not with vs. Forbid him not (*saith Christ*) for he that is not against vs, is with vs. *If we see a* Turke, *or a* Iewe, *or a* Papist, *vpon what pretence soeuer, seeke to drawe any to* Christ, *or to driue the* Deuill *of* Ignorance *out of any, let him alone, forbid him not, mislike him not, for in that point hee is not against vs, nay peraduenture hee may become one of vs. In the* booke *of* Nombers, *word* Numb. 11. *was brought to* Moses, *that* Eldad *and* Medad *prophecied in the hoast. And* Iosua *sayd, My Lord* Moses *forbid them. But* Moses *sayd,* Enuiest thou for my sake? Would God that all the Lords people were Prophets. *And are we angrie, or shall we finde fault, that the* Portingall Priests *being* Papists, *should be reported to*

✲ ✲   *haue*

To the Reader.

haue conuerted the Realme *of* Congo *to the profession of*
Chriſtian Religion? *Shall we enuie them in their well*
doing? I for my part do earneſtly wiſh with all my hart, that
not onely Papiſts *and* Proteſtants, *but alſo all* Sectaries,
and Presbyter-Iohns *men would ioyne all together both*
by word and good example of life to conuert the Turkes, *the*
Iewes, *the* Heathens, *the* Pagans, *and the* Infidels *that*
know not God, *but liue ſtill in darkeneſſe, and in the ſhadow*
of Death. *What a ſingular commendation would it be vnto*
vs, if it might be left in Record, *that we were the firſt con-*
uerters of ſuch a Nation, *and ſuch a people, and firſt brought*
them to the knowledge of God, *and the true profeſſion of his*
glorious Goſpell?

Thus I haue (gentle Reader) *laboured to ſatisfie ſuch*
ſcruples, as may ariſe in thy minde touching this Treatiſe :
which if it ſhall breede either profit or delight vnto thee,
I ſhall reioyce to my ſelfe : If not, I ſhall be ſorie that
I haue employed my precious time ſo idly.
Farewell in Chriſt.

Abraham Hartwell.

A

A REPORTE

OF THE KING-

dome of CONGO, a Region of AFRICA.

And of the Countries that border

rounde about the same.

1. Wherein is also shewed that the two Zones, Torrida & Frigida, are not onely habitable, but inhabited, and very temperate, contrary to the opinion of the olde Philosophers.

2. That the blacke colour which is in the skinnes of the *Ethiopians* & *Negroes* &c. proceedeth not from the Sunne.

3. And that the Riuer *Nilus* springeth not out of the mountains of the Moone, as hath beene heretofore beleeued: Together with the true cause of the rysing and increase thereof.

4. Besides the description of diuers plantes, Fishes and Beastes, that are founde in those Countries,

Drawen out of the writinges and discourses of
Odoardo Lopes a Portingall, by
Philippo Pigafetta.

Translated out of Italian by Abraham Hartwell.

LONDON
Printed by Iohn Wolfe. 1597.

A REPORTE OF

the kingdome of Congo, a Region of *Africa*.

Gathered by *Philippo Pigafetta*, out of the difcourfes of M. *Edwarde Lopes* a Portugall.

Chap. 1.
The iourney by fea from Lifbone to the kingdome of Congo.

N the yeare one thoufande fiue hundreth threefcore and eygh- Anno Dom. 1578. teenth, when *Don Sebaftian* king of *Portugall*, embarked himfelfe for the conqueft of the kingdome of *Marocco*: *Edwarde Lopes* borne at *Beneuentum* (a place xxiiii. myles diftant from *Lisbone*, neere vpon the South fhore of the riuer *Tagus*) fayled likewife in the moneth of Aprill towardes the hauen of *Loanda*, fituate in the kingdome of *Congo*, in a fhippe called S. *Anthony*, belonging to an vncle of his, and charged with diuerfe marchandifes for that kingdome: And it was accompanied with a *Patache* (which is a fmall veffell) whereunto the fhip did continually yeelde good guarde, & miniftred great reliefe, conducting and guiding the fame with lightes

Patache 1. a Brigandine or a Pinniffe.

A 3   in

in the night time, to the ende it ſhoulde not looſe the way, which the ſhip it ſelfe did keepe. He arriued at the Iſlande of *Madera*, belonging to the King of Portugal, diſtant from *Lisbone* about ſixe hundred myles, where he remained xv. dayes, to furniſh himſelfe with freſhe vittaile and wine; which in great aboundance groweth in that Iſlande, yea and in mine opinion the beſt in the world, whereof they carry abroad great ſtore into diuers countries, & eſpecially into England. He prouided there alſo ſundry other confections & conſerues of Sugar, which in that Iſlande are made and wrought both in great quantity, and alſo of ſingular excellency. From this Iſlande they departed, leauing all the *Canaries* belonging to *Caſtile*, and tooke hauen at one of the Iſlandes of *Capo verde*, called S. *Anthony*, without hauing any ſight thereof before they were come vpon it: and from thence to another Iſlande called *Saint Iacopo*, which commaundeth all the reſt, and hath a Biſhoppe and a Chaplen in it, that rule and gouerne them: and here they prouided themſelues againe of victuailes.

The Iſland of Madera.

The Canaries.

Iſle of S. Anthony.

Iſle of S. Iames

I doe not thinke it fitte in this place to tell you the number of the Canarie Iſlands, which indeede are many: nor to make any mention of the Iſlandes of *Capo verde*, nor yet to ſet downe the hiſtory and diſcourſe of their ſituations, becauſe I make haſt to the kingdome of *Congo*: and the ſhippe ſtayed here but onely for paſſage, and eſpecially for that there doth not want good ſtore of Reportes and hiſtories, which in particularity doe make relation of theſe countries: Onely this I will ſay, that theſe Iſlandes of *Capo verde* were eſtabliſhed by *Ptolomee* in the tables of his *Geography*, to be the beginning of the Weſt, together with the Cape or Promontory

The Iſlandes of Capo Verde.

tory

torie which he termeth *Cornu vltimum*, or the Iflandes *Macarie* or *Bleſſed*, which we commonly call *Fortunate*. In theſe Iflandes of *Capo verde* the Portugalles do often arriue, and in thoſe countries do trafficke with ſundry marchandiſes, as little balles of diuers coloured glaſſe, & other ſuch things, wherein thoſe people do greatly delight, and Hollande cloth, and cappes and kniues, and coloured clothes : In exchaunge whereof they bringe back againe, ſlaues, wax, hony, with other kind of food, and cotton-cloth of ſundry colours. Moreouer, right ouer againſt them within the lande are the countreyes & riuers of *Guynee*, and of *Capo verde*, and *Sierra Leona*, that is to ſay the Mountain *Leona*, which is a huge great mountaine and very famous.

From the foreſaide Iflande of *San Iacopo*, they directed their fore-decke towards Breſil: for ſo they muſt do to gaine the winde, and taking ſuch harboroughes as were conuenient for the ſeaſons that raigne in thoſe places, to arriue at the ende of their voyage. Two are the waies, whereby they ſaile from the Iſle of *San Iacopo* to *Loanda* a hauen in the kingdome of *Congo*: the one is by the coaſt of *Africa*, the other by the mayne Ocean, ſtill enlarging their courſe with the North winde, which very much ruleth there in thoſe Monethes, and for the moſt parte is called North, euen by the Portugalles themſelues, & by the Caſtilians, & by the French, and by all thoſe people of the North ſea. And ſo turning their foreſhippe to the South, and ſouth-eaſt, they holde on forwarde till they be neere the Cape of *Good-Hope*, leauing behind them the kingdome of *Angola*; for by that way they muſt afterwardes returne : & then they come to the altitude of betweene **xxvij.** and xxix.

Two waies from S. Iacopo to Loanda. The firſt way.

A 4   degrees

degrees beyond the equinoctiall, quite opposite to our
Pole, which South Pole in this writing shall be called
the Antarctike, that is to say, contrary to the Arctike,
which is our North Pole, and so the Antarctik is opposite thereunto towardes the South.

The Antarctik
is the South
Pole.

In that altitude then of the contrary Pole, the Saylers vse to meete with certaine windes that they cal *Generali*, which doe blowe there almost all our Sommer,
and are termed by them *Northeast*, and *Northeastes* in
the plural number, and by vs Italians, *Li venti dal Græco*,
that is to say, the windes betweene the Northeast, and
the Easte in the spring time: which peradventure the
Venetians in their proper speech doe call *Leuantiere*,
that is to say, easterly, & the Greekes and Latines terme
them *Etesii*, that is to say, such winds as euery yeare do
ordinarily blow in their certayne and accustomed seasons.

And thus sayling euen to xxix degrees of the Antarctik, with the North winde, there falleth out an
admirable effect. For diuers saylers, perceyuing the
first Generall windes when they blowe, doe straight
turne their sailes about, and set their fore-ship directly
on the way to *Angola*, and so very oftentimes they fayle
and are deceyued. But better it is for him that desireth
to arriue at his wished hauen to go much further, & to
expect a lustie winde, and after to returne backwarde:
wherin it is to be noted for a most memorable accidēt,
that the windes do blow very strong from the North,
euen vnto xxix. degrees beyond the Equinoctiall, and
then they meete with other winds, which being more
fierce & furious then they are, doe driue them backe a-
gaine. And this is vsuall and seasonable there for sixe
                                                    monethes

monethes in the yeare.

Now the ſhip called *S.Anthony*, holding on his foreſaid courſe, met with the ſaid Generall windes, & then
turned their prowe and their ſayles, by North and by
Northweſt on the right hand towardes the kingdome
of *Congo.* And ſayling onwardes cloſely with the halfe
ſhippe, they came in twelue dayes and twelue nightes,
to the Iſlande of *S. Elena,* not looking for the ſame, nor
thinking of it. This Iſlande was ſo called, becauſe
on the feaſt day of *S. Helene,* which falleth vppon the
thirde day of May, it was by the Portugalles firſt deſcried. And as it is very ſmal, ſo is it (as it were) ſingular
by it ſelfe; for being ſituate in the height of xvi. degrees
towardes the Antarctike, it contayneth in compaſſe
nine miles about, & is farre diſtant from the firme land.
As you ſayle by ſea, it may be diſcouered thirty myles
of, through certayne hilles: and it is a great miracle of
nature, that in ſo vnmeaſurable an Ocean, being all a-
lone and ſo little as it is, it ſhoulde ariſe (as it were) out
of a moſt tempeſtuous and deep ſea, & yet yeeld a moſt
ſafe harborough, and moſt aboundant ſtore of reliefe
and victuaile, for ſhippes that are forewearied, and ready to periſhe for thirſt, which come out of the Indies.

The woodes of it are very thicke, and full of Ebene
trees, whereof the Mariners do builde their boates. In
the barkes of theſe trees you may ſee written the names
of an infinite number of Saylers, which paſſing by that
Iſlande, doe leaue their names cut and carued in the
ſayde barkes, the letters whereof doe grow greater and
greater, as the bodies of the trees doe waxe greater in
bignes. The ſoyle (euen of it ſelfe) bringeth forth very

B

excellent

excellent fruites. For there groweth the vine, (which was in deede at the firſt brought thether by the Portugalles) and eſpecially in the arbours and walkes that are about the little Church, and in the lodgings that are there for ſuch as ſayle thether. You ſhall ſee there alſo huge wild woodes, of Orenges, of Citrones, of Limons and other ſuch Apple trees, that all the yeare long doe carry flowers & fruites both ripe and vnripe. And likewiſe Pomegranates, great and ſweete, and of a good indifferent taſte, with kernelles great and redde, and ful of pleaſant iuyce, and the ſtones within them very ſmal: and ripe they are at all ſeaſons of the yeare, as the Orenges are: and figges very great both in quantity and aboundance: which naturall gift and property (of being ripe all the yeare long) *Homere* noted to bee in diuers fruites of the Iſle of *Corfu*.

Ouer all the countrey they take Goates, and wilde Kiddes, that are very good to eate, and Boares and other foure-footed beaſts, and Partriches, and wild hens and Pigeons, and other kindes of foules, both great & ſmall. All which beaſtes and fowles are ſo ſecure and ſo tame, that they feare not a man, becauſe they doe not know in what daunger they are to be killed. So that the people which dwell there doo take of them dayly, and poulder them with ſalte, that is congealed on the banks of the Iſlande in certaine caues and holes of the rockes, that are naturally made hollow and eaten by the waues of the ſea. And the fleſh thereof being thus preſerued, they giue to the Saylers that arriue at the Iſland.

The earth is as it were crommeled like aſhes, of colour redde, very fat and fruitfull beyond meaſure, and ſo ſoft, as if ye treade on it with your foote, it will ſinke
like

Vine trees

Fruites.

Odyſſ. H.

Victuailes.

The Soyle.

like fande, and the very trees will fhake with the force
of a man. And therefore it needeth no labour or tillage:
for when it raigneth the fruites doe prefently fpring vp
out of the olde feede. It beareth rootes of Radifh as
bigge as a mans legge, and very good to eate. There
growe alfo Colewortes, and Parfley, and Lettife, and
Goordes, and Chiche-peafon, and Fafelles, and other
kindes of Pulfe, naturally: which being ripe doo fall into the fruitfull grounde, and multiply of themfelues,
and fpring agayne without any tilling. Euery fhippe
that commeth thether, bringeth with it fome fruyte or
garden hearbe, which being planted taketh roote prefently: and bountifull nature yeeldeth a courteous re-
warde and vfury, by referuing the fruite thereof for the
Saylers when the fhip returneth againe.

Rootes and hearbes.

There are certaine little Riuers in this Iflande, that
runne in diuerfe partes of it: whofe water is good
and wholefome, and wherein are fundry fafe places for
fhips to ryde in, as if they were hauens. But the principall of them is in a place, where they haue erected a
little Church, wherein are kept the ornamentes of the
Altar, and the prieftes veftimentes, and other neceffaries
for Maffe. And when fhippes paffe that way, the Religious perfons go downe vnto them to celebrate diuine feruice.

Riuers.

There is alfo in the fame place a little cottage, wherein for the moft parte fome Portingalles doo remayne,
fometimes three, fometimes two, yea and fometimes
but one alone, being left there, eyther by reafon of
fome infirmitie, or for fome offence committed, or
elfe euen voluntarily, becaufe they doe defire by this
meanes to leade the life of an Heremite in that wilder-

B 2   neffe

neſſe, and ſo to doe penaunce for their ſinnes.

Fiſhe.

Moreouer, in the ſame place there is ſo great aboundaunce of fiſh, as if the ſea were very neere vnto them: ſo that you ſhall not need but onely to caſt your hooks into the water, and you ſhall preſently drawe them out againe loaden with fiſh.

Why the Iſland of *S. Elena* is not fortified

I once demanded the queſtiõ, what reaſon there was, why the Portingals did neuer make any accompt, nor had any care to fortifie this Iſland, conſidering it was ſo fit and neceſſary for ſaylers, and founded there (as it were by the prouidence of God) for the reliefe of the Portingals which paſſe that way, as *Granata* doth largely diſcourſe vpon the Creede, firſt written by him in Spaniſhe, and ſince tranſlated by my ſelfe into Italian : But aunſwere was made vnto mee, that there was no need ſo to doo: for that the Iſlande ſerueth to no purpoſe for the voyage into the Indies, becauſe there is another way for that paſſage, and it is alſo a very harde matter to finde it out : but in returning from thence it lyeth full in the way, and is very eaſily deſcried. So that it woulde not quite the'coſt to beſtow money & time in maintayning ſouldiers therein without any profite, ſeeing none other veſſels come thither but onely the Portugals. And when I replyed, that the Engliſh had

This ſlaunderous terme vſed here by this Portugal, cannot impeach the credite of theſe two honourable gentlemen

nowe twice entred into thoſe ſeas, once vnder the conduct of *Drake*, and ſecondly this year 1588. vnder another Pirate, being alſo an Engliſh man and more valiant then hee, called *Candiſh*, who is returned home ful of great richeſſe : It was aunſwered, that yet for all that it coulde not poſſibly bee brought to paſſe to fortifie the ſame within a ſea being ſo farre off, and ſeeing that all the prouiſion which ſhould build there, muſt of neceſſity ceffity bee brought out of Europe.

To be fhort, befides all thefe naturall good giftes aboue rehearfed, the climate is temperate, the ayre pure, cleane and holefome, and the winds which blow there are very pleafaunt. So that ficke perfons, and fuch as were halfe deade with the difeafes of the fea, arry-uing at this Ifland, haue beene prefently healed, and recouered their former ftrength, through the benigni-ty of this Country.

From the Iflande of *S. Helena*, they made fayle with the fame weather, and fo within the fpace of xvij. dayes came to the hauen of *Loanda*, which is in the prouince of *Congo*, the windes being fomewhat more calme then they were afore. This is a very fure, and a great hauen, fo called of an Iflande of the fame name, whereof wee fhall fpeake hereafter.

I told you before, there were two courfes of fayling from the Iflands of *Capo verde* to *Loanda*; the one of thē is now declared, which beeing neuer vfed afterwardes, was at the firft attempted and performed by the fame fhip wherein *Signor Odoardo* went, being then guided by *Francefco Martinez* the kings Pilot, a man very great-ly experienced in thofe feas, and the firft that euer con-ducted veffell by that way: the other is atchieued by paffing along the coaft of the firme lande.

From the Ifland of *San Iacomo*, they come to *Capo* *dos Palmas*, and from thence direct themfelues to the Iflande of *San Thomas*, which lyeth vnder the Equino-ctial, fo called becaufe it was difcouered vpon that day, wherein the feaft of that Apoftle is vfed to bee celebra-ted. It is diftant from the firme lande CLxxx. myles, right againft the riuer called Gaban, which is fo termed

B 3 becaufe

becaufe it is in fhape very like to that kinde of vefture that it is called a Gaban or a cloake.

The hauen thereof is fore-clofed with an Ifland that raifeth it felfe in the chanell of the riuer, whereunto the Portingalles do fayle with fmall barkes from *S. Thomas* Iflande, carrying thether fuch thinges as vfually they carry to the coaft of *Guinea*, and from thence carrying backe with them Iuory, waxe & hony, Oyle of Palme, and blacke-More flaues. Neere to the Iflande of *S. Thomas* towardes the North lyeth another Iflande, cal-

led the Ifle of the Prince, diftant from the firme lande an hundred and fiue miles, being of the fame condition and trafficke, that the Ifle of *S. Thomas* is, although in circuite fomewhat leffe. This Iflande of *S. Thomas*

is in fafhion almoft rounde, and in breadth contayneth Lx. miles, and in compaffe Clxxx. Very rich it is and of great trafficke, difcouered at the firft and conquered by the Portingalles, at fuch time as they began the conqueft of the Indies. It hath diuers hauens, but the principal and chiefeft of all, whereinto the veffelles arriuing there, doe withdraw themfelues, is in the place, where the Cittie ftandeth.

The Iflande breedeth an infinite deale of Sugar, & almoft all kinds of victuals. In the Citty there are fome Churches, and a Bifhoppe, with many Clerks and one Chaplen or Priefte. There is alfo a Caftell, with a garrifon and Artillary in it, which beat vpon the hauen, being a very great and a fafe Port, where many fhippes may ride. But a very ftraunge and admirable thing it is, that when the Portugals did firft come thether, there was no fugar there planted, but they brought it thether

from other Countreys: as they did Ginger alfo, which
tooke

tooke roote,& grew there in moſt aboundant manner.
The ſoyle in deed is moyſt,and as it were appropriated
to foſter the Sugar Cane,which without any other watering, multiplyeth of it ſelfe,and fructifieth infinitely:
the reaſon whereof is , becauſe the dewe falleth there
like rayne and moiſteneth the earth.

There are in this Iſland aboue Lxx.houſes or preſſes
for making of Sugar,and euery preſſe hath many cottages about it as though it were a village, & there may
bee about ſome three hundred perſons that are appointed for that kinde of worke:They do euery yeare loade
about fortie great ſhippes with ſugar. True it is indeed
that not long ago the wormes (as it were a plague to
that land) haue deuoured the rootes of the Canes, and
deſtroyed the fruites of their ſugar, in ſuch ſort, as now
of the forty ſhippes, they do not load aboue fiue or ſixe
veſſels with that marchandiſe. And therevpon it commeth that ſugar is growen ſo deare in thoſe Countreyes.

The Iſland of S.Thomas holdeth trafficke with the
people that dwell in the firme lande, which do vſually
reſort to the mouthes or entries of their Riuers : The
firſt whereof (to begin withal) is named the riuer of
Fernando di Poo, that is to ſay, of Fernando Pouldre,who
did firſt diſcouer the ſame, and lieth in fiue degrees towardes our Pole. Right againſt the mouth of it, ryſeth
an Iſland of the ſame name, lying thirty and ſixe miles
diſtant from it. The ſeconde Riuer is called Bora, that
is to ſay, Filth. The thirde La riuiera del Campo: The
fourth , di San Benedetto, and the fifth, that of Angra,
which in the mouth of it hath an Iſlande called di Coriſco,that is to ſay Thonder.All theſe doe trafficke the ſame

(margin notes:) 70. houſes to make ſugar in, — The Riuer & Iſland of Fernando Poo. — R, Bora. La Riuiera del Campo. R.di San. Benedetto. R di Angra. The Iſle of Coriſco.

B 4   marchan-

marchaundifes, which we mentioned before.

The Cape of
Lupo Gonzale.

But to returne to the voyage of *S. Thomas* : Departing from thence towardes the South, wee found the
Cape of *Lupo Gonzale*, which ftandeth in the altitude
of one degree beyonde the Equinoctiall towardes the
Pole Antarctike, a hundred & fiue miles diftant from
the forefaid Ifle. And from thence they fayle with land
winds, creeping ftil all along the coaft, and euery day
cafting ancre in fome fafe place, either behynde fome
point, or elfe in fome hauen, vntill they come to the
mouth of the greateft Riuer in *Congo*, called in their

Zaire the grea-
teft Riuer of
Congo.

tongue *Zaire*, which fignifieth in Latine *Sapio*, (in
Englifh *I knowe.*) From whence if ye will go through
to the hauen of *Loanda*, yee muft faile the length of an
hundred and fourefcore miles.

*T*hefe bee the two voyages by fea, that bee vfed
from the Iflande of *San Iacomo*, which is one of thofe
Iflandes, that before wee tolde you were the Iflandes
of *Capo verde*, & was but a little while ago firft begun to
be frequented.

And nowe it is time to intreate of the kingdome of
Congo, and all the conditions thereof.

Chap.

Chap. 2.

Of the temperature of the ayre of the kingdome of Congo,
and whether it bee very colde or hote : whether the men
be white or blacke : whether are more or lesse blacke they
that dwell in the hilles , or those that dwell in the playnes :
Of the winds and the raynes, and the snowes in those quar-
ters, and of what stature and semblaunce the men of that
Countrey are.

He Kingdome of *Congo* in the middle part therof, is distant from the Equinoctiall towardes the Pole Antarctike (iust where the Cittie called *Congo* doth lie) seuen degrees and two thirdes: so that it standeth vnder the Region which auncient writers thought to be vnhabitable, and called it *Zona Torrida,* (that is to say, *a Cincture or Girdle of the earth, which is burnt by the heat of the Sun*) wherin they are altogether deceiued. For the habitation there is excee-ding good, the ayre beyonde all credite temperate, the winter nothing so rough, but is rather like Autumne in this Region of *Rome.* The people vse no furres, nor chaunge of apparell: they come not neere the fire: nei-

The situation of Congo.

The tempera-ture of the kingdome.

C   ther

ther is the colde in the toppes of the Mountaines greater then that which is in the plaines : but generally in
Winter time the ayre is more hote then it is in fommer, by reafon of their continual raynes, and efpecially
about two houres before & after Noone, fo that it can
hardely be endured.

The men are blacke, & fo are the women, and fome
of them alfo fomewhat inclyning to the colour of the
wilde Oliue. Their hayre is black & curled, and fome
alfo red. The ftature of the men is of an indifferent bignes, and excepting their blacknes they are very like to
the Portingalles. The apples of their eies are of diuerfe
colours, blacke and of the colour of the fea. Their lips
are not thicke, as the *Nubians* and other Negroes are :
and fo likewife their countenaunces are fome fat, fome
leane, and fome betweene both, as in our countreyes
there are, and not as the *Negroes* of *Nubia* and *Guinea*,
which are very deformed. Their nights and their daies
doo not greatly differ : for in all the whole yeare yee
fhall not difcerne the difference betweene them to bee
more then a quarter of an houre,

The Winter in this countrey (to fpeake at large) beginneth at the fame time, that our Spring here beginneth, that is to fay, when the Sun entreth into the Nor-
thern fignes, in the Moneth of *March*. And at the fame
time that we haue our winter, whē the Sun entreth into the Southern Signs in the moneth of *September*, then
beginneth their fommer. In their winter it rayneth 5.
monethes almoft continually, that is to fay, in *April*,
May, Iune, Iuly & *Auguft*. Of faire daies they haue but a
few, becaufe the raine falleth fo greatly, & the drops of
it are fo big, as it is a wonder to fee. Thefe waters doe
marüel-

maruelloufly fupple the grounde, which is then very
drie, by reafon of the heate of the Sommer paft, wherein it neuer rayneth for the fpace of fixe monethes together, and after the ground is full and as it were ingor-
ged with water, then do the riuers fwell beyond all credite, and are fo replenifhed with troubled waters , that
all the countrey is furrounded by them.

The windes which blow in thefe Moones through
all this region, are the very felfe fame that *Cefar* calleth
by a Greeke worde *Etefÿ*, that is to fay, *Ordinary euery*
yeare: whereby are meant thofe winds that in the *Cearde*
are noted from the North to the Weft, and from the
North to the Nertheaft. Thefe windes doo driue the
cloudes to the huge and high mountaines, whereupon
they rufh with very great violence, and being there ftai-
ed of their owne nature , they are afterwardes melted
into water. So that when it is likely to raine, you fhall
fee the cloudes ftanding (as it were) vpon the toppes of
their higheft hils. *The winds in this Country, in winter time.*

And hence arifeth the encreafing and augmentati-
on of the riuers that fpring in *Æthiopia*, and efpecially
of *Nilus* and others, that difcharge themfelues into the
eaft and weft Ocean : And in the kingdome of *Congo*
and *Guinea*, through which runneth the riuer *Nigir*, fo
called by the auncient writers, and by the newe termed
Senega, you fhall fee the faide riuer encreafe at the very
felfe fame time that *Nilus* doth; but in deed carrieth his
waters towards the weft, directly againft the Iflandes
of *Capo Verde*, whereas *Nilus* runneth by the Ifle of *Me-*
roe in *Egipt* towardes the North, refrefhing and watering all thofe Regions that are full of fcorching heates,
and wilderneffes and deferts. Now for as much as in *The caufe of the encreafe of Nilus, and other riuers in Ethiopia.* *The Riuer Nigir or Se-nega, runneth weftwarde.* *Nilus run-neth north-warde,*

C 2   the

the regions of *Congo* and *Æthiopia* it is alwaies wont to rayne euery yeare at a certaine set tyme, the swelling and ouerflowing of the riuers there, is of no great consideration, nor any straunge accident to make accompt of.

It neuer rayneth in Egypt but onely in Alexandria. But in the Countries, that are farre distant and very drie, as in *Ægypt*, where it neuer raineth (sauing onely in *Alexandria* and the territories thereof) it is accounted a maruellous matter, to see euery yeare so great a quantity of thicke troubled water come vppon them, from places so remote, at a certaine set tyme, without missing: which water doth quicken the grounde, and ministreth foode both to man and beast. And therevpon the auncients did sacrifice to that riuer, calling it αγαθὸς δαίμων, the *good God*, as *Ptolomy* noteth in his fourth booke. Yea and some of our Christians at this day doo hold it for a miracle. So that without these waters they shoulde perish for hunger, because their liues do depende vpon this increase of the water, as *S. Chrysostome* saith.

Thus these windes called by *Cesar Etesij*, and by the Portugalles *Generali*, do blow with vs in Sommer, but with them in winter, and carry the cloudes vnto the toppes of those huge mountaines, which make them to melt into raine. And so it falleth out that by reason of these raines, their winter (as it is aforesaid) is nothing so colde, because the waters do engender a certayne kind of warmth in those hot regions. This is then the cause of the increase of *Nilus*, & other riuers in that Climate, whereof the ancients of old times made so great doubt, and inuented so many fables and errours

But in their sommer, which is our winter, there blow other

other windes that are quite oppofite to the former, e-
uen in *Diametro,* and are noted in the *Carde,* from the
South to the foutheaft, which out of all queftion muft
needes be colde, becaufe they breath from the contrary Pole Antarctike, and coole all thofe countreyes, euen
for all the worlde as our windes in Sommer doo coole
our countreyes. And whereas, there with them, thefe
windes do make the ayre very fayre and cleere, fo doo
they neuer come vnto vs, but they bring with them
great ftore of raine. And this commeth to paffe by a
certain naturall difpofition of the earth which is gouerned by the Heauens and the Clymates thereof, and
by the foueraigne prouidence of God, who hath
parted the heauen, and the courfe of the funne and of
the other planets in fuch fort, that euery countrey vpon
the face of the earth, doth inioy the vertue of their
lightes, both in heate, and in colde, and alfo in all other
feafons of the yeare, by a moft fingular meafure and
proportion. And certainly if the breath of thefe winds
did not refrefh and coole thefe countries of *Æthiopia* &
Congo, and other places neere about them, it were not
poffible for them to endure the heate, confidering that
euen in the night tyme they are conftrayned to hange
two coueringes ouer them to keep away the heat. The
fame cooling and refrefhing by windes, is common alfo
to the inhabitants of the Ifle of *Candie,* & of the Iflandes
in *Arcipelago,* and of *Cyprus,* and of *Afia* the *leffe,* and of
Soria, and of *Ægypt,* which doe liue (as it were) with
this refrefhing of the forefaid winds of the Northweft,
and of the Weft: fo that they may well be called as they
are in Greeke *Zephyri quafi* ζωηφόροι, breeders of life.
     Let it bee alfo remembred, that in the mountaines of
         C 3   Æthi-

Æthiopia, and of *Congo* & the regions neere adioyning, there falleth no snow, neither is there any at all in the very toppes of them, sauing onely towardes the Cape of *Good-Hope*, and certaine other hilles, which the Portugalles call, *Sierra Neuada*, that is to say, the *Snowie mountaines*. Neyther is there anye ice or snow to bee founde in all the Countrey of *Congo*, which would bee better esteemed there then golde, to mingle with their drinkes: So that the riuers there doo not swell and increase by melting of snow, but because the raine doth fall out of the cloudes for fiue whole Moones continually together, that is to say in *April, May, Iune, Iuly*, & *August*: the first raine sometimes beginning on the xv. day, and sometimes after. And this is the cause why the newe waters of *Nilus*, which are so greatly desired & expected by the inhabitaunts there, do arriue sooner or later in *Ægipt*.

Chap. 3

Whether the children which are begotten by Portugalles, being of a white skinne, and borne in those Countries by the women of Congo, bee blacke or white, or Tawney like a wilde oliue, whom the Portugals call Mulati.

The true cause of white & blacke in the bodies of the inhabitantes of these countries.

AL the auncient writers haue certainly beleeued, that the cause of blacke colour in men is from the heate of the Sun. For by experience it is founde, that the neerer wee approach to the cuntries of the *South*, the browner & blacker

blacker are the inhabitants therein. And contrariwise, the farther you go towardes the north, the whiter shall you finde the men, as the *French*, & the *Dutch*, & the *English*, and others. Notwithstanding it is as certaine a thing as may be, that vnder the *Equinoctiall*, there are people which are borne almost all white, as in the kingdome of *Melinde* & *Mombaza* situate vnder the *Equinoctial*, & in the Isle of *San Thomas* which lieth also vnder the same Clymate, and was at the first inhabited by the Portingalles, though afterwardes it was disinhabited, and for the space of a hundred yeares and vpwardes their children were continually white, yea and euery day still become whiter and whiter. And so likewise the children of the Portingals, which are borne of the women of *Congo*, do incline somewhat towards white. So that *Signor Odoardo* was of opinion, that the blacke colour did not spring from the heate of the Sunne, but from the nature of the seede, being induced thereunto by the reasons aboue mentioned. And surely this his opinion is confirmed by the testimony of *Ptolome*, who in his discription of the innermost partes of *Lybia* maketh mention of white *Ethiopians* which hee calleth in his language Λευκαιθιοπες; that is to say, white Moores, and in another place also of white Elephants, which are in the same countrey.

C 4   Chap.

Chap. 4.

Of the circuite of the Kingdome of Congo, *and of the bor-*
ders and confines thereof. And firft of the Wefterne coaft.

He Kingdome of *Congo* is diftingui-
fhed by foure borders: The firft, of the
Weft, which is watered with the O-
cean fea: the feconde of the North:
the thirde of the eaft, & the laft which
is towardes the South.

And to beginne with the border lying vpon the fea,
the firft part of it is in the Bay, called *Seno delle Vacche,* &
is fituate in the height of 13.degrees vpon the Antarctik
fide, and ftretcheth all along the coaft vnto 4. degrees
and a halfe on the North fide, neere to the Equinoctial;
which fpace contayneth 630. miles. This *Seno delle vac-*
che is a hauen but of a moderate bignes, and yet a good
one & able to receiue any fhip that arriueth. It is called
Seno delle vacche, that is to fay, the Bay of *Cowes,* becaufe
thereabouts there are pafturing very many heardes of
that kind of Cattel: The country is plain, & aboundeth
with all manner of victuailes: and there you fhall find
fome kinde of mettels to be publikely folde, efpecially
filuer, and it is fubiect to the King of *Angola.*

A little more forwarde lyeth the Riuer *Bengleli,*
where a certaine Lorde, being fubiect to the King of
Angola doth fpecially commande: and about the faid
Riuer

The wefterne
border of
Congo.
The Bay of
Cowes.

The Riuer
Bengleli.

Riuer is a great compasse of countrey, much like to the
former.   And a little further runneth the riuer *Songa*,
so called by the Portingalles: wherein you may sayle
25.miles vpwardes in a country also like to the former.
Then followeth the riuer *Coanza*, which issueth out of
a little lake, fedde by a certaine riuer that floweth out
of a great lake, being the chiefe and principal spring or
head of *Nilus*, wherof in the other part of this discourse
we shall haue occasion to write. *Coanza* at the mouth
of it is two miles broade, and you may sayle with small
barkes vpwardes against the streame about 100. miles,
but hath no hauen. And here it is to be noted, that all
this Country which we haue here described,was wont
to be subiect to the king of *Congo*: but a while ago the
Gouernour of that countrey is become the absolute
Lorde thereof, and professeth himselfe to bee a friende
to the king of *Congo*, but not his vassall : and yet sometimes he sendeth the King some present, in manner of
a tribute.

   Beyond the Riuer *Coanza* is the haue of *Loanda* being
in ten degrees, made(as it is said) by a certaine Island
called *Loanda*,which signifieth in that laguage,*Bald* or
Shauen, because it is a Countrey without any hilles and
very low : for indeed it scarce rayseth it selfe aboue the
sea. This Island was framed of the sand and durt of the
sea, and of the riuer *Coanza*, whose waues meeting together,and the filthy matter sinking downe there to the
bottome,in continuance of time it grew to be an Island.
It may be about 20. miles long, and one mile broade at
the most, and in some places but onely a bowshoote.
But it is a maruellous thing,that in such a sandy ground
if you shall digge to the depth of two or three hande-
D   breadthes

breadthes, you shall finde sweete water , the best in all those Countreyes. Wherein also there is a very strange effect, that when the *Ocean* ebbeth , this water becommeth somewhat salte , but when it floweth to the top, it is most sweete. A thing that falleth out also in the Islande of *Calis* in *Spayne,* by the report and testimony of *Strabo.*

The money of *Congo.*

This Islande is the *Mine* of all the money which the King of *Congo* spendeth, and all the people thereaboutes. For vppon the shores you shall haue certayne women, that vse to diue and ducke into the sea, two yardes deepe and more, and fill their baskets with sand, and afterwardes diuide the grauell from certayne smal *Shel-fishes* that are among it, which are called *Lumache:* & when these *Lumache* are seuered by themselues, then doe they picke out the *Males* from the *Females,* which they may easily do, because the *Female* is more fine then the *Male,* and greatly esteemed for her colour, which is very neat, bright and pleasant to the sight.

The *Lumache* of *Loanda.*

These *Lumache* doo breede in all the shores of the kingdome of *Congo,* but the best of all are those of *Loanda,* because they looke very fine, and of a very bright colour, some gray or ashecoloured , and some of other colours not so precious. And here you must note that gold and siluer and mettell is not of any estimation, nor in vse of money in these countreyes, but onely these *Lumache:* so that neither with golde nor siluer, in masse or in coine you shal buy any thing there, but with these *Lumache* you shall buy both golde and siluer, or any thing els.

In this Islande there are 7. or 8. *Townes,* called in that Country language, *Libata,* the principal whereof

Kingdome of Congo. 23

of is *Spirito sancto* : and therein dwelleth the Gouernour which is sent from *Congo*, to minister iustice, and to gather the treasure of the moneyes of these *Lumache*. Here are also *Goates*, and *Sheepe*, and *Boares* in great numbers, which being tame at the first, do afterwardes become wilde and liue in the woods. Here groweth also a tree called *Enzanda*, which is a great one and alwaies greene, and endued with a singular qualitie. For from the bowes of it that sproute vpwardes, there hang downe certaine threedes (as it were) which creeping into the earth do take roots, & out from these roots do rise other trees, & so they multiply. And within the outmost barke thereof, there groweth a certaine kind of pil like fine linnen, which being beaten and cleansed, they spreade out in length and in breadth, and therewith they cloath their men and women, that are of the basest sort.

In this Islande they haue certaine vessels, made of the bodies of *Palme-trees*, ioyned together and framed after the manner of our boates, with a prowe and a sterne, wherin they passe from place to place, both with oares and sayles. In these boates they vse to fish about the riuers, which are indeede exceeding full of fish, and sometime also they will go ouer to the firme lande.

In that part of this Islande, which is towardes the maine land, in certaine lowe places there grow certaine trees (which when the water of the *Ocean* ebbeth) discouer themselues : and at the feet thereof you shal find certaine other *Shel-fishes* cleauing as fast to the trees as may bee, hauing within them a great fish as bigge as a mans hande, and very good meate. The people of the countrey know them very well, and call them *Ambizia-*

D 2   *matare*

Ambiziama-
tare.

matare, that is to fay, the *Fifhe of the Rocke.* The Shels of thefe fifhes, they vfe to burne, and thereof make very good lime to builde withall. And being like the corke or barke of the tree which is called *Manghi*, they dreffe their Oxe hydes withall, to make their fhooe foles the ftronger.

To be briefe this Ifland bringeth forth neither corne What kind of
money is vfed
in fundry
countries. nor wine, but there is great ftore of victuaile brought thether from all parts thereaboutes, to fetch away thefe *Lumache.* For as in all other places all things may be had for money of mettell, fo all things here are had for *Lumache.* Whereby may bee noted, that not onely here in this kingdome of *Congo*, but alfo in her neighbour *Ethiopia* and in *Africa*, and in the kingdomes of *China*, & certaine others of the *Indies*, they vfe moneyes of other matter then of mettall, that is to fay, neyther golde, nor filuer, nor copper, nor any other mixture tempered of thefe. For in *Æthiopia* their money is *Pepper:* and in the kingdome of *Tombutto*, which is about the Riuer *Nigir*, otherwife called *Senega*, their money is *Cockles* or *Shelfifhe:* and among the *Azanaghi* their moneyes are *Porcellette:* and in the kingdome of *Bengala* likewife they vfe *Porcellette* and mettall together. In *China* they haue certaine *Shelfifhes*, called alfo *Porcellette*, which they vfe for their money: & in other places *Paper* ftamped with the kings feale, and the barks of the tree called *Gelfomora:* Whereby it appeareth, that the money which is payed for euerie thing is not mettall, all the worlde ouer, as it is in *Europe*, and in many and fundry other countries of the earth.

This Iflande in the ftraiteft part of it, is very neere to the firme lande, and the people do oftentimes fwimme

ouer

ouer the channell there. In this ſtraite there ariſe out of
the *Ocean* certaine *Iſlettes*, which ſhewe themſelues Certaine *Iſlettes*.
forth from the water when it ebbeth, and are couered a-
gaine when it floweth. And in thoſe Iſlettes you ſhall
ſee great trees, and moſt excellent *Shelfiſhes* cleauing
faſt to the bodies of them, ſuch as I tolde you of before.

Neere to this Iſlande towardes the outwarde coaſt Great ſtore of *Whales*
to the ſea, there ſwim an innumerable ſorte of Whales,
that looke blacke, and fighting one with another doe
kill themſelues: which afterwardes being by the waues
caſt vp vpon the ſhore, as bigge as a midling marchants
ſhippe; the *Negroes* goe forth with their boates to
fetch them, and to take the oyle out of them, which being mingled with pitch they vſe to trimme their veſſels
withall. Vpon the ridges or backes of theſe creatures,
there growe many *Shelfiſhes*, made like *Snailes*, *Cockles*
and *Whelkes*: whereof *Signor Odoardo* affirmed, that hee
had ſeene great ſtore. He was alſo of opinion that *Am-*
ber commeth not from theſe fiſhes. For ouer all the
coaſt of *Congo*, where there is an infinite number of *Amber* commeth not from the *Whales*.
them, you ſhal not finde either *Ambregriz*, or any other
Amber, blacke or white in any place. And yet if it ſhould
come from theſe creatures, there muſt haue beene of
neceſſity great ſtore of it founde vpon theſe Shores.

The principall hauen of this Iſland hath his entrance *The hauen of Loanda.*
towardes the North, and on that ſide it is halfe a mile
broade, and of a very great depth. Vpon the firme land
directly ouer againſt the Iſland is a towne called *villa di* *Villa di San Paulo.*
San Paulo, altogether inhabited with Portingalles, and
their wiues, which they brought with them out of
Spaine: and yet it is not fortified.

D 3   All

All this channell is very full of fiſh,eſpecially of *Sar-*

Store of fiſh. *dinæs,* and of *Anchioues*:whereof there is ſo great ſtore, that in the winter time they will of themſelues leape vp to land. Other kindes of moſt excellent fiſhes there are, as *Soles* and *Sturgeons* and *Barbelles,* and all manner of dainty fiſh: and great *Crabbes*, in ſtraunge aboundance, and all very wholeſome: ſo that the greateſt parte of the people that dwel about the banks there, do liue vp-on them.

Into this channell runneth the Riuer called *Bengo,*

The R. *Bengo*. which is a very great one, & nauigable vpwardes xxv. miles. This Riuer with that other of *Coanza* , whereof I tolde you before,doe make the Iſle of *Loanda,* becauſe when their waters do meete together, they leaue their ſande and filth behind them, and ſo increaſe the Iſland. There runneth alſo into it a other great Riuer called

The R . *Dande* *Dande,*which wil receiue veſſels of an hundred tunne :

The R.*Lembe*. & then another Riuer called *Lemba,* which neither hath Hauen , neyther do any Shippes enter into it. Very

The R.*Ozene*. neere vnto this there is alſo another Riuer called *Ozone,* which iſſueth out of the ſame *Lake* , whence *Nilus* like-wiſe ſpringeth, and it hath a hauen. Next to *Ozone,*there is another called *Loze,* without any hauen: and then a-

The R. *Loze*.
The R.*Am-
briz*,
The L. *Lelun-
da*. nother great one with a hauen called *Ambriz,* which runneth within foure leagues neere to the Royall Citty of *Congo*. Laſt of all is the Riuer *Lelunda,* which ſignifi-eth a *Trowt fiſh,*and watereth the rootes of that great hil,

The *Oteiro* of
Congo. wheron the pallace of *Congo* ſtandeth,called by the Por-tingalles the *Oteiro*. This Riuer *Lelunda* ſpringeth out of the ſame *Lake* , from whence *Coanza* iſſueth, and ta-keth into it by the way another Riuer, that commeth from the great *Lake* : and when it doth not raine, then

you

you may paſſe ouer *Lelunda* on footе, becauſe it hath ſo little ſtore of water in it.

Next vnto this is the *Zaire,* a huge Riuer and a large, *The R,* Zaire. and in deed the greateſt in all the kingdome of *Congo.* The original of this Riuer commeth out of three *Lakes:* one is the great *Lake* from whence *Nilus* ſpringeth, the ſecond is the little *Lake* aboue mentioned, and the third is the ſecond great *Lake* which *Nilus* engendreth. And certainely, when you will conſider the aboundance of water that is in this Riuer, you will ſay, that there was no nede to haue any fewer or leſſer ſpringes to make ſo huge a ſtreame as this carrieth. For in the very mouth of it, which is the onely entraunce into it, the Riuer is 28. myles broad, and when it is in the height of his increaſe, he runneth freſh water. 40. or 50. miles into the ſea, and ſometimes 80. ſo that the paſſengers doe refreſh themſelues withal, & by the troubleſomnes of the water they know the place where they are. It is nauigable vpwardes with great barkes about 25. miles, vntill you come to a certaine ſtraite betweene the rockes, where it falleth with ſuch a horrible noiſe, that it may be hearde almoſt 8. miles. And this place is called by the Portingalles *Cachiuera,* that is to ſay a *Fall,* or a *Cataracte,* like to the *Cataractes* of *Nilus.* Betweene the mouth of this Riuer, and the fall thereof, there are diuers great Iſlands Certaine Iſlandes. well inhabited, with townes and Lordes obedient to the king of *Congo,* which ſometimes for the great enmitie that is among them doo warre one againſt another in certaine boates, hollowed out of a ſtocke of a tree, Boates. which is of an vnmeſurable bignes, & theſe boats they call *Lungo.* The greateſt boates that they haue, are made of a certaine tree called *Licondo,* which is ſo great, that The tree Licondo.

ſixe

fixe men cannot compaffe it with their armes, and is in
length of proportion aunfwerable to the thickneffe, fo
that one of them will carrie about 200. perfons. They
rowe thefe boates with their oares, which are not tyed
to any loopes, but they holde them at libertie in their
handes, and moue the water therewith at pleafure. E-
uery man hath his oare and his bowe, and when they
fight together, they lay downe their oare and take their
bowe. Neyther do they vfe any other Rudders to turne
and gouerne their boates, but onely their oares.

The firft of thefe Iflandes, which is but a little one,
is called the Ifle of *Horfes*, becaufe there are bredde and
brought vp in it great ftore of thofe creatures that the
Greekes call *Hippopotami*, that is to fay, *Water-horfes*. In
a certaine village within this Iflande doe the Portingals
dwel, hauing withdrawen themfelues thether for their
better fecuritie. They haue their veffelles to tranfporte
them ouer the water to the firme lande, vpon the fouth

banke of the Riuer, which lande is called the hauen of
Pinda, where many fhippes doe ryde that arriue therein.

In this Riuer there are liuing diuerfe kinds of creatures, and namely mighty great *Crocodiles*, which the
Countrey people there call *Caiman*, and *Water-horfes* a-
boue named: And another kind of creature, that hath
(as it were) two hands, and a taile like a Target, which

is called *Ambize Angulo*, that is to fay a *Hogge-fifhe*, becaufe it it as fat as a *Porke*. The flefh of it is very good,
and thereof they make Larde, and fo keepe it: neyther
hath it the fauour or tafte of a fifh, although it bee a
fifhe. It neuer goeth out from the frefh water, but feedeth vpon the graffe that groweth on the banks, & hath
a mouth

a mouth like the mozell of an Oxe. There are of thefe
fifhes, that weigh 500. poundes a peece. The fifhermen
vfe to take them in their little boates, by marking the
places where they feed, and then with their hookes and
forkes, ftriking and wounding them, they drawe them
dead forth of the water : and when they haue cut them
in peeces, they carry them to the king: For who foeuer
doth not fo, encurreth the penaltie of death, and fo doe
they likewife that take the *Trowt*, and the *Tenche*, and
another Fifhe called *Cacongo*, which is fhaped after the
likenes of a *Salmon*, fauing that it is not red : but indeed
fo fat it is, that it quencheth out the fire whiles it is rofted or broiled. Other fifhes alfo there are that are called
Fifhes Royall, which are carried to the king, vpon very
feuere and rigorous punifhmentes, by open proclama-
tion to be inflicted on fuch as fhall do the contrary, befides other kindes of fifhes that are taken in this Riuer,
the names whereof we thinke it fuperfluous here to re-
cite.

Cacongo, a fifh like a Salmon.

 Beyonde this Riuer of *Congo*, there commeth downe
another Riuer, which the Portingalles call, *La Baia de-
las Almadias*, that is to fay, the Golfe of *Barkes*, becaufe
there are great ftore of them, that are made there, by
reafon of the aboundance of woods & trees that growe
thereabouts, which are fit for that vfe, and wherewith
all the Countries round about do furnifh themfelues.
At the mouth of this Bay there are three Iflandes, one
great Ifle in the middle of the Channell, which maketh
a conuenient hauen for fmall veffelles, and two other
leffe, but none of them inhabited.

La Baia de las Almadias.

 A little higher runneth another ftreame, not verye
great, which is called *De las Barreras Roffas*, of the redde
    E   Clay-

The R. de las Barreras Vermeglias.

Clay-pittes, becaufe it floweth from among certaine Rockes of hils, whofe earth is died with a redde colour: where alfo there is a very high mountain, called by the *Portingals*, *La Sierra Complida*, that is to fay, *The long Mountaine.*

And yet going vp a little further, there are two *Golfes* of the fea in the likeneffe of *a paire of Spectacles*, where-

Baya d Aluaro Gonzales. in is a good hauen, called *La Baia d' Aluaro Gonzales*, that is the Golfe of *Aluaro Gonzales*. Beyonde all thefe are certaine hilles and fhoars, not worth the remembrance, vntill you come to the *Promontorie* that is called by the Portingalles *Capo de Caterina*, which is the border of the

Capo di Caterina. kingdome of *Congo* towardes the *Equinoctiall*, and is diftant from the *Equinoctiall* line two degrees and a halfe, which is 150. *Italian* miles.

Chap. 5.

Of the North coaft of the Kingdome of Congo, *and the confines thereof.*

The Northren border of Congo.

 Ow from *Capo de Caterina* on the *North* fide beginneth another border or Coaft of the kingdome of *Congo*, which *Eaftwarde* ftretcheth it felfe to the place where the Riuer *Vumba* ioyneth with the Riuer *Zaire*, contayning the fpace of 600.

600. miles and more. Beyonde this coaſt of *Congo* towardes the North, and vnder the *Equinoctiall* lyne vpon the ſea ſhoare, and about 200. miles within lande, comprehending in that reckoning the foreſaide *Golfe of Lope Gonzales)* the people called the *Bramas* doo inhabite in a Countrey, that is nowe called the kingdome of *Loango,* and the king thereof *Mani-Loango,* that is to ſay, the King of *Loango.* The Countrey hath great aboundance of *Elephantes,* whoſe teeth they exchange for iron, whereof they make their arrowe heades, their kniues, and ſuch other inſtrumentes. In this Countrey alſo, they weaue certaine cloath of the leaues of *Palme* trees, in ſundry ſorts: as wee ſhal tell you in ſome other place of this narration. The *Bramas.*
The kingdom of *Loango.*

The king of *Loango* is in amity with the King of *Congo,* and the report is, that in times paſt he was his vaſſaile. The people are circumciſed after the manner of the *Hebrues,* like as alſo the reſt of the nations in thoſe countries vſe to be . They do traffick together one with another, & ſometimes make war againſt their neighbors, & are altogether of the ſame nature, whereof the people of *Congo* are. Their armour are long targets, which couer almoſt all their bodies, made of very hard & thicke hides of a certaine beaſt called *Empachas,* ſomwhat leſſe then an *Oxe,* with hornes like the hornes of a *Coate :* (this Creature is alſo bred in *Germanie,* and is called a *Dante.)* The hides thereof are tranſported out of theſe countreyes, and out of the kingdome of *Congo* into *Portingale,* and from thence into *Flanders,* where they are dreſſed; and then they make ierkens of them as good as breaſtplates and corſelets, which they call iackets of *Dante.* Their weapons offenſiue are dartes with long The people of *Loango* circumciſed.
Their armour, *Empachas.*

and

and large heads of iron, like Partizans, or like the auncient Roman *Pilum* or *Iauelin :* the ſtaues whereof are of
proportionable length to caſt, hauing in the middeſt of
them a certaine peece of wood, which they take in their
hands, and ſo with greater force and violence diſcharge
their dartes. They carry alſo certaine daggers, which
are in ſhape much like to the heads of their dartes.

The countrey of *Anzicos.*

Beyond the kingdome of *Loango,* are the people called *Anzigues,* of whom wee ſhall deliuer vnto you a hiſtory, which in truth is very ſtrange, and almoſt incredible for the beaſtly and cruell cuſtome, that they vſe in
eating mans fleſh, yea and that of the neereſt kinſefolkes
they haue : This countrey towards the ſea on the *Weſt,*
bordereth vpon the people of *Ambus:* and towardes
the *North,* vpon other nations of *Africa,* and the wilder-
nes of *Nubia:* and towardes the *Eaſt,* vpon the ſeconde
great Lake, from whence the Riuer of *Congo* ſpringeth, in
that parte which is called *Anzicana:* and from the kingdome of *Congo,* it is diuided by the Riuer *Zaire,* wherein there are many Iſlandes (as before is tolde you) ſcat-
tered from the lake downewardes, & ſome of them belonging to the dominion of the *Anzigues,* by which Riuer alſo they do trafficke with the people of *Congo.*

Sanders.

In this kingdome of the *Anzigues* there are many
Mines of *Copper,* and great quantitie of *Sanders* both
redde and graie: the red is called *Tauilla,* and the graie
(which is the better eſteemed) is called *Chicongo,*
whereof they make a poulder of a verie ſweet ſmell, and
diuerſe medicines. They do alſo mingle it with the
oyle of *Palme* tree, and ſo annoynting all their bodyes
ouer withall, they preſerue themſelues in health. But
the Portingalles vſe it being tempered with Vinegar,
                                                    which

which they lay vpon their pulfes, & fo heale the French
Pockes, which they call in that language *Chitangas.*

Some doe affirme, that this gray *Sanders* is the very
Lignum Aquilæ, that groweth in *India :* and *Signor Odoardo* affirmed, that the Portingals haue proued it for the
heade ake, by laying it on the coales, and taking the
fmoake of it. The pith and innermoft parte of the tree
is the beft, but the vtter parte is of no eftimation.

They make great ftore of linnen of the *Palme* tree,
born of fundry fortes and coloures, and much cloth of
filke, whereof we will difcourfe more hereafter. The
people are fubiect to a king, that hath other princes vnder him: they are very actiue and warlike :   They are
ready to take armes, and doo fight on foote. Their weapons are different from the weapons of all other people
rounde about them: for their bowes are fmall and fhort,
made of wood, and wrapped about with ferpents skins
of diuers colours, and fo fmoothly wrought, that you
woulde thinke them to be all one with the wood. And
this they doo, both to make the bowe ftronger, and alfo
to holde it the fafter.   Their ftringes are of little woodden twigges, like reedes, not hollow within, but found
and pliable, and very dainty, fuch as the *Caualieros* of
Portingale do carry in their handes to beat their palfries
withall.   They are of an afhe colour, and of a Lion tawney, fomwhat tending to blacke.   They growe in the
Countrey of the *Anzigues,* and alfo in the kingdome of
Bengala, through which the riuer *Ganges* runneth. Their
arrowes are fhort and flender, and of a very hard wood,
and they carry them on their bow hande.   They are fo
quicke in fhooting, that holding xxviij. fhaftes or moe
in their bow-hand, they will fhoote and difcharge them
E 3   all,

all, before the firſt arrow light on the grounde : yea and
ſometimes there haue beene ſeene diuers ſtout archers,
that haue killed birds as they flie in the ayre.

   Other weapons alſo they make, as *Axes* and *Hat-*
chets, which they vſe and frame after a ſtrange manner.
For the handle is ſhorter by the halfe then the iron is,
and at the loweſt end of it there is a pommell, for the fa-
ſter holding of it in the hand, and all couered ouer with
the foreſaid skinne of a ſerpent. In the vppermoſt ende
of it, is the iron very bright and ſhining, faſtned to the
woode with plates of *Copper*, in the manner of two
nailes, as long as the handle: it hath two edges, the one
cutteth like a hatchet, and maketh a wounde after the
faſhion of a halfe Roundell: the other is a hammer.
When they fight with their enemies, or defende themſelues from their arrowes, they are ſo exerciſed with a
wonderful ſpeed and nimbleneſſe to manage their weapons, that whirling them rounde about, as it were in a
circle, they keepe all that compaſſe of the ayre which is
before them, ſo that when the enemie ſhooteth, & the
arrowe beginneth to fall, it lighteth vpon the hatchet,
being ſo ſwiftly and vehemently whirled about, that it
breaketh the force of the arrowe, and ſo it is repulſed :
Then do they hang the *Hatchet* vpõ their ſhoulder, & be
gin to ſhoot themſelues. They haue alſo certaine ſhort
daggers, with ſheathes of the ſerpents skins, made like
kniues with a haft vnto them, which they vſe to weare
a croſſe. Their girdles are of diuers ſorts, but the men of
war haue their girdles of *Elephants* skin, 3.good fingers
broad: & becauſe they are at the firſt 2.fingers thicke, &
very harde to handle handſomly, by the heate of the fire
they bow thẽ round, & ſo with certain buttons tie them
             ouerthwart

ouerthwart about them. The men are very actiue and nimble, and leape vp and downe the mountaines lyke *Goates.* Couragious they are and contemne death: men of great fimplicitie, loyalty and fidelitie, and fuch as the Portingalles doo truft more then any other. In fo much as *Signor Odoardo* was wont to faye, that if thofe *Anzichi* woulde become Chriftians, (being of fo great fidelity, fincerity, loyalty and fimplicity, that they wil offer themfelues to death, for the glory of the world, and to pleafe their Lordes will not fticke to giue their owne flefh to bee deuoured) then woulde they with a farre better harte and courage endure martirdome, for the name of our redeemer *Iefus Chrift,* and would moft honourably maintaine our faith and religion, with their good teftimony, and example againft the *Gentiles.*

The nature of the *Anzicos.*

Moreouer, the faid *Signor Odoardo* did likewife affirme, that there was no conuerfing with them, becaufe they were a fauage and a beaftly people, fauing onely in refpect that they come and trafficke in *Congo,* bringing thether with them flaues both of their owne nation, & alfo out of *Nubia* (whereupon they do border) & linnēcloth (whereof we will tell you hereafter.) & *Elephantes* teeth: in exchange of which chaffare they recarry home with thē *Salt* & thefe *Lumache,* which they vfe in fteed of their money & coine; and another greater kinde of *Lumache,* which come from the Ifle of *S. Thomas,* and which they vfe to weare for brooches to make themfelues fine & galiant withal. Other marchaundifes alfo they carry backe with them which are brought out of *Portingall,* as filks, and linnen, and glaffes, & fuch like.

Their marchandife.

They vfe to circumcife themfelues : and another foolifh cuftome they haue, both men and women, as

E 4   well

well of the nobilitie, as of the commonalty, euen from

their childhood to mark their faces with fundry flafhes made with a knife, as in due place fhal be further fhewed vnto you.

 They keepe a fhambles of mans flefh as they do in thefe countryes for beefe and other victuailes. For their enemies whom they take in the warres, they eate, and alfo their flaues, if they can haue a good market for them, they fell : or if they cannot, then they deliuer them to the butchers to be cut in peeces, and fo folde, to be rofted or boyled. And (that which is a maruellous hiftory to report) fome of them being weary of their liues, and fome of them euen for valour of courage, and to fhew themfelues ftout and venturous, thinking it to be a great honour vnto them, if they runne into voluntary death, thereby to fhewe that they haue a fpeciall contempt of this life, will offer themfelues to the butchery, as faithfull fubiectes to their Princes, for whofe fakes, that they may feeme defirous to doe them notable feruice, they do not onely deliuer themfelues to be deuoured by them, but alfo their flaues, when they are fat and well fed, they doe kill and eate them. True it is that many nations there are, that feede vpon mans flefh as in the eaft *Indies,* and in *Brefill,* and in other places :

but that is onely the flefh of their aduerfaries and enemies, but to eat the flefh of their owne frendes and fubiectes and kinfefolkes, it is without all example in any place of the worlde, fauing onely in this nation of the *Anzichi.*

 The ordinary apparel of thefe people is thus: The cómon fort go naked from the girdle vpwards, & without any thing vpon their heades, hauing their hayre truffed
vp and

vp and curled. The noble men are apparelled in filkes
and other cloath, and weare vpon their heades blewe
and red, and blacke colours, and hattes and hoodes of
Portingale *Veluet* , and other kindes of cappes vfuall in
that countrey.   And indeede they are all defirous to
haue their apparell handfome and neat as their hability
will fuffer them.   The women are all couered from top
to toe, after the common manner of *Africa*. The poorer
fort of them doe girde themfelues clofe from the girdle
downewards. The noble women and fuch as are of
wealth, do weare certaine mantelles, which they caft
ouer their heades, but keepe their faces open and at libertie: & fhooes they haue on their feet, but the poore
go barefoote. They go very quicke and lightfome :
Their ftature is comely, and their conditions fayre and
commendable.

    Their language is altogether different from the lan- *Their lan-*
guage of *Congo*, and yet the *Anzichi* will learne the lan- *guage.*
guage of *Congo*, very foone and eafily, becaufe it is the
plainer tonge: but the people of *Congo* do very hardely
learne the language of the *Anzichi*.   And when I once
demaunded what their religion was, it was tolde mee
they were Gentils, and that was all that I could learne
of them.

Chap. 6.

Of the Eaſt coaſt of the Kingdome of Congo, *and the confines thereof.*

The Eaſterne border of *Congo.*

He Eaſt Coaſt of the kingdome of *Congo*, beginneth (as we haue tolde you) at the meeting of the Riuer *Vumba*, and the Riuer of *Zaire*; and ſo with a line drawen towardes the South in equall diſtance from the Riuer *Nilus*, which lyeth on the left hande, it taketh vp a great mountaine which is very high, & not inhabited in the toppes thereof, called the mountaine

The mountaine of *Chry-ſtall.*
The mountaines of the *Sunne.*

of *Chriſtal*, becauſe there is in it great quantity of *Chriſtal* both of the mountaine and of the cliffe, and of all ſorts. And then paſſing on further includeth the hilles that are called *Sierras de Sol*, that is to ſay, the hilles of the *Sunne*, becauſe they are exceeding high. And yet it neuer ſnoweth vpon them, neyther doe they beare any thing, but are very bare and without any trees at all : On the

The mountains of *Sal-Nitrum.*

leaft hand there ariſe other hils, called the hilles of *Sal-Nitrum*, becauſe there is in thē great ſtore of that *Mineral*. And ſo cutting ouer the riuer *Berbela*, that commeth **out**

out of the firſt Lake, there endeth the ancient bound of the kingdome of *Congo* on the Eaſt.

Thus then the eaſt coaſt of this kingdome is deriued from the meeting of the two foreſaid riuers *Vumba* and *Zaire*, vntill you come to the lake *Achelunda*, and to the Countrey of *Malemba*; contayning the ſpace of ſixe hundred miles. From this lyne, which is drawen in the eaſterne coaſt of *Congo* to the riuer *Nilus*, and to the two Lakes (whereof mention ſhalbe made in conuenient place) there is the ſpace of 150. miles of ground wel inhabited, and good ſtore of hils, which do yeeld ſundry mettalles, with much linnen, and cloth of the *Palme* tree.

And ſeeing wee are now come to this point of this diſcourſe, it will be very neceſſary to declare vnto you the maruellous arte which the people of this countrey, and other places thereabouts do vſe in making cloathes of ſundry ſortes, as *Veluets* ſhorne and vnſhorne, cloth of *Tiſſue*, *Sattens*, *Taffata*, *Damaskes*, *Sarcenettes* and ſuch like, not of any ſilken ſtuffe, (for they haue no knowledge of the Silkewormes at all, although ſome of their apparell bee made of ſilke that is brought thether from our Countreys.) But they weaue their cloathes aforenamed of the leaues of *Palme* trees, which trees they alwayes keepe vnder and lowe to the grounde, euery yeare cutting them, and watering them, to the ende they may grow ſmal and tender againſt the new ſpring. Out of theſe leaues being cleanſed & purged after their manner they drawe forth their threedes, which are all very fine and dainty, and all of one euenneſſe, ſauing that thoſe which are longeſt, are beſt eſteemed. For of thoſe they weaue their greateſt peeces. Theſe ſtuffes

F 2   they

they worke of diuers fashions, as some with a nappe vpon them like *Veluet* on both sides, and other cloath called *Damaskes*, braunched with leaues, and such other
thinges; & the *Broccati*, which are called *High* and *Lowe*,
and are farre more precious then ours are. This kinde
of cloath no man may weare but the king, and such as it
pleaseth him. The greatest peeces are of these *Broccati*:
for they contayne in length fower and fiue spannes,
and in breadth, three and foure spannes, and are called
Incorimhas, by the name of the countrey where it groweth, which is about the Riuer *Vumba*. The *Veluettes* are
called *Enzachas* of the same bignesse, and the *Damaskes*
Insulas, and the *Rasi Maricas*, and the *Zendadi Tangas*, &
the *Ormesini Engombos*. Of the lighter sort of these stuffes
they haue greater peeces which are wrought by the *An-*
zichi, and are sixe spannes long, and fiue spannes
broade, wherewith euery man may apparell himselfe
according to his habilitie. Besides that, they are very
thicke and sounde to keepe out the water, and yet very
light to weare. The Portingalles haue lately begun to
vse them for tents and boothes, which do maruellously
resist both water and winde.

The Riuer
Nilus.   This coast then shutteth vp the kingdome of *Congo*,
which lyeth *Westwarde* of it : and from this Coast with
a line of equall distance somwhat more towardes the
East runneth the riuer *Nilus*, about 150. miles, contayning within it a Countrey that aboundeth with all the
commodities aboue rehearsed, possessed by sundrye
Lordes, some subiect to *Prete Gianni*, and some to the
mighty King *Moënemugi*.   In all which Countrey
there was nothing worth the noting, sauing that from
Nilus towards the *West*, the people do trafficke with the
king-

kingdome of *Congo*, and the riuers of that fea: and from thence towardes the Eaſt they goe through the kingdomes of *Moenemugi*, euen to the ſea of *Mombaza* and *Mozambiche*.

Chap. 7.

Of the confines of the kingdome of Congo *towardes the South.*

His Eaſterne Coaſt (as it is before ſet downe) endeth in the mountain called *Serras de Plata*, that is the mountaines of ſiluer, and there beginneth the fourth and laſt border of the kingdome of *Congo*, towardes the South, that is to ſay, from the foreſaide mountaine to the Bay of *Cowes* on the Weſt, contayning in length the ſpace of foure hundred & fifty miles. And this Southerne line doth parte the kingdome of *Angola* in the middle, and leaueth on the left hand of it, the foreſaide mountaines of *Siluer*, and further beyond them towardes the South the Kingdome of *Matama*, which is a great kingdome, very mighty, and abſolute of it ſelfe, and ſometimes in amity, and ſometimes at vtter enmitie with the kingdome of *Angola*.

The king of *Matama* is in religion a Gentile, and his

The Southern Coaſt.
The mountain of *Siluer*.

The K. of *Matama*.

F 4 king-

kingdome ſtretcheth towardes the *South* to the riuer *Brauagal*, and neere to the mountains commonly called the *Mountaynes of the Moone*, and towardes the eaſt bordereth on the *Weſterne* bankes of the riuer *Bagamidri*, and ſo croſſeth ouer the riuer *Coari*.

This countrey aboundeth in vaultes of *Chriſtall* and other mettalles, and all manner of victuaile, and good ayre. And although the people thereof, & their neighbour borderers do trafficke together : Yet the King of *Matama*, and the king of *Angola* doo oftentimes warre one againſt the other, as we told you before : And this riuer *Bagamidri* diuideth the kingdome of *Matapa* from the kingdome of *Monomata*, which is towardes the *Eaſt*, and whereof *Iohn de Barros* doth moſt largely diſcourſe in the firſt Chapter of his tenth booke.

Towardes the ſea coaſt there are diuers Lordes, that take vpon them the title of kinges: but indeed they are of very baſe and ſlender eſtate : Neyther are there any portes or hauens of any account or name in the riuers there. And nowe foraſmuch as wee haue oftentimes made mention of the kingdome of *Angola* , this will be a very conuenient place for vs to intreate thereof : becauſe it hath beene heretofore ſaide , that the king of *Angola*, being in times paſt but a Gouernour or Deputy vnder the king of *Congo*, although ſince that tyme he is become a good Chriſtian, yet hath he made himſelfe a free and an abſolute Prince, and vſurped all that quarter to his owne iuriſdiction, which before hee had in regiment and gouernement vnder another. And ſo afterwards in time conquered other countries thereabouts, inſomuch as he is now growen to bee a great Prince, & a rich, and in power little inferiour to the king of *Congo* himſelfe

himfelfe, and therefore eyther payeth tribute, or refu-
feth to pay tribute vnto him, euen at his owne good
pleafure.

It came to paffe, that *Don Giouanni* the fecond, being
king of *Portingall,* planted the chriftian religion in the
Kingdome of *Congo,* and thereupon the king of *Congo*
became a Chriftian. After which time the Lorde of
Angola was alwaies in amitie, and (as it were) a vaffall
of the forenamed King of *Congo,* and the people of both
countries did trafficke together one with another, and
the Lord of *Angola* did euery yeare fende fome prefents
to the king of *Congo.* And by licence from the King of
Congo there was a great trade betweene the Portingalles
and the people of *Angola* at the hauen of *Loanda,*
where they bought flaues and chaunged them for o-
ther marchaundifes, and fo tranfported all into the
Ifle of Sainte *Thomas.* Whereby it came to paffe,
that the trafficke was heere vnited with the trafficke
of *S. Thomas:* fo that the fhippes did vfe firft to arriue
at that Iflande, and then afterwarde paffed ouer to *Loan-*
da. And when this trade began in proceffe of time to
increafe, they difpatched their fhippes from *Lisbone* to
Angola of theinfelues, and fent with them a Gouernour
called *Paulo Diaz* of *Nouais,* to whome this bufines did
(as it were) of right appertaine, in regarde of the good
defertes of his auncefters, who firft difcouered this trafficke. To this *Paulo Diaz* did *Don Sebaftiano* King of
Portingale graunt leaue and authority to conquere, for
the fpace of xxxiij. leagues vpwardes along the coaft,
beginning at the Riuer *Coanza* towards the *South,* and
within the iande alfo, whatfoeuer hee coulde get, towardes all his charges for him and his heyres. With

John the fe-
cond, K. of
Portingall, firft
brought chri-
ftianity into
Congo.

Paulo Diaz
the firft difco-
uerer of this
trafficke.

Don Sebaftian
K. of *Portin-*
gall.

G him

him there went many other fhippes that opened and found out a great trade with *Angola*, which notwith-ftanding was directed to the forefaide hauen of *Loanda* where the faide fhippes did ftill difcharge themfelues.

Paulo Diaz buildeth a houfe in *Anzelle*

And fo by little & little he entred into the firme land, & made himfelfe a houfe in a certain village called *Anzelle* within a mile neer to the riuer *Coanza*, becaufe it was the more commodious & nigher to the trafficke of *Angola*.

When the trade here beganne thus to increafe, and marchaundifes were freely caried by the Portingales, &

The authour calleth him *Lord*, becaufe he was then but a petty king.

the people of *Congo* to *Cabazo* a place belonging to the Lorde of *Angola*, and diftant from the fea, 150. miles, there to fell and barter them, it pleafed his Lordfhip to giue out order, that all the Marchants fhould be flaine, and their goods confifcated, alleadging for his defence, that they were come thether as fpies, and to take pof-feffion of his eftate: but in truth it is thought that hee did it onely to gaine all that wealth to himfelfe, confi-dering that it was a people that did not deale in the ha-bite of warriours, but after the manner of Marchants. And this fell out in the fame yeare, that the King *Don Sebaftiano* was difcomfited in *Barbarie*.

When *Paulo Diaz* vnderftoode of this courfe, he put

Paulo Diaz in armes a-gainft the K of *Angola*.

himfelfe in armes againft the King of *Angola*, and with fuch a troupe of Portingals as he could gather together that were to bee founde in that countrey, and with two Gallies and other veffels, which he kept in the riuer *Coanza*, he went forwarde on both fides of the riuer con-quering, and by force fubdued many Lords, and made them his frendes and fubiectes. But the king of *Angola* perceyuing that his vaffalles had yeelded to the obedi-ence of *Paulo Diaz*, and that with all profperous fuc-cefle

ceffe he had gayned much land vpon him, he affembled
a great army to go againft him, and fo vtterly to deftroy
him. Whereupon *Paulo Diaz* requefted the King of
Congo that he woulde fuccour him with fome helpe to
defende himfelfe withall, who prefently fent vnto him
for aid an army of 60 thoufand men, vnder the conduct
of his cofin *Don Sebaftiano Manibamba*, and another captayne with 120. Portingale fouldiers, that were in thofe
countryes, and all of his owne pay for the atchieuing of
this enterprife. This army was to ioyne with *Paulo Diaz*, and fo altogether to warre againft the King of *Angola*: but arriuing at the fhoare, where they were to paffe
ouer the riuer *Bengo*, within 12. miles of *Loāda*, & where
they fhoulde haue met with many barkes to carry the
Campe to the other fhore, partly becaufe the faid barks
had flacked their cōming, & partly becaufe much time
wold haue been fpent in tranfporting fo many men, the
whole armie tooke their way quite ouer the riuer, and
fo going on forwardes they met with the people of the
King of *Angola*, that were ready to ftoppe the fouldiers
of *Congo*, from entering vpon their Countrey.

The military order of the *Mociconghi* (for by that
terme we do call the naturall borne people of the kingdome of *Congo*, as wee call the *Spaniardes* thofe that
are naturally borne in *Spaine*) and the military order of
the people of *Angola*, is almoft all one: For both of them
doo vfually fight on foote, and diuide their armie into
feuerall troupes, fitting themfelues according to the fituation of the field where they doo incampe, & aduan-
cing their enfignes and banners in fuch fort as before is
remembred.

The remoues of their armie are guided and directed

by

*P. Diaz, de-
mandeth fuc-
cour of the K.
of Congo.*

*The millitary
order of the
people of
Congo.*

by certaine feuerall foundes and noyfes, that pro-

How the foul-
diers doo vn-
derftand the
pleafure of
their Generall.
ceede from the *Captayne Generall,* who goeth into the
middeft of the *Armie,* and there fignifieth what is to bee
put in execution : that is to fay, eyther that they fhall
ioyne battell, or els retyre, or put on forward, or turne
to the right hand, and to the leaft hand, or to performe
any other warlick action. For by thefe feueral founds diftinctly deliuered frõ one to another they doe all vnderftande the commandementes of their *Captayne,* as we
heere among vs doo vnderftande the pleafure of our
Generall by the fundrie ftroakes of the *Drumme,* and the

Three kinds
of inftru-
ments vfed in
their wars.
1
Captaines foundes of the *Trompet.*

Three principall foundes they haue which they vfe
in warre: One which is vttered aloude, by great *Rattles*
faftned in certaine woodden cafes, hollowed out of a
tree, and couered with leather, which they ftrike with
2
certaine little handles of *Iuory.* Another is made by a
certaine kinde of inftrument, fafhioned like a *Pyramis*
turned vpwarde : for the lower ende of it is fharpe and
endeth as it were in a point, and the vpper end waxeth
broader & broader like the bottom of a *Triangle,* in fuch
fort that beneath they are narrow & like an *Angle,* & a-
boue they are large and wide. This inftrument is made
of certayne thinne plates of iron, which are hollowe
and empty within, and very like to a bell turned vp fide
downe. They make them ring, by ftriking them with
woodden wandes: and oftentimes they do alfo cracke
them, to the ende that the found fhould be more harfh,
horrible, and warlicke : The thirde inftrument is
3
framed of *Elephants* teeth, fome great, and fome fmall,
hollowe within, and blowen at a certaine hole which
they make on the fide of it, in manner of the *Fife,* and

not

not aloft like the *Pipe*. Thefe are tempered by them in
fuch fort that they yeelde as warlicke and harmonious
muficke as the *Cornet* doth, and fo pleafant and iocund
a noyfe, that it moueth and ftirreth vp their courages,&
maketh them not to care for any daunger whatfoeuer.
Now of thefe three feueral forts of warlick inftruments,
there are fome bigger and fome leffe. For the *Captayne*
Generall carrieth alwaies with him the greater fort, to
the ende that by them he may giue fignification to the
whole *Campe* what they fhall doo.   The particular
bandes and troupes of the armie haue in like manner
their fmaller fort, and euery *Captayne* in his feuerall regiment hath alfo one of the fmalleft, which they ftrike
with their handes. Whereupon it falleth out, that when
they heare the founde of the generall *Rattle*, or *Cornet*,
or the other thirde kinde of inftrument, euery part of
the army doth prefently anfwere in the fame note, figni-
fying thereby that they haue wel vnderftood the good
pleafure of the *Captaine*, and fo confequently the *vnder*
Captaines do the like. Neyther do they onely vfe thefe
inftruments and founds vniuerfally, but alfo when they
are in fight and in fkirmifh, the valiant and couragious
fouldiers go before the reft, & with this kinde of belles,
which they ftrike with their woodden wandes, they
dance, & encourage their fellows, & by the note do fignifie vnto them in what danger they are, and what weapons they haue met withall.

The militarie apparell of the better fort, and of the
Lords of the *Moci-Conghi* is this. On their heades they
carry a cappe, which is garnifhed with fundry plumes
of the feathers of the *Eaftruche*, of the *Peacocke*, of the
Cocke, and of other kindes of birdes, which make them

to feeme men of greater ftature then they are, and terrible to looke vpon. From the girdle vpwards they are all naked, and haue hanging about them from their necks, both on the right fide and on the leaft, euen as lowe as to both their flanks, certaine chaines of iron, with rings vpon them as bigge as a mans little finger, which they vfe for a certaine military pompe & brauery. From the girdle downewardes they haue breeches of linnen, or fendale, which are couered with cloath, and reach downe to their heeles, but then they are folded againe vpwardes and tucked vnder their girdle. Vpon their girdle, which (as we tolde you) is made with exquifite and curious worke, they do fasten certaine belles, very like to the inftruments that are before named, which in moouing of themfelues and in fighting with their enemies, do ring & make a noife, & ad courage vnto them, while they are in combate with their aduerfaries. Vpon their legges they haue likewife their buskins after

Their weapōs. the Portingall fafhion. Their armour we haue already declared, that is to fay, bowe and arrowes, fworde, dagger and Target: but yet with this caueat, that whofoeuer weareth a bowe, he weareth alfo a dagger, but no target: for thofe two weapons may not be worne together, but fword & target they may lawfully weare both at once.

The Military apparell of the tacaner fort. The common fouldiers go all naked from the girdle-ftead vpwardes, and haue the reft of their bodies armed with bowe and arrowes and daggers. Thefe are they that do firft offer the skirmifh, going out before the reft of the armie, as it were feuerally and difperfedly prouoking to fight, and receyuing the fhot from a farre of, they turne and winde this way and that way, and

doo

doo nimbly leape from one fide to another, to the ende
they may auoide the lighting of their enemies arrowes.
Befides thefe there are alfo certaine quicke and gallant
young men that runne out before the reft, which with
the ringing of their bels (as afore is fayde) are as it were
comforters of their fellows, and when they haue fought
fo much, that the Captaine thinketh them to bee euen
weary, then doth he call them backe with the founde of
one of thofe inftruments aboue mentioned: fo that perceyuing the medley to waxe hote, they turne about and
retyre themfelues back againe, & others fucceed in their
places, which courfe is ftill obferued and kept vntill fuch
time, as both the armies do indeed ioyne all their maine
forces together, and fo fight it out.

　In the place aboue defcribed, there were fundry en- The iffue of this battell.
counters on the one fide and on the other. And in the
firft battels the people of *Congo* remayned conquerours:
but afterwards, when they had diuers times fought together with great loffe on both fides, and victuailes began nowe to faile, and confequently men waxed ficke
and died, the Campe of the king of *Congo* was diffolued,
and euery man returned to his owne home.

　In this meane while *Paulo Diaz*, though he coulde P. Diaz at Luiola.
not ioyne his forces with the Armie of his frendes that
came to fuccour him, yet fet himfelfe forwardes, and
paffing ouer the riuer ftayed at *Luiola*, becaufe it was a
place very ftrong & fit to refift the King of *Angola*. The
fituation of *Luiola* is this: The two riuers *Coanza* and
Luiola do ioyne together about 105. miles from the fea
fhore, and a little aboue the faid ioyning together, thefe
Riuers doe feauer themfelues for the fpace of an Arcu-
bufe fhotte, fo that they make as it were an Iflande be-
　　　　　G 4　　　　　　　　tweene

tweene them : In which Iſlande at the meeting of the
two riuers there riſeth a hill, which *Paulo Diaz* ſurpriſed
and fortified for his better ſafety. And whereas in times
paſt there was neuer any habitation there, nowe at this
preſent it is growen to be a prety conntrey inhabited by
the *Portingalles*.

    From this place thus ſurpriſed by *Paulo Diaz*, and
called *Luiola*, you may ſaile along the riuer with certain
ſmall veſſelles, euen to the ſea, and goe by lande without any daunger for the ſpace of one hundred and fiue

The hilles of
Cabambe.

miles. Neere therevnto are the hilles that are called the
hilles of *Cabambe*, producing infinite ſtore of ſiluer :
which the ſaide *Diaz* doth euery day by little and little
endeauour to conquere. And theſe hils are the graund
quarrell betweene him and the people of *Angola*. For
knowing that the *Portingalles* doe eſteeme greatly of
theſe hilles, in regarde of the ſiluer pits which are there
in great aboundance, they doe vſe all the force and skill
they can to keepe the *Portingalles* from them. They
fight alſo with them in diuers other places: for the Portingalles paſſing ouer the riuer *Coanza* doe continually
make inroades into the countries that are ſubiect to the
king of *Angola*.

The weapons
of the people
of *Angola*.

    The weapons of theſe peoples, are bowes ſixe hand-
fulles long, with ſtringes made of the barkes of trees: &
arrowes of woode, leſſe then a mans little finger, and
ſixe handefuls long. They haue iron heads made like a
hooke, and feathers of birdes in the toppes of them: and
of theſe arrowes they vſe to carry to the number of ſixe
or ſeauen vpon their bow hand, without any quiuer at
all. Their daggers are faſhioned with a haft after the
manner of a knife, which they weare at their girdle, on
                             their

their left fide, and hold them aloft in their hands, when
they fight with them. By their *Militarie* actions and proceedinges you may obferue their great fkill and good
order in matter of warre. For in diuers battels that were
betweene them and the *Portingalles*, it was plainly feene
how they coulde choofe their aduantages againft their
enemies, as by affaulting them in the night time, and
in rayny weather, to the ende that their arcubufes and
guns fhold not take fire,& alfo by diuiding their forces
into many troups, to trouble them the more. The king
doth not vfe to go to the warre in his owne perfon, but
fendeth his *Captains* in his fteed. The people are alfo accuftomed to flie & run away incontinently, as foone as
they fee their Captaine flaine, neyther can they be per-
fwaded to ftay by any reafon or argument, but prefently yeelde vp the fielde. They are all footemen, neyther
haue they any horfes at all. And therefore the Captaines if they will not go on foote, caufe themfelues to
be carried on the fhoulders of their flaues, after one of
the three manners, which wee will fhew vnto you hereafter. This nation goeth out to warre in number almoft
infinite, and very confufedly : they leaue no man at
home that is fit to carry a weapon: they make no prepa-
ration of victuailes neceffary for the Campe: but fuch
as perhaps haue any, conuey it with them vpon the fhol-
ders of their feruantes, and yet they haue fundry fortes
of creatures that might bee managed, and ferue their
turnes to drawe and to carry as in the feconde part of
this Treatife fhalbe defcribed vnto you. And thereupon it falleth out, that when they come into any country
with their whole armie, all their foode is quickly quite
confumed, & then hauing nothing leaft to feede vpon,

H   they

they diſſolue their hoaſt euen in the greateſt neceſſity
of proſecuting their enterpriſe, and ſo are inforced by
hunger to returne into their owne countries.

They are greatly giuen to *Diuination* by birdes : If

They are giuē to diuination by birdes. a bird chaunce to flie on their leaft hand, or crie in ſuch
manner, as thoſe which make profeſſion to vnderſtand
the ſame, doe ſay that it fore-ſheweth ill lucke and ad-
uerſity, or that they may go no further forwardes, they
will preſently turne backe and repayre home : which
cuſtome was alſo in the old time obſerued by the ancient *Romanes*, and likewiſe at this day by ſundry other
Pagans.

Why ſo ſmall a number, as Paulo Diaz had with him, was able to reſiſt ſo huge an armie of the K. of Angola. Now if it ſhall ſeeme ſtraunge to any man, that ſo
few *Portingall* ſouldiours as *Paulo Diaz* retayneth there
with him, and others of the *Portingall* nation, which
traffick into the Realme, & relieue him with ſuccours,
being in number but three hundred at the moſt, accounting their ſlaues, and alſo the *Malcontentes*, the
rebelles and fugitiues of *Angola* which dayly reſort yn-
to him, & amount not in al to the quantity of xv. thouſand men, ſhould be able to make ſo gallant a reſiſtance
againſt that innumerable rabble of *Negroes*, being ſubiect to the king of *Angola*, which are gathered there together (as it is ſaid) to the number of a Million of ſoules.
I aunſwere, that great reaſon may bee alleadged for the
ſame. For the armie of the *Negroes* is all naked, and vtterly deſtitute of all prouiſion and furniture for armour
of defence: And as for their weapons of offence, they
conſiſt onely but of bowes and daggers (as I told you.)
But our fewe *Portingalles* that are there, are well lap-
ped in certaine iackets that are ſtuffed and baſted with
bombaſt, and ſtitched and quilted very ſoundly, which
keepe

keepe their armes very fafe, and their bodies downewardes as lowe as their knees: Their heades alfo are armed with cappes made of the fame ftuffe, which doo
refift the fhot of the arrow and the ftroke of the dagger:
Befides that, they are girt with longe fwords,and fome
horfemen there are among them that carry fpeares for
their weapons. Now you muft vnderftande that one
man on horfebacke, is of more worth then a hundred
Negroes, becaufe the horfemen do affray them greatly:
& efpecially of thofe that do difcharge guns and peeces of artillarie againft them, they doo ftande continually in an extreame bodily feare. So that thefe few being well armed,and cunningly and artificially ordered,
muft needes ouercome the other, though they be very
many in number.

This kingdome of *Angola*, is full of people beyonde
all credite: For euery man taketh as many wiues as hee
lifteth, and fo they multiply infinitely: But they doe
not vfe fo to do in the kingdome of *Congo*, which liueth
after the manner of the *Chriftians*. And fo *Signor Odoardo* did affirme and belieue, that the kingdome of *Angola* had a Million of fighting men,by reafon that euery
man taking to him as many wiues as he woulde, begot
many children, and likewife becaufe euery man doeth
willingly go to the warres in the feruice of his Prince.

This kingdome alfo is very rich in mines of *Siluer*, &
moft excellent *Copper*, and for other kindes of mettall
there is more in this kingdome then in any other countrey of the world whatfoeuer. Fruitfull it is in all manner of foode, and fundry fortes of cattell, and fpecially
for great heards of *Kine*. True it is, that this people do
loue *Dogs* flefh better then any other meate: & for that

The Kingdom of Angola very populous.

The commo-dities of Angola.

H 2　　　that

that purpose they feede and fatten them, and then kill them, and sell them in their open shambles. It is con-

A *Dogge* solde for 220. duc- cates, stantly affirmed, that a great dogge accustomed to the *Bull* was solde by exchaunge for xxij. slaues, which af- ter the rate of x. *Duckates* a poll, were worth in all 220. *Duccates*: in so high a price and account do they holde that Creature.

The moneyes that are vsed in *Angola*, are much dif-
The money of *Angola*, ferent from the *Lumache* of *Congo* : for they of *Angola* do vse beades of glasse, such as are made in *Venice* as big as a Nut, and some of lesser quantity, and of diuers and sundry colours and fashions. These doe the people of *Angola* make, not onely to vse them for money, but also for an ornament of their men and women, to weare a- bout their neckes and their armes, and are called in their tongue *Anzolos*: but when they are threeded vpon a stringe lyke a payre of Beades, they call them *Mizanga.*

The Religion of *Angola*. The King of *Angola* is by religion a Gentile, and worshippeth *Idoles*, and so doo all the people in his kingdome. It is true, that hee hath greatly desired to become a Christian, after the example of the King of *Congo.* But because there hath not beene as yet any pos- sibility to sende *Priestes* vnto him, that might illuminate and instruct him, he remayneth still in darkenes. The foresaide *Signor Odoardo* tolde mee that in his time the king of *Angola* sent an Ambassadour to the King of *Con- go*, requesting that he would sende him some religious persons to inform him in the Christian religiō. but the King of *Congo* had none there that hee coulde spare, & therefore coulde sende him none. At this day, both these kinges doo trafficke together, and are in amity

one

one with another, the king of *Angola* hauing now clee-
red and difcharged himfelfe for the iniuries & flaughters that were committed vpon thofe of *Congo*, and vpon the Portingalles at *Cabazo.*

　　The language of the people of *Angola* is all one with
the language of the people of *Congo*, becaufe (as wee
told you before) they are both but one kingdome. Onely the difference betweene them is, as commonly it is
betweene two nations that border one vpon another,
as for example betweene the *Portingalles* and the *Cafti-*
lians, or rather betweene the *Venetians* and the *Calabri-*
ans, who pronouncing their wordes in a diuers manner, and vttering them in feuerall fortes, although it be
all one fpeech, yet do they very hardly vnderftand one
another.

　　Wee haue fignified vnto you heretofore, that the
Bay of *Cowes* doth diuide the kingdome of *Angola* in
the middeft, and hitherto wee haue treated but of the
one halfe thereof: Now we will defcribe vnto you the
feconde parte of it, which lyeth from the faid Bay of
Cowes towardes the *South.*　From this Bay then, to the
black Cape called *Capo Negro*, by the coaft of the *Ocean*
they doe reckon two hundred & twenty miles of fuch
country and foile as the former is, and poffeffed by many Lordes that are fubiect to the king of *Angola.* From
Capo Negro there runneth a line towardes the *Eaft*,
through the middeft of the Mountaynes, that are called
Monti Freddi, that is to fay, the *Cold Mountaines*: which
alfo in fome certaine parts of them, that are higher then
the reft, towardes the *Equinoctiall* are tearmed by the
Portingalles *Monti Neuofi*, or *Snowie Mountaines*, and
fo endeth at the rootes of other Mountaynes that are

　　　　　　　　　　called

called the *Mountaines* of *Chryſtall*. (Out of theſe *Snowie*

Mountains do ſpring the waters of the *Lake Dumbea Zoc-
che.*) This foreſaid line from the mountaine of *Chriſtall*
draweth onwardes towardes the *North* through the
Mountaines of *Siluer*, till you come to *Malemba*, where
wee tolde you the kingdome of *Congo* was diuided, and
parted the Riuer of *Coari* in the middeſt. And this is
the Countrey poſſeſſed by the King of *Angola*, whereof I haue no more to ſay, then is already ſet downe, neither of the qualities of his perſon, nor of his Court.

Chap. 8.

Of the circuite of the Kingdome of Congo *poſſeſſed by the
King that nowe is, according to the foure borders aboue
deſcribed.*

Eginning therefore at the Riuer *Coanza*, and drawing towardes the
Equinoctiall 375. miles, you ſhal find
the Riuer that they call *Las Barreras
Vermellias*, or the *Redde Pittes*, which
are indeed the ragged ruines of certaine rockes worne by the ſea, and
when they fall downe doo ſhew themſelues to be of a
redde colour. From thence by a direct line vpon the

North, that which the King poſſeſſeth is 450. miles.

                                                    And

And thē the said line diuiding it self towards the South *The East 500,*
passeth by the hilles of *Christall* (not those that we told
you before did belong to *Angola,* but others that
are called by the same name) and so by the mountains of *Salnitro,* trauersing the Riuer *Verbela* at the roots
of the Mountaines of *Siluer* it endeth at the Lake *A-* *The South.*
quelunda, which is the space of 500. miles. The fourth *360.*
line runneth along the Riuer *Coanza,* which issueth out
of the said Lake & contayneth 360. miles. So that the
whole Realme now possessed by *Don Aluaro* the king of *The kingdom*
Congo is in compasse 1685. miles. But the breadth there- *of Congo con-*
tayneth in cō-
of beginneth at the mouth of the Riuer *Zaire,* where *passe, 1685.*
the point is, which in the Portingal speech is called *Pa-* *miles.*
draon, and so cutting the kingdome of *Congo* in the middle, and crossing ouer the mountaines of the *Sunne,* and
the mountaines of *Christall,* there it endeth, containing *In breadth*
the space of 6_0. miles, & within 150. miles, neere to the *600. miles.*
Riuer *Nilus.* Very true it is indeed, that in ancient time
the predecessors of this Prince did raigne ouer many
other countreyes thereaboutes, which in processe of
time they haue lost : and although they bee now in
the gouernement of others, yet doo the Kings of *Con-* *The title or*
go retaine still to this day the titles of those regions, as *stile of the*
King of Congo
for example, *Don Aluaro,* king of *Congo,* and of *Abundos,*
and of *Matama,* and of *Quizama,* and of *Angola,* and of
Cacongo, and of the seauen kingdomes of *Congere Amo-*
laza, and of the *Pangelungos,* and Lorde of the Riuer
Zaire, and of the *Anziquos,* and *Anziquana,* and of *Lo-*
ango.

H 4   Chap.

Chap. 9.

The sixe Prouinces of the kingdome of Congo, *and
first of the Prouince of* Bamba.

The first pro-uince is Bam-ba, *and the de-scription of it.* Sebastian *chief Gouernour of* Bamba, *and those that rule vnder him.*

His kingdome is diuided into sixe Prouinces, that is to say, *Bamba, Songo, Sundi, Pango, Batta* & *Pemba.* The Prouince of *Bamba,* (which is the greatest and the richest) is gouerned by *Don Sebastian Mani Bamba,* cosin to the King *Don Aluaro* last deceased, and it is situated vpon the sea coast, from the riuer *Ambrize,* vntill you come to the riuer *Coanza* towardes the *South.* This *Don Sebastian* hath vnder his dominion many Princes and Lordes, and the names of the greatest of them are these, *Don Antonio Mani-Bamba,* who is Lieuetenant and brother to *Don Sebastian,* and *Mani-Lemba* another, and *Mani-Dandi,* & *Mani-Bengo,* and *Mani-Loanda,* who is gouernour of the Island of *Loanda,* and *Mani-Corimba,* and *Mani-Coanza,* and *Mani-Cazzanzi.* All these doo gouerne all the sea coast but within lande, for that parte which belongeth to *Angola,* there are another people called the *Ambundos,* who dwelling on the borders of *Angola* are subiect

to

to the saide *Mani-Bamba*, and they are thefe, *Angazi*, *Chinghengo*, *Motollo*, *Chabonda*, and many others of bafer condition.

Note, that this worde *Mani* fignifieth a Prince or a Lord, and the reft of the word is the name of the coun- *Mani* what it trey and Lordefhippe, where the Lorde ruleth. As for fignifieth. example, *Mani-Bamba* fignifieth the Lord of the countrey of *Bamba*, & *Mani-Corimba* the Lorde of the countrey of *Corimba*, which is a parte of *Bamba*, and fo like- The Confines wife of the reft. This Prouince of *Bamba* confineth with of *Bamba*, *Angola*, on the *South*, & vpon the *Eaft* of it towardes the The country Lake *Achelunda* lyeth the country of *Quizama*, which is of *Quizama*, gouerned like a comon wealth, and is diuided among a number of Lordes, who in deed liuing at their owne libertie, doo neyther obey the King of *Congo*, nor the King of *Angola*. And to bee fhort, thefe Lords of *Quizama*, after they had a long time quarrelled with *Paulo Diaz*, yet at laft they became his fubiects, becaufe they woulde auoide the yoake of the King of *Angola*, and by their good aid and affiftance doth *Paulo Diaz* greatly helpe himfelfe againft the faid King of *Angola*.

Nowe the aforefaid Countrey of *Bamba*, (as wee *Bamba* the haue tolde you) is the principall Prouince of all the principall Prouince of Realme of *Congo*, and in deed the very keye, and the all *Congo*. buckler and the fworde, and the defence thereof, and (as it were) the frontier which oppofeth it felfe againft all their enemies. For it refifteth all the reuoltes and rebellions of thofe quarters, and hath very valorous people in it, that are alwaies ready for to fight, fo that they do continually keep their aduerfaries of *Angola* in great awe: and if it happen at any time that their king ftande in neede, they are alwaies at his commaunde to annoy

I   the

the other countries whenfoeuer. When neede requi-
Bamba yeeld- reth, hee may haue in *Campe* foure hundred thoufande
eth for a men of warre, and yet that number is but onely the fixt
need 400000 parte of the whole kingdome, though indeede it be the
men of warre better parte and the ftronger. The principall Citty of
Panza the this Prouince lieth in the plaine which is betweene the
principall Ci- riuer *Loze* and *Ambrize*, and is called *Panza* (which is
ty of Bamba. a common name for euery towne.) There dwelleth
the Lorde of the Prouince, and it is diftant from the fea
a hundred miles. In this *Signorie* alfo doo the hilles be-
Mines of Sil- ginne, where the mines of *Siluer* and other Mettalles
uer and other are founde, and fo ftretch out towardes the kingdome
mettalles. of *Angola*. It is very rich: for vpon the coaft of the fea
there, they haue great ftore of the *Lumache*, which are
vfed for Moneyes ouer all the kingdome of *Congo*: Befides, there is alfo a greater trafficke & Market for flaues,
that are brought out of *Angola*, then in any place els.
For there are yearely bought by the Portingalles aboue
fiue thoufand head of *Negroes*, which afterwardes they
conueigh away with them, and fo fell them into diuers
parts of the worlde.

Valiāt, migh- The people of this Prouince are in armes the moft
tie & ftrong valiant of all the Kingdome of *Conga*. They go armed
men in Baba. like the *Sclauonians*, with long and large fwords, that are
brought them out of *Portingal*. There are among them
very mighty men, that wil cleaue a flaue in the middeft
at one blowe, and cut of the head of a Bull at one ftroke
with one of thofe fwordes. And (that which is
more, and will peraduenture feeme incredible) one of
thefe valiant men did beare vppon his arme a certaine
veffell of wine, which was the fourth parte of a Butte,
and might waigh about 325.pound, vntill it was cleane
emptied

emptied. Moreouer, they do carry bow and arrowes, whereat they are very quicke and nimble, and withall their long Targets made of the *Dants* skin, whereof we told you before, when we made mentió of the *Anzichi*.

The Creatures that are founde in this Prouince, are firft the Elephantes, which doo breed ouer all the kingdome of *Congo*, but principally in the countrey of *Bamba*, becaufe it aboundeth in VVoodes, in paftures and in waters, more then any of the reft, by reafon of the many riuers that runne through it. And therefore the countrey is (as it were) appropriated to nourifhe and breede fuch a kinde of beafte, as is indeede of an vnreafonable bigneffe. For *Signor Odoardo* tolde me, that hee had oftentimes taken the meafure of an *Elephantes* foot in the duft, & one of them was in plain *Diamteer* fower fpannes broade. Whereby if you frame the whole circle of the foote, accordingly you may by proportion finde out the bigneffe of the whole bodie of the beaft. This foot they cal *Malo-Manzao* that is to fay, the *Foot of an Elephant*. And if in *Portingal*, in *Italy*, & in *Germany*, ther haue been feen in our times, any of thefe creatures that were far leffer in refpect of the aforefaid hugenes, you muft vnderftande that they were but young, and brought into thofe countreyes in their tender age, of purpofe to make them tame. But in thefe quarters they fay that the Elephantes doe liue an hundred and fiftie yeares, and that vntill the middle of their age they continue ftill in growing. And to confirme this truth hee added, that he had feene and waighed diuerfe of their teeth (which are not of horne, as fome thinke) and their waight amounted to 200. pounds a peece after the rate of xii. ounces to euery pound. In the language of *Congo* the

Certain creatures in Bamba Prouince.

Elephantes.

An Elephantes foot 4. fpanne broad.

You may find hereby what the bignes of the whole Elephant was, if you will vfe the Arte of Proportion, as Pithagoras did by the foot of Hercules. Aul. Gellius lib. 1. Cap. 10.

The Elephant liueth 150. yeares.

An Elephantr tooth of 200. waight.

the

the *Elephants* tooth is called *Mene-Manzao*, that is to say, *The tooth of an Elephant* : and their young ones are called *Moana-Manzao*, that is, a young *Elephant*. Their eares are greater then the greatest Targattes that the *Turks* vse to weare, in length sixe spans, in shape like an Eg, & towards their sholders they grow to be narrower & sharper. With their ears, & with their tronke, and with their tayle, they beate away the flies that trouble them: yea and some haue leaft it in writing, that where they cannot reach with their tronke, with their eares, or with their taile, they will gather their skinne together, and so nip the poore flies to death betweene the wrincles.

Certain haires in the *Elephants* taile, very precious. They haue in their taile certaine hayres or bristles as bigge as rushes or broome-spriggs, of a shining black colour. The older they bee, the fayrer and stronger they be, and of great price among them. For the people of that countrey doe greatly esteeme them because the noble men and women of the kingdome of *Angola*, and of the *Ambundi* their neighbours doe vse to adorne and bedecke their neckes withal, & therefore do loue them, for that they are indeede very fayre and rare, and grow vpon so goodly a beast. They are very stronge, and like a twined corde, so that if a man shall striue to breake them asunder with both his handes, hee shall not bee able with all his force and strength to cracke them, but rather spoyle his handes with them. And for the cause lately rehearsed, many there are, which waiting for the *Elephantes*, when they ascend some steepe and narrowe way, doe come behinde them, and with very sharpe kniues cut of their tayles: the poor beast being not able in those straits to turne back to reuenge it selfe, nor with
his

his tronke to reach his enemie. And this they do, onely to haue thofe haires, which they fell for two or three flaues a peece. Other light & couragious perfons there are, that trufting much to their fwiftnes in running, do lie in a waite, and fet vpon the poore beaftes behinde, whiles they are in feeding, and at one blow attempt to cut off their tayles, & fo endeauour to faue themfelues by running away in a rounde. For the greatnes of the beaft is fuch, as outright it is very fwift, becaufe it maketh very large ftrides though in deede but flowe, and in the plaine is farre quicker then any luftie horfe: but in turning rounde it loofeth much time, and fo the huntfeman efcapeth in fafetie. And therefore many haue beene furprifed and flaine by the *Elephantes*, that haue fought to efcape from them by running away outright.

Our Aunceftors, being not well enformed in thefe matters haue leaft in writing, that the *Elephantes* could not ly down vpõ the ground, but that they vfed to lean themfelues againft a tree: which being before weakened or fawed in funder by the hunters, both the *Elephantes* and the tree fel downe to the earth, and fo were taken. But *Signor Odoardo* affirmed vpon his credit, that they lay downe vpon the ground, that they kneeled vpon their knees, and that they woulde with both their fore-feete leape vpon the trees to feede on the leaues, & ftoope downe to drink of the waters, that were in their caues, and that they had their iointes as other creatures haue, fauing that in fome partes they do fomewhat differ from others: as for example, frõ the hoofes of their fore-feete, vp to their fhoulders, you fhall not perceaue that they haue any more then two ioyntes. In their

An errour of ancient writers.

I 3   feeding

feeding: they vſe to ſhake and roote vp the great trees The manner of the *Elephãts* feeding. with the force of their ſhoulders, and ſtrength of their whole backes: But the ſmaller trees they take between both their teeth, and ſo bowe them and plucke them downe, that they may feede vpon the leaues of them: inſomuch as ſometimes they breake one of their teeth with ſo doing. And this is the cauſe why you ſhall find diuers of them in the fieldes that haue loſt their teeth. They chawe their meate with their ſhort teeth, which are not ſeene as their two long tuſkes are: and they carry it to their mouth by their long Snout, or Tronke, which is to them in ſteed of an arme & a hand. The tip of their Tronke is faſhioned & diuided into little ſlits, and (as it were) fingers, wherewith they will take vp very ſmall thinges, as Nuttes, and Strawes, and Berries, & ſo reach them to their mouth, as I *Philippo Pigafetta* haue ſeene my ſelfe at *Lisbone*.

The *Shee-Elephant*. The Females of theſe creatures doe beare their broode in their wombe for the ſpace of two yeares and no more: And foraſmuch as the younge *Elephant* cannot ſo quickly bee brought vp, (for it groweth very ſlowly) the milke is kept from it, and ſo it waxeth apt to feede of it ſelfe. And therefore Mother *Nature* hath prouided that the *Elephantes* are not great with young, but from ſeauen yeares to ſeauen yeares.

The *Elephants* skinne. Their skinne is harde beyond all credite. For being fower fingers thicke, it cannot bee pearced, no not with the ſhot of an Arcubuſe. And *Signor Odoardo* reported, that with a little Gunne, which is called a *Petreraa*, one of them was ſtricken, without any wound making, but indeede he was grieuouſly bruiſed, ſo that he ranne away from that place all in a rage, the ſpace of

three

three daies iourney and there died, after hee had flaine certaine flaues that he met by the way.

The manner of taking the Elephantes.

The people of that Countrey haue not the skill to tame thefe beaftes. Whereby they might reape great commodity and profite, for carrying their ftuffe from place to place for diuerfe other good vfes. But yet they take them; by digging certaine deepe trenches in the places, where they vfe to pafture, which trenches are very narrowe at the bottome, and broade aboue, to the end the beaft may not help himfelfe, & leape out when he is fallen into them. Thefe trenches they couer with Soddes of earth, and graffe, and leaues, becaufe the beaft fhoulde not fee their traine, but paffing ouer them remaine there entrenched. Whereupon the Gentleman beforenamed tolde mee, that hee had feene with his owne eyes a very ftraunge and admirable thing in *Coanʒa,* namely, that a younge *Elephant* following his damme fell downe by chaunce into one of thefe pittes, and after that fhee coulde not with all her skill and ftrength drawe him out of it, fhe buried him therein, and couered him with earth, with branches, and with bowes, infomuch as fhe filled the pit vp to the toppe, to the ende that the hunters fhoulde not enioy her calfe, choofing rather to kill it her felfe, then to leaue it to the mercie of the cruell huntfemen. This louing and kind mother, not fearing the people (that ftood round about her, & fhouted againft her, & threatned her with fundry weapons, & vttered ftraunge clamours and noyfes to affray her, & caft many fiers at her) but affuring her felfe in her owne ftronge and valiant nature, did labour and toyle from morning till night, that fhe might draw her calfe out of the pitte: and when fhee founde that

A ftraunge effect of Nature.

I 4

it

it was not poffible for her to atchieue what fhe defired, then fhee couered it in manner as wee haue tolde you.

The *Elephant* is a very gentle beaft, and trufteth greatly in his natural ftrength. He feareth nothing, nor hurteth any man that doth not trouble him: and haunteth neere to mens houfes without doing any harme at all. If he efpie men that go in his walke, he wil not meddle with them, vnleffe they feeke to moleft him: fauing that fometimes peraduenture hee will gently with his fnowte hoyfe them vpwardes into the ayre, whom he meeteth withall in his way, and that is all the hurt hee will doo vnto them. Thefe *Elephantes* doo greatly delight in waters: and if a man be defirous to fee them, his beft way is to lie fomewhere nigh to the Riuers, and Lakes, where they vfe to haunt about noone tide, to drinke, to refrefh themfelues, and to bathe their bodies in the water: for there they will ftande vp to their bellies, and all the reft of their bodie, that is aboue the water, they will wafh all ouer with the water that they fnuffe vp into their fnout for that purpofe. And becaufe there are fo many foords & paftures (as is faid) in the kingdome of *Congo*, therefore is there very great ftore of thefe creatures in that countrey. For *Signor Odoardo* affirmed, that in the way betweene *Cazanze*, & *Loanda*, in a little graffie valley hee had feene about a hundred of them in a company, olde and young that followed their dammes: and thefe were the firft young ones that euer hee faw till that day. And herewithall you muft vnderftand, that they vfe to go together in heardes, as *Kine*, and *Camelles*, and other fuch like gentle Creatures doo, and not alone like *Lions* and other fuch wilde beaftes. Now the reafon why this country

aboundeth

(margin note: The nature of the Elephant.)

aboundeth so in *Iuory*, is easy to be yeelded. For so many
Elephantes being bredde in that Region, they made no
account of that commodity in times past: but onely after that the *Portingalles* began to trafficke with those
countreyes, it grewe in estimation: and so hauing gathered together in so many ages an infinite quantity
thereof, which they found in their fieldes, they haue
sould them till this day at a very good penniworth.

It is not knowen, whether there be in that countrey *Rinoceros,*
any other beast that is so big as an *Elephant* is, nor whether there breed therein any *Rinoceros*, which is a Creature as bigge indeede as the *Elephant*, and in *India* is called a *Bada*. But yet there are brought into the countries
of the *Anzichi* some of their hornes that growe vpon
their nofes, that are both of great value & estimation, &
also vsed for the help of diuers diseases. So that it is very
credible and likely, that there are some of them to bee
founde in those quarters.

There are in the Region of the *Anzichi Lions* also, *Lyons.*
like the *Lions* that breed in other partes of the worlde,
but they doo not vse to haunt the Region of *Bamba*:
But in *Bamba* there are very great store of *Tigres*,
which are of the very same shape that those in *Florence* *Tygres.*
are, which *Signor Odoardo* saw there, and testified to be
very *Tygres* indeed. He tolde mee also of a notable custome which they haue: And that is, that they will not
set vpon any men that are white, but onely such as are
blacke: And it hath beene found, that when the white
and the blacke haue slept together in the night time,
they haue slayne the blacke to deuoure them, and spa-
red the white. When they are hungry they will bee so
bolde as to fetch cattell euen out of the yardes that

K   are

are about the houfes without any feare at all, when they cannot finde any victuailes abroade in the fieldes. They are very daungerous and hurtfull to all kindes of Creatures whatfoeuer they be, and in that language they are called *Engoi*. They are as fierce and cruell beaftes as the *Lion*, and roare as the *Lion* doth. They are alfo altogether like the *Lion*, fauing onely in the colour of their haire; for the *Tygre* is fpotted, but the *Lyon* is all of one colour. They vfe to take and kill thefe *Tygres* after diuers manners. For befides that, which hath beene before fpoken, they poyfon them with *Sublimate* or fome other venome, mingled with flefh which is laid for them. Or els they tie young *Goates* at certaine lines made like fnares, and faftned about the ftocke of a tree, fo that when the beaft commeth to her pray, the engine openeth it felfe, and the more the beaft ftriueth withall, the more it is intangled, and fo at laft is hanged therein. Another way they haue to kill them, that is with arrowes, with Iauelins, and with Arcubufes. It is a Creature very harmeful, both to the *Negroes* themfelues, and alfo to their flockes of fheepe and heards of cattell. Notwithftanding *Signor Odoardo* tolde me, that he had gotten one of them, that was fifteene dayes old, and he brought it vp with Goates milke: which being afterwardes growen bigger would followe him like a dogge: and although it were very taine, yet it would not willingly fuffer any other to touch it befides his maifter. He woulde alfo roare mightily, and when he was angry, his eies wold looke very terribly & fearfully. But in proceffe of time this *Tygre* killed a *Dogge*, belonging to the houfe, and alfo a *Zebra*, that were very deare to their maifter, and thereupon, perceiuing how perillous

The manner of taking the tame Tygres.

A tame Tyger.

lous

lous a beaſt it was. hee ſlewe it with an Arcubuſe-ſhot.
He reported moreouer, that the *Moſtacchios* of the *Ty-*
gre are helde in that Region to be mortall poyſon: for
being giuen in meates, it procureth a man to die, as it
were in a madneſſe: And therefore the king doth pu-
niſh all thoſe that bring him a *Tygres* ſkinne without the
Moſtacchios.

There breedeth likewiſe in this Countrey another
Creature, which they call a *Zebra,* commonly founde
alſo in certaine Prouinces of *Barbary* and *Africa:* which
although it be altogether made like a great *Mule,* yet is
not a *Mule* indeed, for it beareth young ones. It hath
a moſt ſingular ſkinne, and peculiar from all other creatures. For from the ridge of the chine downe towards
the bellie, it is ſtraked with rowes of three colours,
blacke, white, and browne Bay, about the breadth of
three fingers a peece, and ſo meet againe together in a
circle, euery rowe, with his owne colour. So that the
necke, and the head, and the Mane (which is not great)
and the eares, and all the legges are ſo interchaunged
with theſe colours, and in ſuch manner and order, as
without all faile, if the firſt ſtrake beginne with white,
then followeth the ſecond with blacke, & in the thirde
place the Bay: & ſo another courſe beginning in white
endeth ſtill in Bay. And this rule is generally and infal-
libly obſerued ouer all the body. The tayle is like the
tayle of a *Mule,* of a Morell colour, but yet it is well coloured, and hath a gliſtring gloſſe. The feet like the feet
of a *Mule,* and ſo are the hooffes. But touching the reſt
of her carriage and qualities, ſhe is very luſty and plea-
ſaunt as a horſe: and ſpecially in going, and in running
ſhe is ſo light & ſo ſwift that it is admirable. In ſomuch
as

as in *Portingale* and in *Caftile* alfo , it is commonly vfed
(as it were for a prouerbe) *As fwift as a Zebra*, when they
will fignifie an exceeding quickenes. Thefe creatures
are all wilde, they breede euery yeare, and are there in
fuch aboundance that they are innumerable. If they
were made tame, they woulde ferue to runne and to
drawe for the warres, and for many other good vfes, as
well as the beft horfes that are. So that Mother *Nature*
feemeth to haue fufficiently prouided in euery country
for the commodity and neceffity of man, with diuers
fortes of Creatures, of nourifhments, and temperature
of ayre , to the ende hee fhoulde want nothing. And
therefore they hauing no horfes at all in the whole
Kingdome of *Congo*, nor any skill to vfe their oxen
to the yoke , or to the packfaddle, that they might eyther be drawen or carryed, nor to tame their *Zebraes*
with bridle and faddle, or any other way to take the be-
nefite of their beaftes, that might tranfport them from

*The manner
of the carry-
ing of the
Moci-Conghi.*

place to place: Euen very neceffity hath taught them to
vfe men in fteed of labouring cattel. For either they lay
thefelues al along in certain Litters (as it were) or els fet
themfelues vpright, with fhadows ouer them to keepe
them from the Sunne, and fo they caufe themfelues to
be carried too and fro, by their flaues, or by other men
that for wages are alwaies ready at Pofte-houfes to that
purpofe. They that meane to iourney with fpeede, do
take with them many flaues , and when the firft number are weary, then do the feconde number vndertake
the burden, and fo fucceffiuely chaungeone after another, as the *Tartarians* and *Perfians* vfe to do with their
horfes : and thefe men being thus accuftomed to thefe
labours, (and fo often chaunging) will go as faft, as any
　　　　　　　　　　　　　　　　　　　Poftilion

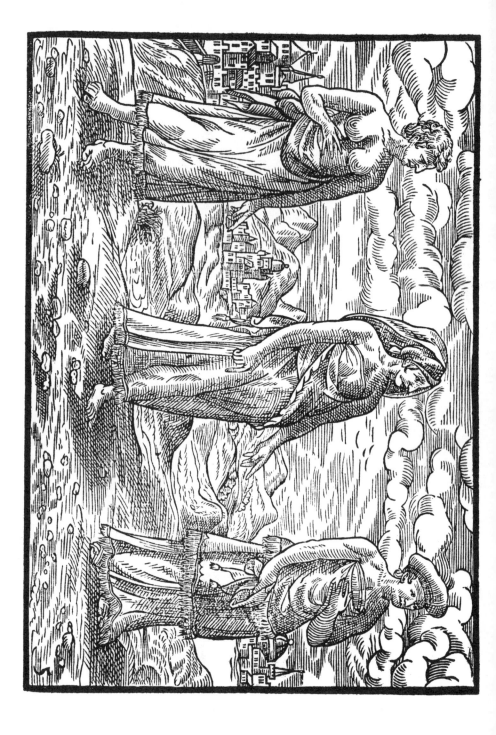

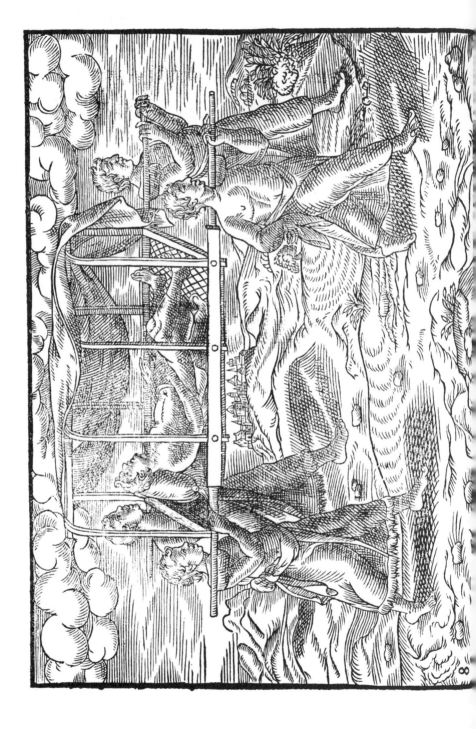

Poſtilion gallop. Of all which faſhions of carrying or going in iourney, we haue ſet down the pictures as alſo of
the *Zebra*; of the apparel both of the men & women, of
the ſouldiers, and of the Military Inſtrumentes or *Cornets.*

    There are alſo to bee founde in this countrey cer-
taine other foure-footed beaſtes, ſomewhat leſſe then *The Dante.*
Oxen, of colour red, with hornes like *Goats* horns, which
are very ſmooth and gliſtering, and enclining to black:
whereof they make diuers prety knackes, as they doe
likewiſe of the *Buffes* hornes. They haue their heades
and their haires, like the heads and haires of *Oxen*: and
their skinnes are of great eſtimation : & therefore they
are carried into *Portingall,* and from thence into *Germany,* to be dreſſed, and then they are called *Dantes.* The
king of *Congo* is very deſirous to haue ſome men that
had skill to cleanſe them and dreſſe them, and to make
them fit for vſe, to the end hee might employ them for
Armour of defence. And yet thoſe nations doo already vſe them for ſhieldes and Targats; and do find that
they will reſiſt the blowe of a weapon, and eſpecially
the ſhot of an Arrow. They kill them with Arcubuſes
and with arrowes. But if they doe eſpy the huntſman,
they wil ſet vpon him, and being by nature very fierce,
and couragious, they will ſo knocke him and thumpe
him with their feete and their Muzzle (becauſe they
cannot do him any harme with their hornes) that they
wil leaue him either halfe deade or ſtarke dead. There *Wilde Buffes.*
is alſo an infinite number of wilde *Buffes,* that go wan- *Wilde Aſſes.*
dring about the deſerts in the kingdoms of the *Anzichi,*
and wilde *Aſſes* likewiſe, which the *Greekes* call *Ona-
gri.*

M 2   There

There are befides thefe, other beafts called *Empalan-*
ga, which are in bigneffe and fhape like *Oxen*, fauing
that they holde their necke and heade aloft, and haue
their hornes broade and crooked, three handbreadthes
long, diuided into knots, and fharp at the endes, whereof they might make very faire *Cornets* to found withall:
and although they liue in the forrefts, yet are they not
noyfome nor harmefull. The skinnes of their neckes
are vfed for fhoo-foles, and their flefh for meate. They
might likewife bee brought to drawe the plough, and
doo good feruice in any other labour, and tilling of
the ground. Moreouer they feed great heards of *Kine*,
and tame *Oxen*, tame *Hogges* and wilde *Boares*, flockes of
Sheepe and *Goates*. *Signor Odoardo* affirmed, that the
Goates and the *Sheepe* doo bring forth two, and three, &
foure lambes or kids at a time, and two when they haue
feweft, and neuer one alone at any time. And becaufe
their pafture is fo fat, they do all fucke, and milke their
owne dammes, which hee proued himfelfe to be true
in his owne houfe, where hee had very great ftore of
that Cattell.

There are *Wolues* alfo which loue the oyle of *Palmes*
beyonde all meafure, and haue a great fent: a propertie
that *Virgile* attributeth to *Dogges*, *Odora Canum vis*, *The*
fmelling fent of Dogges. They will fmell this oyle a farre
off, and fteale it in the night time out of their houfes of
ftrawe, and fometimes from thofe that carry it by the
way, whiles the poore foules doe reft themfelues and
fleepe. The oyle (as fhall be tolde you) is made of the
Palme tree: it is thicke and harde like Butter. And it is
a maruell to fee, how thefe *Wolues* do take a bottle that
is full of this liquor betweene their teeth, & fo caft it
on

Empalanga.
Other fruitful Cattell.
Wolues.

on their fhoulders and run away withall, as our *Wolues* here doo with a *Sheepe.* There are very great ftore of *Foxes,* that fteale *Hennes* as our *Foxes* doo. And further *Foxes.* in this country of *Bamba,* there is an innumerable quantity of hunting game, as *Stagges, Fallow-Deere, Roebucks,* Hunting and *Gazelles,* whereof he affirmed that he had feene exceeding great heardes, as alfo of *Conies* and *Hares,* becaufe there were no hunters to kill them.

In the Region of *Pemba* there are many wilde *Ciuet-* In *Pemba, Ci-Cattes,* which the *Portingales* call *Algazia,* and fome of *uet Cattes.* thefe the people of that countrey had made tame, that they might inioy their *Ciuet,* in the fmell whereof they doo greatly delight. But this was before the *Portingals* did trafficke with thofe Countryes. And in *Manibatta* there are caught many *Sables,* with very white hayres In *Batta, Sa-* and exceeding fine, called *Incire :* but no man may *bles.* weare thefe skinnes, vnleffe the Prince permit him fo to do : for it is helde in great eftimation, and euery *Sa-ble* is worth a flaue. Towardes the *Anzichi* they catch *Marterns* alfo, wherewith they apparrell themfelues, as In *Anziqua Marternes.* in due place we will note vnto you.

Apes, Monkeyes, and fuch other kinde of beaftes, In *Sogno, Apes* fmall and great of all fortes there are many in the Region of *Sogno,* that lyeth vpon the Riuer *Zaire.* Some of and *Monkeyes.* them are very pleafant and gamefome, and make good paftime, and are vfed by the Lordes there for their recreation and to fhew them fport. For although they be vnreafonable Creatures, yet will they notably counterfait the countenances, the fafhions, & the actions of men. In euery one of thefe Regions abouenamed, there are fome of the aforefaid Creatures, in fome places mo, and in fome places fewer.

Of *Adders*, and *Snakes* in these countries there bree-deth a certaine kinde, that in respect of our countryes is very straunge, and of an excessiue greatnesse. For you shall finde some that are xxv. spanne long, and fiue span broade: and the bellie and the mouth so large, that they can swallow and receiue into their bellie a whole *Stag*, or any other creature of that bignesse. And it is cal-led   that is to say a great *Water-Adder*. It wil go forth of the water vp to the land to prey for his victuails, and then returne into the riuers againe, and so it liueth in both the Elements. It wil get it self vp vpon the bows & braunches of trees, and there watch the cattell that feed thereaboutes, which when they are come neere vnto it, presently it will fall vpon them, and wind it selfe in many twines about them, and clappe his tayle on their hinder partes, and so it strayneth them and biteth so ma-ny holes in them, that at last it killeth them. And then it draweth them into some woode or other solitary place, where it deuoureth them at pleasure, skinne, hornes, hooffes and all. Now it falleth out, that when it is thus full, and (as it were) great with so monstrous a meale, it becommeth almost drunke & very sleepie, so that any child may kil it. And in this sort wil it remaine full & satiffied for the space of 5. or 6. daies together, & then returne againe to prey. These *Adders* do change their skinnes in their ordinarie seasons, yea and some-times after they haue eaten so monstrously, and the said sloughes, when they are found, are gathered vp and re-serued for a shew of so vnmeasurable a Creature. These *Adders* are also greatly esteemed by the *Pagan Negroes*, for they do vse to rost them, and eate them for meat, & make more account of them then they doo of *Hennes*,

or

Adders and *Snakes* of a huge scantling

The Author doth not set downe the name.

or any such delicate flesh. They find great store of them
when they haue occasion to burne their thicke woods:
for there they shall haue them lying on the ground, ro-
sted with the fire.

Besides these there are *Vipers* also, well knowne vnto
that people. Which *Vipers* are so venemous, that such
as are bitten by them doe die within the space of xxiiii.
houres : But the *Negroes* are acquainted with certaine
hearbes that will heale their woundes.

There are also certaine other Creatures, which being as big as *Rams*, haue wings like *Dragons*, with long
tailes and long chappes, and diuerse rowes of teeth, &
feede vpon raw flesh. Their colour is blew and greene,
their skinne bepaynted like scales, and two feete they
haue but no more. The *Pagan Negroes*, do vse to wor-
shippe them as *Goddes*, and at this day you may see diuers of them that are kept for a maruaile. And because
they are very rare, the Chiefe Lordes there doo curi-
ously preserue them, and suffer the people to worship
them, which tendeth greatly to their profite, by reason
of the giftes and oblations which the people offer vnto
them.

There are there also to be found *Chameleons*, which
haue fower feete, and breede vpon the rockes, and liue
of the winde and the aire, of the bignesse and likenesse
of an *Efte*, with a sharpe heade, and a tayle like a sawe.
They are for the most parte of the colour of the skie,
but somewhat more duskie and greenish, and if you
stand to looke a while vpon them , you shall see them
chaunge themselues into diuers colours. They dwell
much vpon high rockes and trees, to the ende they may
take aire, wherewith they are nourished.

M 4 Other

Vipers.

Another
strange crea-
ture.

Chameliens.

Other ferpentes there are that are venemous,
that carrie vpon the tippe of their taile a certaine little
roundell like a bell, which ringeth as they go, fo as it
may be hearde. It may be it was there fet by nature, of
purpofe, that people fhould beware of them, and it is
founde by experience that thefe belles and the heades
of the ferpents are very good remedies againft an ague,
and againft the trembling of the hart. Thefe kindes and
fortes of lande-Creatures are to be founde in thefe regions, befides others alfo that are commonly to be had
in other countries.

It refteth now, that we fpeake fomewhat touching
Birdes, and firft of all of the *Eaftriche*, becaufe it is bigger then all the reft. Thefe *Eaftriches* are found in thofe
partes of *Sundi* and of *Batta*, that are towardes the *Mu-
zambi*. The young *Eaftriches* doo fpring out of their
egges, being warmed and difclofed by the eye & heate
of the *Sunne*. Their feathers are vfed in fteede of *Enfignes* and *Banners* in warre, mingled with fome plumes
of the *Peacocke*, and are fafhioned in the likeneffe of a
fhadowe againft the Sunne. And forafmuch as I am
fallen into the fpeech of *Peacockes*, I muft tell you by the
way, that in the partes of *Angola*, there are *Peacockes*
brought vp priuately in a certaine woode that is compaffed about with walles : and the king will not fuffer
any other bodie to keepe thofe birdes but onely himfelfe, becaufe they are for the *Royall Enfignes*, as I tolde
you before. And it is read in auncient hiftories of *A-
lexander the Great*, that he did alfo priuiledge this Birde,
at fuch time as he firft faw it in *Europe*.

There are alfo *Indie-Cockes* and *Hens*, and *Geefe*, and
Duckes of all fortes both wilde and tame : *Partriches* fo

many

A ftraunge
Serpent.

The *Eaftrich*.

Peacocks.

Fowles of
diuers forts.

many as children take them with ginnes. Other birdes
they haue likewife, as *Pheafantes*, which they call *Gallig-*
noles, *Pigeons*, *Turtles*, and of thefe fmall birdes called
Becca-fichi an infinite number. Birdes of prey, as *Eagles-*
Royall, *Faulcons*, *Gerfaulcons* and *Sparhaukes*, and others,
great ftore, which notwithstanding the people neuer
vfe to hauke withall. Birdes of the fea, as *Pellicanes* (for
fo the *Portingalles* do call them) white and great, which
fwimme vnder the water, and haue their throates fo
wide, that they will fwallow a whole fifh at once. This
bird hath fo good a ftomacke, and naturally fo hot, that
it eafily digefteth the fifh that it fwalloweth whole, and
the skinne of it is fo hoat, that the people of that countrey do vfe to weare them, and to warme their colde
ftomackes withall, and therefore make great reckoning
of them.

There are many white *Herons* and *Gray Bittours*, that
feede in the wafhes there, and are called *Royall Birdes*.
Other *Fowles* there are of the likeneffe of a *Crane*, with
a red bill and redde feete, as bigge as *Storkes*, and their
feathers for the moft part redde and white, and fome
darke graye. Goodly birdes they are to looke too, and
the people of the countrey doo call them *Flemminges*,
becaufe they doo much refemble them, and are good
meat to eate.

They haue *Parrattes* of gray colour, great and very
talkatiue: & others of greene colour, but they are little
ones & not fo talkatiue: They haue likewife certaine
fmal little birds, which they call *Birds of Muficke*, and yet
greater thē the *Canarie Birds*, of feather & bill red: fome
greene, with their feet & bill only black: fome all white:
fome gray or dunne: fome all blacke, and this kinde is
N   more

more sweet in their notes then all the rest aforenamed:
for you woulde thinke that they talked in their singing.
Others there are of diuers colours: but they do all sing
in sundrie sorts, so that the chiefe Lords of those countreyes, from auncient times to this day, haue continually kept them in cages, and greatly esteemed them for
their song.

Chap. 10.

*Of the Prouince of Sogno, which is the Countrey
of the Riuer Zaire, and Loango.*

 His Countrey is bounded with the
Riuer *Ambrize*, towardes the *North* in
seauen degrees and a halfe, and so trauersing the Riuer *Lelunda*, and the Riuer *Zaire* it endeth at the Rockes called
Barreuras Vermellias, that is to say, the
Redde pittes, which are in the borders of the Kingdome
of *Loango*. In the middest of this Prouince there is a
certaine *Territory*, called by the same name *Sogno*, where
the Gouernour of the Countrey dwelleth. The chiefe
Lordes that rule this Prouince are called *Mani-Sogno*,
that is *Princes of Sogno*, and are commonly of the blood
Royall. The Prince that gouerneth there at this day is
called

The second
Prouince *Sog-
no*, and the de-
scription
thereof.

Sogno the chief
towne of this
Prouince.

called *Dõ Diego Mani.Sogno.* He hath vnder his dominiõ
many other petty Lords, & other prouinces, that in olde
time were free and liued by themſelues, as the people of
Mombalas, ſituate ſomwhat neere to the Cittie of *Congo,*
which are now ſubieƈt to this gouernement. And on
the other ſide of the Riuer *Zaire* towardes the *North* is
the Prouince of *Palmar,* that is to ſay of *Palmes,* becauſe
there is great ſtore of *Palme trees* growing therein. O-
ther Lordes there are, that border vpon the King of
Loango, who was ſometime ſubieƈt to the King of *Congo,* but in proceſſe of time he became a free Lord, and
now profeſſeth himſelfe to be in amity with the king of
Congo, but not to be his vaſſall. The people that are vnder theſe Lords in thoſe borders, are called the *Bramas:*
and they reach within land, vnder the *Equinoƈtiall* line
towardes the *Eaſt* to the boundes of *Anzicana,* all along
the Mountaines which diuide them from the *Anzichi*
vpon the *North.* They are called by the people of *Loango, Congreamolal,* becauſe they were ſubieƈt to *Congo.*

 In this Countrey of *Loango* there are many *Elephants*
and great ſtore of *Iuory* which they doo willingly exchaunge for a little iron, ſo that for the naile of a ſhippe
(be it neuer ſo ſmall) they will giue a whole *Elephantes*
tooth. The reaſon thereof is either becauſe there groweth no iron in that place, or els they haue not the ſkill
to get it out of the mines where it groweth: But all the
iron they can get they employ for heading of their arrowes, and their other weapons, as we told you, when
we ſpake of the *Bramas.*

 They make great ſtore of cloth of the *Palme* trees,
whereof wee made mention before: but theſe are leſſer
and yet very fine. They haue greate aboundance of

N 2 kine

Don Diego
chiefe Gouer.
nour of *Sogno,*
& thoſe that
rule vnder
him.

The *Bramas.*

The commo-
dities of *Sogno*

The manner
of the life of
the inhabi-
tants.

Kine and of other cattell before named. They are in Religion *Pagans*: their apparell after the fashion of the people of *Congo*: They maintaine warre with their bordering neighbours, which are the *Anzichi* and the inhabitants of *Anzicana*, & when they enterprise warre against the *Anzichi*, then they craue aide of the people of *Congo*, and so they remaine halfe in freedome, and halfe in daunger of others. They worship what they list, and hold the *Sunne* for the greatest *God*, as though it were a man, and the *Moone* next, as though it were a woman. Otherwise euery man chooseth to himselfe his owne idol, and worshippeth it after his owne pleasure. These people would easily embrace the Christian Religion: For many of them, that dwell vpon the borders of *Congo* haue beene conuerted to Christendome: and the rest, for want of Priestes and of such as should instruct them in true religion, do remaine stil in their blindnes.

Chap. 11.

Of the third Prouince called Sundi.

The third prouince Sundi, & the description thereof.

His Prouince of *Sundi* is the neerest of all to the Citty of *Congo*, called *Citta di San-Saluatore*, the Citty of *Saint Sauiours*, and beginneth about 40. miles distant from it, and quite out of the territory thereof, and reacheth to

the

the riuer *Zaire*, and so ouer the same to the other side where the *Caduta* or *Fall* is, which wee mentioned before: and then holdeth on vpwardes on both sides towards the *North*, bordering vpon *Anzicana* and the *Anzichi*. Towardes the *South* it goeth along the said riuer *Zaire*, vntill you come to the meeting of it with the Riuer *Bancare*, and all along the bankes thereof, euen to the rootes of the mountaine of *Chriſtall*. In the bounds of the Prouince of *Pango*, it hath her principall Territory, where the Gouernour lyeth, who hath his name from the Prouince of *Sundi*, and is seated about a daies iourney neere to the *Fall* of the Riuer, towardes the *South*.

The chiefe towne of *Sundi*.

This Prouince is the chiefeſt of all the reſt, and (as it were) the Patrimony of all the kingdome of *Congo*: and therefore it is alwaies gouerned by the Kinges eldeſt Sonne, and by thoſe Princes that are to ſucceede him. As it fell out in the time of their firſt Chriſtian King, that was called *Don Iohn*: whoſe eldeſt ſonne, that was Gouernour here ſucceeded him, and was called *Don Alfonſo*. And euer ſithence, the Kinges of *Congo* haue ſucceſſiuely continued this cuſtome, to conſigne this Gouernement to thoſe Princes which are to ſucceede in the kingdome: As did the king that nowe is called *Don Aluaro*. who was in this Gouernment before *Don Aluaro* the King his father died, and was called *Mani-Sundi*.

This prouince of *Sundi* is alwaies gouerned by the heire apparent of the K. of *Congo*.

And here by the way you muſt note, that in all the Kingdome of *Congo* there is not any perſon, that poſſeſſeth any proper goodes of his owne, whereof hee may diſpoſe, and leaue to his heyres: but all is the Kinges, & he diſtributeth all offices, all goodes, and all landes, to

In al the kingdome of *Congo*, no man hath any thing of his owne whereof hee may diſpoſe, or leaue to his heyres: but all is the Kinges.

N 3   whom

whomfoeuer it pleafeth him. Yea and to this law, euen
the Kinges owne fonnes are fubiect. So that if any
man do not pay his tribute yearely (as hee ought) the
King taketh away his Gouernement from him, and giueth it to another. As it happened to the king that now
liueth, who at the time that *Signor Odoardo* was at the
Courte, being of his owne nature very liberall, and
bountifull beyond meafure, and one that beftowed
much vpon his feruants, could not difcharge thofe im-
pofitions that the king had layed on him. Whereupon
he was by the king depriued of his reuenews, of his gouernement, and of his royall fauour, that is to fay in
that language, hee was *Tombocado*, as we will declare
more at full in the feconde part of this difcourfe.

Many Lords there are that are fubiect to the Gouernour of *Sundi*. The people do trafficke with their neighbour Countries, felling and bartering diuers things. As
for example, falt, & clothes of fundry colours, brought
from the *Indies*, and from *Portingale*, and *Lumachette* to
ferue for their coine. And for thefe commodities they
doo exchaunge cloth of *Palme* trees, and *Iuory*, and the
skinnes of *Sables* and Marternes, and certaine girdles
wrought of the leaues of *Palme* trees, which are greatly efteemed in thofe partes.

There groweth in thefe countries great ftore of *Chri-
ftall*, and diuers kinds of mettall: but *Iron* they loue a-
boue all the reft, faying that the other mettalles are to
no vfe: for with Iron they can make kniues, and weapons, and hatchets, and fuch like inftruments, that are
neceffary and profitable for the vfe of mans nature.

Chap.

Chap. 12.

Of the fourth Prouince called
Pango.

He Prouince of *Pango* in auncient time was a free kingdome,
that was gouerned of it felfe, &
bordereth on the *North* vppon
Sundi, on the *South* vpon *Batta*,
on the *Weſt* vpon the Countie
of *Congo*, and on the *Eaſt*, vpon
the mountaines of the *Sunne*.
The principal Territory, where the Gouernours dwelling is, hath the fame name that the Prouince hath, viz.
Pango. It ſtandeth vpon the Weſterne ſide of the Riuer *Barbela*, and in olde time was called *Pangue-lungos*,
and in time afterwardes the worde was corrupted and
chaunged into *Pango*. Through the middeſt of this
Prouince runneth the riuer *Berbela*, which fetcheth his
originall from the great *Lake* (whence the riuer *Nilus*
alſo taketh his beginning) and from another leſſer *Lake*
called *Achelunda*, and ſo diſchargeth it ſelfe into *Zaire*.

The fourth prouince Pan-go, and the deſcription ther-of,

Pāgo the chief town of this Prouince.

N 4   And

And although this be the least Countrey of all the rest, yet doth it yeeld no lesse tribute then the rest.

This Prouince was conquered after the Countrey of *Sundi*, and made subiect to the Princes of *Congo*: and is now all one with it, both in speech and manners, neither is there any difference at all betweene them. The *Don Francisco* present Gouernour thereof is called *Don Francesco Ma-* *chiefe Gouer-* *ni-Pango*, and is descended from the most auncient no-*nour of Pango* bilitie of all the Lordes of *Congo* : and in all consultations touching the State he is sent for, because he is nowe an olde man, and of great wisedome. For hee hath remained in the gouernment of this region for the space of fiftie yeares, and no man euer complained of him, neither did the king at any time take his gouernement from him.

The trafficke of this Prouince is like the trafficke of *Sundi.*

Chap. *13.*
Of the fift Prouince called Batta.

The fift Pro
uince *Batta*
& the descrip-
tion thereof.

He boundes of this Prouince are towards the *North*, the Countrey of *Pango*: on the *East* it taketh quite ouer the Riuer *Barbela*, and reacheth to the Mountaines of the *Sunne*, and to the foote of the mountains

Mountaines of *Sal-Nitre.* And on the *South* from the said Mountains, by a line paſſing through the meeting of the riuers *Barbela* and *Cacinga,* to the mountaine *Bruſ-ciato,* that is to ſay *Scorched.*

Within theſe boundes is *Batta* contayned, and the Principall Cittie, where the Prince dwelleth, is likewiſe called *Batta.* In auncient time it was called *Aghirimba,* but afterwardes the word was corrupted, and it is now called *Batta.* It was in old time a very ſtrong and a great Kingdome, & voluntarily of it ſelfe, without any war it ioyned it ſelfe with the kingdome of *Congo,* peraduen-ture becauſe there was ſome diſſention among their Lords: and therefore it hath more preheminence then the reſt of the Prouinces of the kingdome of *Congo,* in priuiledges and liberties. For the Gouernment of *Batta* is alwaies aſſigned to one, that is of the bloode of the Kings of that countrey at their choiſe and pleaſure, ha-uing no more reſpect to one then to another, ſo that he be of the ſtocke and bloud Royall, neyther to the eldeſt ſonne nor to the ſecond. Neither yet goeth this Go-uernement by inheritaunce, but the king of *Congo* (as is told you before) doth diſpoſe it at his own pleaſure to whō he thinketh beſt, to the end they ſhold not vſurpe it by way of ſucceſſion, or by rebellion. Hee dwelleth neerer the king then any other Gouernour or Lorde of the kingdom of *Congo,* & is the ſecōd perſon therin, nei-ther may any man gainſay his arguments & reaſons, as they may any of the reſt, for it is ſo decreede among them. Nowe if the line of the king of *Congo* ſhould chaunce to faile, ſo that there were none of that blood to ſucceed, the ſucceſſion ſhall fall vpon the gouernour of *Batta.* Hee that now gouerneth there, is called *Don Pedro*

Batta the chiefe towne of all *Batta.*

The Preemi-nence of the Gouernour of *Batta.*

Don Pedro chiefe Gouer-nour of *Batta.*

Pedro Mani-Batta.

Sometimes he eateth at the kinges owne table, but yet in a bafer feat then the kinges feat is, and that alfo not fitting, but ftanding, which is not graunted to any other Lord of *Congo,* no nor to the fons of the king him-felfe. His Court and his traine is little leffe then the Court & traine of the king of *Congo.* For he hath *Trom-pets* and *Drummes* and other inftrumentes going before him, as becommeth a Prince, and by the *Portingalles* he is commonly called the *Prince of Batta,* becaufe (as it is faid) if the fucceffion fhoulde faile in the bloode of the kinges of *Congo,* the empire of the whole kingdome muft light vpon fome one of this ftocke.

Hee doth holde continuall warres with the *Pagans* that border vpon him: and hee is able to gather toge-ther about 70. or 80. thoufand fighting men. And be-caufe hee doth ftill mayntaine warre with the people that are next him, he hath liberty graunted vnto him to entertaine Arcubufiers, that fhall bee of his owne natu-rall fubiectes. For the king of *Congo* will not fuffer any other Gouernour of any other Prouinces, nor any of their children, to haue any Arcubufiers, that are borne within their Countrey, but onely the *Portingalles.* Sig-nor *Odoardo* demaunding once of the King, why he did not giue leaue to his other Gouernours to retaine fhot about them: the King aunfwered, that if peraduenture they fhould rebell againft him with a thoufand, or two thoufande Arcubufiers, he fhould not haue any poffi-bility to make them refiftance.

And forafmuch as wee haue told you, that the King hath graunted licence, onely to the prince of *Batta,* to entertaine Arcubufiers in his owne countrey, it is fitte
                                    you

The K. of *Cō-go* wil not fuf-fer any natural borne fubiect in *Congo,* to haue an Arcu-bufe.

The reafon why the K. of *Congo* permit-teth *Mani-*

you fhould vnderftand, that hee doth it vpon very ne-ceffary occafion. For towardes the *Eaft* of *Batta,* be-yond the mountaines of the *Sunne,* and of *Sal-Nitre,* vp-on the bankes of the *Eaft* and *Weft* of the riuer *Nilus,* & in the borders of the Empire of *Mohenhe-Muge* there liueth a nation, which by the people of *Congo,* are called *Giaquas,* but in their own language they are called *Agag:* Very fierce they are and warlicke, much giuen to fight and pillage, and make continuall inroades into the Countries neere adioyning, and fometimes among the reft into the Prouince of *Batta.* So that this Countrey muft needes be in continuall Armes, and ftande vpon good guarde, and maintaine Arcubufiers to defende themfelues from them.

Batta to haue Arcubufiers in his Prouince.

The Giacas.

  The Prince of *Batta* hath many Lordes vnder him: and the naturall people of this Prouince are called *Mon-fobos,* and their language is well vnderftoode by the in-habitants of *Congo.* They are farre more rude and ru-fticall then the *Moci-Conghi,* and the flaues that are brought from thence, doo proue more obftinate and ftubborne, then thofe that come from other Coun-tries.

The conditi-ons of the people of Batta.

  Their trafficke is the fame, that the trafficke of the other countreyes are, whereof we haue laft intreated. And the profite which the king receyueth from *Batta,* amounteth to double afmuch, as he receiueth out ofa-ny two of the other Prouinces before mentioned.

Their traffick,

Chap. 14.

*Of the sixt and last Prouince called
Pemba.*

The sixt Pro-
uince *Pemba*,
and the situa-
tion thereof.

Don Antonio
cheife Gouer-
nor of *Pemba*.

He Prouince of *Pemba* is seated in the heart and middle of the King-dome of *Congo*, compassed and comprised within the boundes before described, whose Gouer-uernour is called *Don Antonio Mani-Pemba*, seconde sonne to King *Don Aluaro*, that dead is, and brother to the king that raygneth at this present. And forasmuch as his father did loue him dearely, he assigned vnto him this Gouernement, because he knew not what better thing to giue him, sauing the Realme it selfe: which in deed he would willingly haue bestowed on him, for that he was more like vnto him in quality & nature then his el-dest son was. But it would not be by reason of the lawe of the Kingdome, which wold not haue yeelded there-vnto.

This countrey is the very *Center* and middest of all the state of *Congo*, and the originall of all the auncient Kings, and the Territorie where they were borne, and the chiefe and principall seat of all the other Prouinces

and

Kingdome of Congo. 105

and Principalities. And therefore the chiefe and royall Citty of all that Empire is assigned to this Prouince, whereof we will heareafter deliuer you a full information. The Gouernour of *Pemba* dwelleth in a Territorie of the same name, situate at the foote of the *Scorched Mountaine*, along the Riuer *Loze*, which riseth out of the *Lake*, and runneth through the Region of *Bamba* into the sea.

The Courtiers, and Lordes, and seruitors belonging to the king of *Congo*, haue their goods and possessions, and reuenewes in this Prouince, because it is neerest to the Court, & very conuenient for the conueighing of their victuailes, and their other stuffe vnto the Court. Some of these Lordes, in that parte specially, that bordereth vpon the aforesaid Prouince of *Bamba*, haue much a doo to keep fight and defende themselues from the people of *Quizama*, because they are neerest vnto them. For this people (as wee tolde you) did rebell against the king of *Congo*, and reuolted from him, and doe professe that they will bee at libertie, and gouerned of themselues.

And here will we end the first booke, which consisteth of the description of the kingdome of *Congo* in generall, and of his borders, and in particular of all the sixe Prouinces thereof. Now it remayneth that wee proceede forwarde to the second booke: Wherein we will treate of the situation of the Cittie of *Congo*, and of the Territorie therevnto belonging, of the first christening of the king, of his manners, of his Court and of other conditions appertayning to the politicke and militarie Gouernment of these people. And afterward we will describe vnto you the kingdomes neere adioyning

The chiefe Cittie of all Congo is situate in this prouince of Pemba.

The Courtiers &c. dwel for the most part in Pemba.

Conclusion of this booke.

The contents of the seconde booke.

ioyning, and all the regions thereaboutes towardes
the *South*, euen till you come to the *Cape* of *Good Hope*,
and the riuers and countries of the *Ocean* that is right a-
gainſt *India*: and within land the kingdomes of *Presbi-
ter Iohn*, touching alſo by the way the ſpring and
original of *Nilus*, and the cauſes of his wonderful encreaſe, which ſundry fooles
doe account to bee a
Miracle.

The

THE SECOND
BOOKE.

Chap. 1.

*Of the situation of the Royall Cittie of the
Kingdome of Congo.*

Lthough the chiefe and Royall Cittie of the Kingdome of *Congo* bee after a sort comprehended within the Prouince of *Pemba*, yet notwithstāding forasmuch as the gouernement thereof, and the territorie therevnto belonging, which may in compasse amount *The Territory of the chiefest Cittie in all* Congo *contayneth in compasse 20. miles about.* to the space of twenty miles about, doeth depende wholly of the king of *Congo* himselfe, wee will place it in a seuerall regiment, and intreate of it by it selfe.

This cittie is called *San Saluatore*, or *Saint Sauiours*, and in times past in that country language it was called *The chief Citty called San-Saluadore.*

O 4 *Banza*

Banʒa, which generally fignifieth the Court, where the king or the Gouernour doeth ordinarily foiourne.

The fituation of the Citty. It is feated about 150. miles from the fea, vpon a great and a high Mountaine, being almoft all of a rocke, but yet hauing a veyne of iron in it, whereof they haue greatvfe in their houfing. This mountaine hath in the toppe of it a great plaine, very well manured and fur-

The moun-taine where-vpon it ftan-deth. nifhed with houfes and villages, contayning in circuite about ten miles, where there doeth dwell and liue the number of a hundred thoufand perfons.

The foile is fruitfull, and the ayre frefh, holefome

The foile, the ayre, the wa-ters and the cattell. and pure: there are great ftore of fpringes, of indiffe-rent good water to drinke, and at certaine times doo not harme any man: and of all fortes of cattell great aboundance. The toppe of the mountaine is feuered and diftinguifhed from all the reft of the hill which is about it, and therefore the *Portingalles* doe call it *The*

The *Otheiro.* *Otheiro,* that is to fay, *a Viewe,* or a *Watch Tower,* or a *Singular height,* from whence you may take a fight of all the Champeigne round about. Onely towardes the *Eaft,* and towardes the Riuer, it is verye fteepe and rockie.

For two caufes did the firft Princes of this King-

The reafon why they built in this place. dome place this habitation in the forefaide *Height* of this Mountaine. Firft, becaufe it lyeth in the very middeft and (as it were) in the *Center* of all the Realme, from whence he may prefently fend ayde to any part of his Kingdom that may ftand in neede of reliefe: & fecondly becaufe it is fituated in a Territory that is by Nature mounted aloft, hauing a very good ayre, and of greate fafetie: for it cannot be forced. By the chiefe common high way, that goeth vp to the Citie, and

looketh

looketh towardes the Sea, being diftant from thence
150. Miles (as hath bene told you) which way is very
large and competent, though it go fomewhat about
in compaffe, you fhall afcende fiue Myles from the
bottom to the toppe of the Mountayne. At the foote
thereof on the Eaft fyde there runneth a Riuer, wherevnto the women doe defcend by the fpace of a myles
walke to wafhe their clothes. In diuerfe other partes
thereof there are fundry valleyes planted & manured:
neyther do they fuffer any part of the countrey thereaboutes to be left vntilled or vnvfed, becaufe it is the
countrey where the Court remaineth.

The Cittie is feated in a corner or angle of the hill
towards the *Southeaft*, which *Don Alfonfo* the firft chriftian king did compaffe about with walles, and gaue
vnto the *Portingalles* a feuerall place for themfelues, fhut
vp likewife within walles. Then did he alfo inclofe his
owne pallace and the Kinges howfen with another
wall, and in the middeft betweene thefe two enclofures
left a great fpace of ground where the principal Church
was built, with a faire market place before it. The
doores and gates afwell of the lodginges of the Lords,
as of the *Portingalles* inhabitations, do open on the fide
of the faid Church. For in the vppermoft ende of the
market place do diuers great Lords of the Court dwel,
and behinde the Church doeth the market place runne
into a narrow ftreet, where there is alfo a gate, and beyond that gate many houfes towardes the *Eaft*. Without thefe walles, (which do inclofe the kinges houfes,
and the Cittie of the *Portingalles*) there are a number
of other buildinges, erected by diuers Lordes, e-
uery man making his feuerall choice of the place

P   which

Fiue miles frō the bottome of the hill to the toppe.
A riuer at the hill foote

The particu-cular fituation of the Cittie.
A feuerall place for the *Portingalles.*
The K. pallace
The principall Church and market place.

which he thinketh moſt fit & conuenient for his dwelling neere vnto the Court. So that the greatnes of
this Citie cannot well be determined or limited. Beyond theſe walles alſo, that thus do compaſſe this Citty; there is a great champaigne plaine, full of villages,
and ſundry pallaces, where euery Lorde poſſeſſeth (as
it were) a whole Towne within him ſelfe. The circuite
of the *Portingalles* cittie contayneth about a mile : and
the kings houſen as much. The walles are very thick :
the gates are not ſhutte in the night time, neyther is
there any watch or ward kept therein.

Good ſtore of
water. And although that plaine doeth lie verie high &
aloft, yet is there great aboundance of waters in it, ſo
that there is no want thereof. But the Court and the
Portingalles Cittie do al drinke of a certaine fountaine,
that ſpringeth continually, towardes the *North*, and
lyeth downe the hill, as farre as a Gunne will ſhoote:
And from hence they doe fetch all their water, and
bring it to the Cittie in veſſelles of wood, of earth and
of leather, vpon the backes of their ſlaues.

The plaine
very fruitfull.
Seuerall ſortes
of graine.

Luco. All this plaine is very fruitfull, and well manured :
It hath meadowes full of graſſe, and trees that are al-
wayes greene. It beareth ſundrie ſortes of graine, but
the principall and beſte of all is called *Luco*, which
is very like to *Muſtardſeede*, but that it is ſomewhat bigger. When it is grinded with *Hand-Quernes* (for ſo
they vſe to doe) it yeeldeth a very white meale, whereof they make bread, that is both white, and alſo of a very good ſauour, and holeſome withall: neyther doth
it giue place to our wheat in any ſort, ſauing that they
doe not celebrate the *Sacramente* with it. Of theſe
graines there now is great ſtore ouer all the Kingdom
of

of *Congo* : but it is not long fince that this feede was brought thether from that parte of the riuer *Nilus*, where it falleth into the fecond *Lake*. There is alfo a white kinde of *Millet*, called the *Mazza* of *Congo*, that is to fay, *the Corne of Congo*: and another graine which they call *Maiz*, but they make no account of it, for they giue it to their hogges : neyther doe they greatly e- fteeme of *Rice*. The forefaid *Maiz* they commonly terme by the name of *Mazza-Manputo*, that is to fay, the *Portingalles Corne*: for they call a *Portingall Man- puto*.

White *Millet* called the *Mazza* of *Congo*.
Maiza

There are moreouer diuerfe and fundry fortes of trees, that beare very great ftore of fruites, infomuch as the greatteft parte of the people doe feede vppon the fruites of the Countrey, as *Citrons*, *Limons*, and fpecial- ly *Orenges*, very ful of liquour, which are neither fweet nor fower, & are ordinarily eaten without any annoy- ance or harme at all. And to fhewe the fruitfulneffe of this countrey, the faid *Signor Odoardo* reported, that hee had feene from a kernell of the fruit of a *Pome- Citrone*, which was leaft within the rinde thereof, there fpronge vp within the fpace of fower daies a prettie tall fprigge. Other fruites there are, which they call *Banana*, and we verily thinke to be the *Mufes* of Ægypt and *Soria*, fauing that in thofe countreyes they growe to be as bigge as trees, but here they cut them yearely, to the end they may beare the better, The fruit is ve- ry fweet in fmell, and of good nourifhment. In thefe plaines there growe likewife fundry kindes of *Palme- trees*: one that beareth *Dates*, and another that beareth the *Indian Nuttes*, called *Coccos*, becaufe they haue with- in them a certaine fhell, that is like to an *Ape*: and

Diuers kinds of trees bea- ring fruit.

Banana

Diuers kindes of *Palme-trees*

there-

therevpon they vſe in *Spaine* to ſhewe ʒheir children a
Coccola when they wold make them afraide. Another
Palme tree there groweth alſo very like to the former,
but of a more ſtraunge and ſingular property : For it

The oyle of
Palme. yeeldeth *Oyle, Wyne, Vineger, Fruite,* and *Breade.*   The
Oyle is made of the Shale of the fruite, and is of the co-
lour and ſubſtance of butter, ſauing that it is ſomewhat
greeniſhe.   They vſe it, as other people do vſe *Oyle*
and butter, and it will burne like oile.   They annoint
their bodies withall, and beſides it is very good to eate.
They preſſe it out of the fruite, as oyle is preſſed out of
the *Oliues,* and then they boyle it, and ſo preſerue it.

The bread of
Palme The bread is made of the ſtone of the fruit it ſelf, which
is like to an *Almond,* but ſomewhat harder: and within
the ſame is there a certaine kernell or pith, which is
good to eate: very holeſome and of good nouriſh-

The fruit of
the *Palme*. ment.   The whole fruit, together with the vtter ſhale
is greene, and they vſe to eate it both raw and roſted.

The wine and
Vineger of
Palme. The Wine is drawne from the toppe of the tree, by
making a hole therein, from whence there diſtilleth a
liquor like milke, which at the firſt is ſweet, but afterwardes ſowre, and in proceſſe of time becommeth very *Vineger,* to ſerue for ſallets.   This wine they drinke
colde, and it moueth to vrine very much: ſo that in
thoſe countries, there is not a man that is troubled
with grauell or ſtone in the bladder. It will make them
drunke, that drinke too much of it: but in deede it is of
a very good nutriment.

There are other trees, that beare a certaine fruite
The fruit *Cola* called *Cola,* as bigge as a *Pyne-apple,* which hath within
it other fruites like *Cheſt-nuttes,* wherein are foure ſeuerall ſhales or skinnes, of redde and Carnation colour.
                                                                 Theſe

Thefe they vfe to holde in their mouthes, and chawe them, and at laft to eate them, for the quenching of their thirft, and better relifhing of their water. They comforte and preferue the ftomacke, but aboue all other qualities they are fingular good againft the difeafes of the liuer. And it is faide, that the liuer of a *Henne* or of any other like birde, which is putrified and ftinketh, being fprinkled ouer with the matter of this fruit, returneth into his former eftate, and becommeth frefh and founde againe. This foode is commonly and generally vfed among them all, and there is very great aboundance of it: and therefore it is good cheape. Other kindes of wilde *Palme-trees* there are, which yeeld diuers fruites that are eaten: and their leaues referued to make mattes, wherewith their houfes are couered, and baskets and fkeppes, and fuch other like inftrumentes, that are neceffary for their dayly vfes. Other trees there are likewife, called *Ogheghe* which beare a fruit which is like a yellow *Plumme*, and is very good to eate, and hath a very fweete fmell withall. Of thefe trees they cut off the bowes, and plant them fo thicke together, that they touch one another, and ftand clofely all in a ranke, fo that when they are growen great, they make a ftrong fenfe or wall about their houfen, which being afterwardes couered with mattes, it refembleth a handfome Court or cloffe, wherein they vfe to walke, (as it were) in an arbour that maketh a great fhaddow, and defendeth them from the heate of the Sunne. In the middeft of thefe enclofures they vfe to build certaine houfing of woode, couered with ftraw, & diuided into fundry conuenient rooms, all on the ground without any ftories or Sollers aboue them:

Other kindes of *Palme-trees*

Trees called *Ogheghe.*

P 4 Thefe

These they do line with very faire and delicate mattes, and furnish them with other ornaments in very hand-some manner.

Wherein you must note that they doe not builde thus rustically and shepheard-like for want of stuffe to builde withal.   For in the moun-taines of the Realme of *Congo*, there are a number of places, that yeelde most exquisite fine stone of diuers kindes: From whence you may digge out whole pil-lers, and principalles, & Bafes, and other peeces as big as you lift, if ye be difpofed to build.   Infomuch as it hath beene confidently affirmed, that there are to bee found among them many maffes and lumpes of ftone, which are of fuch thickneffe and hugeneffe, that you may cut out a whole Church, euen of one whole peece, yea and of the fame kinde of ftone, whereof the *Obelifco* is made, that is erected before *Porta del Po-polo* in *Rome*. Befides this, there are whole Mountains of *Porphyrie*, of *Iafper*, and of white Marble, and of other fundry colours, which here in *Rome* are called *Marbles of Numidia*, of *Africa*, and of *Æthiopia*: cer-taine pillers, whereof you may fee in the Chappell of *Pope Gregorie*.   Other Stone there is, that is fpeckled with graines or ftrakes, but among all the reft, that kind is moft admirable, which hath in it faire *Iacinthes*, that are good iewelles.   For the ftrakes being difpearfed like vaynes ouer all the bodie of their *Mother-Stone*, if you fhall diuide them and plucke them out as you would picke the kernels out of a *Pomegranate*, they wil fall into graines and little peeces of perfect *Iacynth*: But if you pleafe to make pillers, or *Obeliskes*, or other fuch like Memorialles, of the whole Maffe, you fhall fee

them

Great ftore of ftone to build with all.

them shine and sparkle, full of most faire and goodly
iewels. There are also other kinds of rare stones, which
make a shew of mettell in them, as of *Copper*, and of sundry other colours, that are very fresh, and bright, and
smooth, whereof you may make Images, or any other
worke of singular beautie. And therefore it is not the
scarcitie of matter or stuffe, that is the cause of this
their simple building, seeing that their mountains haue
such plenty of the foresaid stone, yea and perhaps more
store of other kindes, then is to be founde in any other
place of the whole worlde, besides lime, and trees for Lime & tim-
beames, and cattell both for carryage and drawing in ber, and cattel
the cart, and all other manner of prouision, that is re- to carry and
quisite for building.   True it is in deede, that they Want of
want Masons, & Cutters, and Plaisterers, and Carpen- workmen to
ters, and other such artificers: for when the Churches, build.
and the walles, and the other fabrickes in those countries were built, the workemen were brought thether
out of *Portingall*.

There are also *Tamarindes*, and *Cassia*, and *Ceders* in Stuffe for
such multitudes growing all along the Riuer of *Congo*, building ships
besides other trees of an vnmeasurable length and & housing.
thicknesse, that an infinite number of shippes and houses may be builded of them.   Their gardens do beare
all manner of hearbes and fruites, as *Pompions*, *Melions*, Hearbs and
Cocombres, *Colewortes*, and such like, besides other sorts fruites.
that doo not agree with our *Climates* of *Europe*.

Q   Chap.

Chap. 2.

Of the Originall beginning of Chriſtendome in the
Kingdome of Congo, and how the Portin-
galles obtained this trafficke.

The firſt tra=
fficke of the
Portingalles
into *Congo.*

He K. of *Pertingal Don Giouanni* the ſecōd, being deſirous to diſcouer the *Eaſt Indies*, ſent forth diuers ſhips by the coaſt of *Africa* to ſearch out this Nauigation, who hauing founde the *Iſlands* of *Capo Verde*, and the Iſle of Saint *Thomas*, and running all along that coaſt, did light vpon the Riuer *Zaire*, wherof we haue made mention before, and there they had good trafficke, and tryed the people to bee very courteous and kinde. Afterwards he ſent fourth (for the ſame purpoſe) certaine other veſſelles, to entertaine this trafficke with *Congo*, who finding the trade there to be ſo free and profitable, and the people ſo frendly, leaft certaine *Portingalles* behinde them, to learne the language, and to trafficke with them : among whom one was a Maſſe-prieſt. Theſe *Portingalles* conuerſing familiarly with the Lorde of *Sogno*, who was vncle to the

Mani Sogno
the K. vncle
entertaineth
the *Portingals.*

the King, and a man well ſtroken in yeares, dwelling at that time in the Port of *Praza* (which is in the mouth of *Zaire*) were very well entertained and eſteemed by the Prince, and reuerenced as though they had beene earthly *Gods*, and deſcended downe from heauen into thoſe Countries. But the *Portingalles* told them that they were men as themſelues were, and profeſſors of *Chriſtianitie*. And when they perceyued in how great eſtimation the people held them, the foreſaide *Prieſt* & others beganne to reaſon with the Prince touching the Chriſtian religion, and to ſhew vnto them the errors of the Pagan ſuperſtition, and by little and little to teach them the faith which wee profeſſe, inſomuch as that which the *Portingalles* ſpake vnto them, greatly pleaſed the Prince, and ſo he became conuerted.

Mani-Sogno conuerted & become a Chriſtian.

With this confidence and good ſpirit, the prince of *Sogno* went to the Court, to enforme the King of the true doctrine of the Chriſtian *Portingalles*, and to encourage him that he would embrace the Chriſtian Religion which was ſo manifeſt, and alſo ſo holeſome for his ſoules health. Herevpon the king commanded to call the Prieſt to Court, to the end he might himſelf treat with him perſonally, and vnderſtand the truth of that which the Lord of *Sogno* had declared vnto him. Whereof when he was fully enformed, he conuerted and promiſed that he would become a Chriſtian.

The King of Congo promiſeth to becom a Chriſtian.

And nowe the *Portingall* ſhippes departed from *Congo*, and returned into *Portingall*: and by them did the King of *Congo* write to the King of *Portingall*, *Don Giouanni* the ſecond, with earneſt requeſt, that he would ſend him ſome Prieſtes, with all other orders and ceremonies to make him a Chriſtian. The Prieſt alſo

Q 2   that

that remayned behind, had written at large touching this bufines, and gaue the King ful information of all that had happened, agreeable to his good pleafure.

The K. of Por- tingall fendeth Prieftes to the K. of Congo to inftruct him.
And fo the King tooke order for fundry religious perfons, to be fent vnto him accordingly, with all ornaments for the Church and other feruice, as *Croffes* and *Images*: fo that hee was throughly furnifhed with all thinges that were neceffary and needefull for fuch an action.

Mani-Sogno promoteth the Chriftian Religion.
In the meane while the Prince of *Sogno* ceafed not day and night to difcourfe with the Portingall prieft, whom he kept in his owne houfe, and at his owne table, afwell that hee might learne the Chriftian faith himfelfe, as alfo inftruct the people therein : fo that he began to fauour chriftianitie with all his power. And forafmuch as the Chriftian Religion had nowe taken roote and begun to bud in thofe Countries, and for that both the people, & alfo the king himfelfe did continue in their earneft defire to purge themfelues from that abhominable fuperftition, he did inftantly deale with the Prieft, that he wold proceed in the fowing & difpearfing of the Chriftian doctrine, as much as hee could. And in this good affection did they wait for the *Portingall* fhippes, that fhoulde bring them all prouifion for baptifme; and other thinges therevnto appertayning.

The fhips re- turne from Portingall. 1491. Mani-Sogno & his traine entertayneth the Portingals,
At the laft the fhippes of *Portingall* arriued with the expected prouifions (which was in the yeare of our faluation 1491) and landed in the port which is in the mouth of the Riuer *Zaire.* The Prince of *Sogno* with all fhewe of familiar ioy, accompanied with all his gentlemen ran downe to meete them, and entertained
the

the *Portingalles* in moſt courteous manner, and ſo con-
ducted thē to their lodgings. The next day following
according to the direction of the Prieſt that remayned
behinde, the Prince cauſed a kinde of **Church** to bee
builded, with the bodies and braunches of certayne
trees, which he in his owne perſon, with the helpe of
his ſeruantes, moſt deuoutly had felled in the woode.
And when it was couered, they erected therein three
Altars, in the worſhippe and reuerence of the moſt holy *Trinitie,* and there was baptiſed himſelfe and his
young ſonne, himſelfe by the name of our Sauiour, *E-
manuel,* and his child by the name of *Anthonie,* becauſe that Sainte is the Protector of the Cittie of
Lisbone.

    Now if any man here demande of me, what names
the people of theſe Countries had, before they receyued Chriſtianitie: of a truth it will ſeeme incredible
that I muſt anſwere them, that is to ſay, that the men
and women had no proper names agreeable to reaſo-
nable Creatures, but the common names of Plantes, of
Stones, of Birdes and of Beaſtes. But the Princes &
Lordes had their denominations from the places and
ſtates which they gouerned. As for example the foreſaid Prince, which was the firſt Chriſtian in *Congo,* was
called *Mani-Sogno,* that is to ſay, the *Prince of Sogno,* &
when hee was chriſtened, was called *Emanuel,* but at
this day they haue all in generall ſuch Chriſtian names
as they haue learned of the *Portingalles.*

    After a Maſſe was celebrated and ſonge, one of the
Prieſtes that came from *Portingall* went vp, and made
a briefe Sermon in the *Portingall* language, declaring
the ſumme of the new Religion, & faith of the Goſpel

Q 3   which

Mani-Sogno buildeth a Church.

Mani Sogno & his ſonne baptized.

What names the people of *Congo* had before they were chriſtened.

A ſermon cõtayning the ſumme of Chriſtian Religion.

which they had receiued.   This fermon, the Prieſt
that was left behinde, hauing nowe learned the *Congo*
fpeech, did more at large expounde to the Lords that
were in the Church: for the church could not poſſibly
holde the innumerable multitude of the people that

Mani Sogno were there gathered together, at the conuerſion of
rehearfeth the their Prince: who afterwardes came abroade vnto
Sermon to his
people. them, and rehearſed the whole fermon, with great loue
and charitie, mouing and exhorting them to imbrace
likewiſe the true beliefe of the Chriſtian doctrine.

　　When this was done, all the *Portingals* put themſelues
The *Portingals* on their way towards the Court, to baptiſe the King,
go to the who with a moſt feruent longing attended the ſame.
Court to bap-
tiſe the king. And the Gouernour of *Sogno* tooke order that many of
his Lordes ſhould wait vpon them with Muſicke, and
ſinging, and other ſignes of wonderfull reioyſing, beſides diuers ſlaues which he gaue them to carry their
ſtuffe, commanding alſo the people, that they ſhould
prepare all manner of victuaill to be ready in the ſtreets
for them.   So great was the number of people, that
ran and met together to beholde them, as the whole
Champaigne feemed to be in a manner couered with
them, and they all did in great kindnes entertaine and
welcome the *Portingall Chriſtians,* with ſinging and
ſounding of Trompets, and Cimballes, and other inſtrumentes of that Countrey.   And it is an admirable
thing to tell you, that all the ſtreetes and high wayes,
that reach from the *Sea,* to the Citty of *Saint Sauiours,*
being one hundred and fiftie miles, were all cleanſed
and ſwept, and aboundantly furniſhed with all manner of victuaile and other neceſſaries for the *Portingals.*
In deede they do vſe in thoſe countries, when the king

　　　　　　　　　　　　　　　　　　　　　　　　or

or the principall Lordes go abroade, to cleanſe their
waies and make them handſome : and therefore much
the rather vpon this ſpeciall occaſion, when the *Portingals*, whom they reuerenced as though they had bene
ſome of the old *Heroes*, did purchaſe for their King the
Iewell of Religion, and ſaluation of his ſoule, and generally for euery one of them the cleere knowledge of
God, and of eternall life.

    Three dayes iourney from the place whence they The Courtiers of *Congo* meet the *Portingals*.
departed, they deſcried the kinges Courtiers, that
came to meet them, to preſent them with freſh victuailes, and to doe them honour : and ſo from place to
place they encountred other Lordes, that for the ſame
purpoſe were ſent by the King to receiue the Chriſtians, who were the meſſengers and bringers of ſo great
a ioy. When they were come within three miles neere
to the Cittie, all the Court came to entertaine and welcome the *Portingalles*, with all manner of pompe and
ioyfulnes, and with muſicke and ſinging, as in thoſe
countreyes is vſed vppon their ſolemneſt feaſt-daies.
And ſo great was the multitude of people, which a-
bounded in the ſtreets, that there was neyther tree, nor
hillocke, higher then the reſt, but it was loaden with
thoſe that were runne forth and aſſembled to viewe
theſe ſtrangers, which brought vnto them this newe
law of their ſaluation. The King himſelfe attended
them at the gate of his pallace, in a Throne of eſtate e- The king him ſelfe receyueth them
rected vpon a high ſcaffold, where hee did publikely
receiue them, in ſuch manner and ſorte as the auncient
kinges of that Realme accuſtomed to doe, when any
Embaſſadours came vnto him, or when his tributes
were paied him, or when any other ſuch Royall cere-
Q 4 monies

monies were performed.

And firſt of all, the Embaſſador declared the Embaſſage of the King of *Portingall*, which was expounded
and interpreted by the foreſaid Prieſt, that was the
principall authour of the conuerſion of thoſe people.
After the embaſſage was thus deliuered, the King rayſed himſelfe out of his ſeate, and ſtandinge vpright
vppon his feete, did both with his countenaunce and
ſpeech ſhew moſt euident ſignes of the great ioy, that
he had conceyued for the comming of the Chriſtians,
and ſo ſate downe againe.   And incontinently all the
people with ſhouting, and ſounding their trumpets, &
ſinging, and other manifeſt arguments of reioycing,
did approue the kinges wordes, and ſhewed their exceeding good liking of this Embaſſage.   And further
in token of obedience, they did three times proſtrate
themſelues vpon the grounde, and caſt vp their feete,
according to the vſe of thoſe kingdomes, thereby al-
lowing and commending the action of their king, and
moſt affectionately accepting of the Goſpell, which
was brought vnto them from the Lorde God by the
handes of thoſe religious perſons.

Then the king tooke view of all the preſentes that
were ſent him by the King of *Portingall*, and the *Ve-
ſtimentes* of the *Prieſtes*, and the Ornamentes of the
Altar, and the *Croſſes*, and the *Tables*, wherein were de-
painted the *Images* of *Saintes*, and the *Streamers*, and
the *Banners*, and all the reſt, and with incredible atten-
tion, cauſed the meaning of euery one of them to bee
declared vnto him, one by one.   And ſo withdrewe
himſelfe, and lodged the *Embaſſadour* in a pallace
made ready of purpoſe for him, and all the reſt were
placed

The *Portingal* Embaſſadour declareth his Embaſſage.

The K. reioy-ceth at the Embaſſage.

The people reioyce at it.

The K. view-eth the Pre-ſents ſent vnto him by the K. of *Portingall*.

placed in other houſes of ſeuerall Lordes, where they were furniſhed with all plentie and eaſe.

The day following the King cauſed all the *Por-* tingalles to bee aſſembled together in priuate : where they deuiſed of the courſe that was to be taken for the chriſtening of the king, and for effecting the full conuerſion of the people to the chriſtian faith. And after ſundry diſcourſes, it was reſolued and concluded, that firſt of all a *Church* ſhoulde be builded, to the end that the chriſtening, and other ceremonies therevnto belonging, might be celebrated therein with the more ſolemnity : and in the meane while the king and the Court ſhould be taught and inſtructed in the *Chriſtian Religion.* The king preſently commaunded, that with all ſpeed prouiſion ſhould be made of all manner of ſtuffe neceſſary for this building, as *Timber, Stone, Lime* and *Bricke,* according to the direction and appoiutment of the *Worke-maiſters* and *Maſons,* which for that purpoſe were brought out of *Portingall.*

Conſultation among the Portingals for the Chriſtening of the K. & for the building of a Church.

But the *Deuill* who neuer ceaſeth to croſſe all good and holy proceedinges, rayſed new diſſentions, and conſpiracies, and lettes againſt this promoting of the *Chriſtian Faith,* which in deede began to ouerthrowe, and deſtroy the power that hee had long helde in that Realme, and in ſteed thereof to plant the moſt healthfull tree of the *Croſſe,* and the worſhip of the *Goſpell.* And this hee did by procuring a rebellion among certaine people of the *Anzichi,* and of *Anzicana,* which dwell vpon both the bankes of the Riuer *Zaire,* from the foreſaid falles vpwardes, to the great *Lake,* and are ſubiect and belonging to the King of *Congo.* Now this monſtrous Riuer being reſtrained and kept backe by

An inſurrection raiſed by the Deuill, to hinder the progreſſe of Chriſtian Religion.

R   theſe

thefe falles, doeth fwell there mightily, and fpreadeth it felfe abroade in a very large and deepe channell. In the breadth whereof there are many *Iflandes,* fome fmall and fome great, fo that in fome of them, there may be maintayned about thirtie thoufande perfons. In thefe *Iflandes* and in other places adioyninge to the riuers thereaboutes, did the people make an infurrecti-on, and renounced their obedience to the king, and flew the Gouernours that hee had fent thether to rule.

And all this was done by the *Deuill,* of purpofe to interrupt the propagation of Chriftianity, which was now begunne, and to hinder it by the meanes of this rebellion.   But the King, by the infpiration of God, prouided a good remedy for this mifchiefe, and fent thether his eldeft fonne, called *Mani-Sundi,* within whofe Prouince that countrey lyeth.   And yet after-wardes the trouble and tumult fell out to be fo great & daungerous, that the king muft needes go himfelfe in perfon to pacifie thefe broyles : howbeit hee refolued to be baptifed before his going, and fo was enforced to forbeare the building of the *Church* of *Stone,* and with all fpeed in fteed thereof to erect one of timber, which *Church* hee in his owne perfon with the aduice of the *Portingalles,* did accomplifh in fuch manner and fort as it ought to be, and therein did receiue the *Sacrament* of holy *Baptifme,* and was named *Don Giouanni,* and his wife *Donna Eleonora,* after the names of the king and Queene of *Portingall,* and the Church it felfe intituled and dedicated to S. *Sauiour.*

But here it is to be noted, that all thefe ftirs and re-bellion of the people aforefaide, arofe by the cunning fleight & inftigation of the Deuill, & not of the poore
foules

Mani-Sundi goeth againft the rebelles.

The K. build-eth in hafte a Church of timber.

The K. & Q. of *Congo* Chriftened. The Church of S. *Sauiours.*

ſoules themſelues, that dwell in thoſe *Iſlandes* of the *Great Lake*: (as it is written in the firſt booke of the hiſtories of the *Indies* lately ſet forth in latine). For the *Lake* is diſtant from the confines of the Cittie of *Congo*, about two hundred miles, neyther had the inhabitants thereaboutes any knowledge of *Congo*, but onely by heareſay in thoſe dayes, and very little they haue of it as yet, at this day. And beſides that, the booke is faultie in the name of that people that rebelled : for it calleth them *Mundiqueti*, whereas in deede the *Portingalles* do rightly call them *Anziqueti*. *The Latine hiſtorie of the Indies doth report amiſſe of this rebellion.*

The ſame day, wherein the king was baptiſed, diuers other Lords following his example were baptiſed likewiſe, hauing firſt learned certaine principles of the *Chriſtian Fayth*. And when all this was done, the kinge went in perſon to diſpearſe the turbulent attemptes of his aduerſaries, againſt whom he found the Prince his ſonne, and the Lorde of *Batta* already fighting with a formall Armie. But at the arriual of the king, the enemies yeelded, and ſubmitted themſelues to the obedience which before they performed: and ſo he returned in triumph to the Cittie of *Congo*, and the Prince his ſon with him, who preſently was deſirous to become a *Chriſtian*, and was chriſtened by the name of the firſt Prince of *Portingall*, called *Alfonſo*: and with him alſo were chriſtened many gentlemen and *Caualieros*, and other of his ſeruantes, that came with him out of his Prouince. *Diuers Lordes baptiſed.* *The K. goeth in perſon againſt the rebels, and diſcomfiteth thē.* *Mani-Sunai chriſtened and many other with him.*

But ſee the *Deuill* once againe, the vtter enemy of *Chriſtian Religion*, howe hee proſecuted his former intent to hinder *Chriſtianitie* among theſe people. For when hee perceyued that hee preuayled nothing by

theſe

Mani-Pango resisteth the Gospell.

these wars, he incensed the mind of the *Kings second Son*, that hee woulde not agree to receiue the new *Religion* which his *Father*, his *Mother*, his *Brother* & so many other Lords had imbraced, sowing his Cockle & Darnel not onely in him, but also in many other Lordes that fauoured him, who being addicted rather to the sensualitie of the flesh, then the puritie of the minde, resisted the Gospel, which beganne now to be preached, especially in that Commaundement, wherein it is forbidden that a man should haue any mo wiues but one. A matter that among them was more harde and difficult to be receyued, then any other Commandement whatsoeuer, because they were vsed to take as many wiues as they would. And thus the two brethren being diuided betweene themselues, eyther of them did stiffly maintaine his seuerall opinion. The eldest brother *Don Alfonso*, did with great feruencie, defende *Christianitie*, & burned all the *Idoles* that were within his Prouince. The second brother (called *Mani-Pango*, because he was Gouernour of the Countrey of *Pango*) did resist it mightely, and had gotten the greatest part of the principall Lordes of *Pango* to bee on his side. For there were diuers of the newe christned Lordes, whose Ladies seeing themselues seperated, and forlorne of their *Husbande-Lordes* by force of the *Christian Lawe*, did take it as a great iniury and scorne done vnto them, and blasphemed and cursed this new Religion beyond all measure. These Lords vnited themselues together with others, and began to plot treachery against *Don Alfonso*, hoping that if they could ridde him out of the world, the Christian Faith would vtterly cease of it selfe. And therefore *Mani-Pango* and his

Mani-Pango and his complices accuse Mani-Sundi to his father,

his complices gaue intelligence to his Father, that the
Prince *Don Alfonso* fauoured the Chriſtian faction, onely to the end that vnder the colour of his countenance
and fauour they might rayſe an inſurrection and rebellion againſt him, and to driue him out of his kingdome.

The king gaue credite to their informations, and
depriued his ſonne of the Gouernement wherein hee
was placed: But the prouidence of God which reſer-
ued him for a greater matter, did relieue him by the
good mediation and counſell of his frendes, who entreated the *King* his Father, that he would not be moued to anger, before he had examined the anſweres &
reaſons of the Prince his ſonne.   Wherein the Kinge
was eſpecially perſwaded by *Mani-Sogno,* who (as we
tolde you) was before chriſtened, and called *Don Ema-*
nuel, and by good happe was in Court at that preſent.
This man (being the auncienteſt *Courtier* and Lorde
of that time, ſingularly well beloued of the king and
all his people) did with ſound reaſons and dexterity of
wit, procure the king to reuoke the ſentence that was
giuen againſt the Prince *Don Alfonſo,* ſo that the Kinge
being afterwardes throughly informed both of the ho-
neſt mind and actions of his ſonne, perceiued that the
accuſations plotted againſt him, were falſe and mali-
ous, and therevpon reſtored him againe to his former
gouernement, with a ſpeciall charge, that hee ſhoulde
not proceed with ſuch rigour againſt the Gentiles, for
the propagation & exaltation of the chriſtian Religion.
But he being full of feruent charity, and godly ſpirit,
ceaſed not (for all that) to aduance the faith of the *Go-*
ſpell, and to put the commandements of God in execu-

R 3   tion

The K. depri-
ueth *Mani-*
Sundi of his
gouernment.

Mani-Sogno
maketh inter-
ceſſion for his
brother.

Mani-Sundi
reſtored.

tion.

    Wherevpon his aduerfaries who neuer refted from their former attempt, were continually at the Kinges elbowe, and fought by all cunning fhifts and fecret de-uifes, to deftroy that which the good prince had build-ed, efpecially when they faw that the Prince of *Sogno* was departed from Court, and returned into his Go-uerne ment. So that no body being now leaft to pro-tect & defend the *Chriftian Religion*, the King began to doubt of the faith, which with fo great zeale he had before embraced: and therefore fent to his fonne, that he fhould come againe to the Court, to make account of thofe *Reuenues* that hee had gathered within the Countrey of his Gouernement, with a full intent and meaning indeed to depriue him, when his accountes fhoulde be finifhed.   But hee being illumined by his good *Angell*, and difcouering the treacheries of the e-nemies of God and himfelfe, delayed and delayed the matter fo long, that in the meane while, his Father be-ing an old man, did by meanes of a naturall infirmity departe out of this life.   And his mother who alwaies perfeuered conftant in the *Catholicke Faith*, louinge her eldeft fonne moft entirely, concealed the Kinges death for the fpace of three daies, being therein aided and affifted by fome of her truftie frendes, and gaue it out, that the King had taken fuch order as no man might come vnto him to trouble him. In the meane feafon fhe did fecreatly fignifie to her Sonne the death of his father, which fhe would keepe clofe till his com-ming, and charged him without any delay, and in all hafte to fpeede him to the Court.   This fhe did by ceitaine *Runners*, that from place to place in conueni-ent

Marginal notes:

The K. waue-reth in Religi-on, & calleth *Mani-Sundi* to account, of purpofe to de-priue him.

The K. dyeth.

The Queene Mother fen-deth in all haft for her fonne *Mani-Sundi.*

ent diftaunces and iourneyes, are alwayes readie like *Poftes* to conueigh the precepts and commandements of the King ouer all the Realme. Wherevpon he prefently caufed himfelfe to be carryed *Poft* both day and night, by certaine flaues according to the vfe of that Countrey, and in one day and two nightes, with moft exquifite diligence accomplifhed the iourney of two hundred miles, and fo arriued at the Cittie, before he was expected.

Chap. 3.

*Don Iohn, the firft Chriftian King being dead, Don Alfonfo
his fonne fucceeded. Of his warres againft his Brother. Of certaine miracles that were wrought,
and of the Conuerfion of thofe
people.*

Ow together with the death of the king, there was alfo publifhed the fucceffion to the *Crowne* of *Don Alfonfo*, being then prefent, who in his owne perfon did accompanie the corps of his deade Father to the buriall, withall the Lords of the Court, and all the Chriftian *Portingalles*,

The funerall of *K. Iohn*, celebrated by K. *Alfonfo*.

S   which

which was solemnifed after the manner of Chriften-
dome, with feruice and prayers for the dead, and all
this with fuch funerall pompe, as was neuer feene before among thofe people.   But they which heretofore were aduerfaries to this newe King, doubting of
their owne fafetie if they fhould remaine in the Court,
vnited themfelues with *Mani-Pango*, who was nowe
departed into the Prouince of his owne Gouernment,
and while his father liued, was wholly employed in
fighting againft the *Mozombi*, and certaine other people that had rebelled againft him.   When he heard
of the death of his Father, and vnderftoode that his
brother was already placed in the *Seate Royall*, he tooke
truce with his enemies, and gathering together a great
armie beganne to go in armes againft his Brother , and
lead with him almoft all the whole Realme, which in
deed fauoured him, to the number of two hundred
thoufande men. King *Alfonfo* awaited his comming
at the *Royall Cittie* , with a very fmall number, fauing
that he was directed, aduifed and affifted by the good
auncient Lord *Mani-Sogno*, who vniting himfelfe vnto him in the ftrength and vertue of the holy *Chriftian
Faith*, and making a lift of all thofe armed frends, that
he had to defend him againft fo great an enemy,found
by computation that they did not amount to the number of ten thoufand, among which there were but a-
bout one hundred Chriftians, naturall of that Countrey, befides fome few *Portingalles,* which by chance
arriued there at that time.

All thefe people were indeed too few for fuch an
encounter, and therefore not very refolute to abide a-
ny attempt, but became very doubtfull and timorous,
by

Mani-Pango rebelleth againft his brother.

The Kinges power both flender and timerous.

by reafon of the great power, that *Mani Pango* brought
with him. But the king trufting confidently in his
ftrong faith, and in the Celeftiall aide and affiftance:
comforted and ftrengthened his fouldiers by all the
meanes he could, and fo did the good olde Lorde his
vncle, who ceafed not,both night and day,with words
and deeds to encourage that fmal number, which they
had, to expect and endure the affaults of their aduerfaries, with all manhoode and courage, affuring them,
that God would bee their helpe and fuccour.   Thus,
while they attended the procedinges of their enemies,
Mani-Pango and his forces fet forwardes to the be-
fieging of the Cittie, with fo great a noife of warlicke
inftrumentes, and cries, and fhoutinges, and terrible
threatninges, that the poore fewe, which were in the
Cittie,afwel Chriftians as others,fainted in their harts,
and failed in their courage, and came and prefented
themfelues before the king, faying, that hee had not
power enough to refift fo power-full an enemie, and
therefore they thought it better for him to growe to
fome concorde and compofition, and to abandon the
new *Religion*, which hee had lately begun to profeffe,
to the ende hee might not fall into the handes of his
cruell aduerfaries.   But the king being refolute, and The king to
full of religious conftancie, reproued their cowardife, his fouldiers.
and called them daftardes, and bafe people, and willed „
them, if they had any mind or defire to forfake him,& „
go to the enemie,that they fhould fo doe: As for him- „
felfe and thofe few that would follow him, hee did not „
doubt but affuredly truft, though not with the poffibi- „
litie or ftrength of man, yet with the fauour of God,to „
vanquifh and ouercome that innumerable multitude, „

„ And therefore he would not requeſt them eyther to
„ ioyne with him, or to put their liues in hazarde againſt
„ his aduerſaries for his ſake, but onely they might reſt
„ themſelues and expect the iſſue that ſhoulde followe
„ thereon.

But they for all this ſpeech became neuer a whit the
more couragious, but rather waxed more timorous, &
were vtterly determined to forſake the king, and to
ſaue themſelues.   Now they were ſcarſe out of the
Cittie, and on their way homewardes, when by great
good fortune, they met with the good old Lord *Mani-*
Sogno, who with ſome few of his followers had beene
abroade to ſurueigh the enemies Campe, and to make
prouiſion for ſuch thinges as were neceſſary in ſuch an
action: To him they declared all that they had before
declared to the King, *That they thought it to bee a point*
of expreſſe madneſſe, to put their liues and goods in daunger
with ſo fewe people againſt an infinite multitude, and that
without all doubt it were a ſafer way to compounde with the
enemie, and ſo ſaue themſelues.   The good Lorde with
great pietie and Chriſtian valour aunſwered them, that
they ſhould not ſo quickly fall into diſpaire; but (as the
king had tould them before) they ſhould looke vpon
Ieſus Chriſt the Sauiour of the worlde, whoſe faith and
religion they had ſo lately and with ſo great zeale gayned and purchaſed: who alſo moſt aſſuredly and vn-
doubtedly would ſuccour and defend thoſe that were
his. And ſo entreated them, that they woulde not like
raſh headed people chaunge their mindes from that
holy doctrine, which they had with ſuch feruency of
late receyued, adding moreouer, that they had not to
fight with a ſtraunge nation, nor with a people that
came

The Kinges
Souldiers de-
part from
him.

Mani Sogno
meeteth with
them.

came from farre Countries, but with their owne kinf-
men and countreymen, fo that they might alwaies
haue opportunity (if need fo require) to yeelde themfelues, and in all frendfhip and kindneffe to bee embraced.   Behold I pray you (faith *Mani-Sogno*) mine age „
now arriued to a hundred yeares, and yet I beare armes „
for the zeale and defence of the Religion that I haue „
entred, and for the homage and honour that I owe to „
my king. And you that are in the flower of your yeares, „
do you fhew your felues to be fo bafe and feareful, and „
vnfaithfull to your owne narurall king? If algates you „
be not minded to fight your felues, yet incourage your „
vaffals and fubiects, and doo not difmay them.   Let „
vs expect the firft encounter of the enemie, and there- „
vpon we fhall not want fit occafion to take fome other „
courfe and prouide for our fafetie.

   With thefe comfortable wordes, the Lords re- *The Fugitiues*
couered their fpirites that were quailed, and returned *returne and*
backe with him to feeke the king, who was in the *afke the King*
Church at his prayers, befeeching God to fende him *forgiuenes.*
helpe and fuccour.   They waited for him vntill he
came forth, and then kneeled downe vpon their knees
before him, requefting pardon for their fault and want
of dutie, which they had fhewed vnto him being their
Prince, in that they would haue forfaken him when he
was in this extreame daunger, and promifing that they
would put on a new and conftant courage for the defence of him, and of the law and religion which they
had receyued, and that they would fight for thefame
euen vntill death.   But the king who perceyued well
that this comfort and helpe came from God himfelfe, *The K. giueth*
firft gaue him hartie thanks fecretly from the bottome *thankes to*
God.

of his hart, and vowed that he would sacrifice himselfe
for the maintenance of his faith and Gospell. And then
with a cheerefull countenance he saide. I doe beleeue
" (Lord) that thy greatnes is infinite, and that thou canst
" doo all thinges, and canst make of little much, and of
" much little, whenfoeuer it pleafeth thee. Neyther do
" I any thing doubt, but that thou wilt yeeld aide to this
" my weakenes, and affift the fame with thine inuincible
" force, fo that through thy gracious fauour, with thefe
" few and weake perfons I fhall become the conquerour
" not onely of this armie, but alfo of a farre greater, if it
" fhould come againft me. And I promife thee (O my
" God) befides that which I haue already fpoken, that I
" will all the dayes of my life promote and exalt thy
" true faith, thy holy name, and thy moft holefome do-
" ctrine. In teftimony and memory of which his con-
feffion, he did prefently caufe a *Croffe* to bee planted, &
erected in the middeft of the market place right againft
the *Church*, which his father had builded : This *Croffe*
was of a wonderful length, for it was fourefcore fpan
long, and the Croffe-barre in proportion aunfwerable
therevnto. Nowe the eternall God, who knew the
faith from whence this vow of the good king did proceed, vouchfafed to comfort him with a celeftiall vifion, which was a very cleere and admirable light. At
the fhining whereof, hee caft himfelfe vpon his knees,
and wept, and lifted vp his handes and eyes to heauen, but fpake not a word, for that hee was ouercome
with teares, and fighes, and wholly rauifhed in fpirite.
But that which he himfelfe faw, was feene of no body
els, neyther woulde hee euer publifh the fame to any
man. All thofe that were in his company did euen

*The King e-
recteth a
Croffe of a
great length.*

*A vifion ap-
peared to him*

as

as he did, and for a while loſt the ſight of their eyes : and by reaſon of that miraculous light remayned in a traunce.   At the laſt euery man lifted vp his eyes, and perceyued that there were imprinted on him fiue *Swordes*, very bright and cleere, which for the ſpace almoſt of an houre continued vnmoueable (as it were) in a circle, but all they could neyther vnderſtand nor expounde what was the meaning thereof.   The fiue *Swordes* the *King* tooke for his armes, as is to be ſeene in his *Signet Royall*, which hath beene   vſed   euer ſithence that time,   yea euen by the *Kinge* that nowe liueth and raigneth.   The *Croſſe* alſo, that was thus planted by vowe, is to be ſeene in the ſame place, wherein it was erected, at the front of the *Church*, which *Church* was called *Saint Croſſes*, of the *Croſſe* there planted, and of the miracle that there appeared. This *Croſſe* the laſt *King*, that dead is, *Don Aluaro* father to the *King* that now is, renewed and made another of the ſame bignes that the firſt was of, in remembraunce of ſuch a miracle. For the old *Croſſe* was in time decaied and conſumed, and quite fallen downe.

The Armes of the King of Congo.

The aforeſaid viſion did greatly confirme the minds of the Cittizens, which before were quailed, and did wonderfully appall and fully terrifie the enemies, when they vnderſtood the news thereof. Notwithſtanding *Mani-Pango* ſent vnto the *King*, & ſignified vnto him and to all the reſt that were with him,   that if they did not incontinently yeelde themſelues, and deliuer the Cittie vnto him, and create and ſweare him for their *King*, and withall abandon and relinquiſh their newe *Chriſtian Religion*, he would put them all to the edge of the ſworde: but if they would ſo do, hee woulde

The proude meſſage of *Mani-Pango* to the King.

freely

freely pardon them. Herevnto the Lordes that ſtood
on the Kinges parte anſwered,that they were moſt ready to die in defence of their *Prince*, and of the *Chriſtian*
" *Faith.* But in particular the *King* ſent him this meſſage,
" that he nothing feared his terrible threates, but rather
" as his kind brother was very ſory, euen from his hart, to
" ſee that he walkcd in darkenes, and ſtrayed out of the
" way of light: that the kingdome did by law belong vn-
" to him, and was not fraudulently vſurped by him: And
" that the *Religion*, which he had receyued, was aſſured-
" ly deliuered him from God, who no doubt woulde
" protect and maintaine him therein: And withall be-
" ſought him, that he would eſtraunge himſelfe from his
" falſe beliefe and worſhipping of the *Deuill*, wherein he
" had beene nouriſhed and brought vp,and that he wold
" be baptized, for ſo hee ſhoulde become the childe of
" God, and merite the *Glorie Celeſtiall.* Then the *King*
ſent to fetch his iewelles and other rich ornamentes of
houſholde, which he had at home, and the better to
encourage theſe Lordes, that tooke his part, hee moſt
graciouſly diſtributed them amongſt them all: wherewith they remayned very greatly ſatiſſied, and bounde
themſelues to proſecute his enterpriſe and to followe
his enſigne with a moſt ardent courage.

    This being done, the very ſame night, the one halfe
almoſt of the baſe people that were in armes, being ſurpriſed with a very great feare did ſecretly flie into the
Campe of *Pango*, and hauing thus reuolted, gaue *Mani-
Pango* to vnderſtand, that the *King* and all the reſt of
his retinue were vtterly diſmaied and diſcouraged,that
euery man was deuiſing with himſelfe how he might
eſcape, & that they had none other meane to ſaue
themſelues

The Kinges antwere.

The King re- wardeth his followers.

Certain timo- rous fugitiues runne to the Campe of Mani-Pango.

themfelues but onely by taking the lane that leadeth downe to the Riuer, which (as wee haue tolde you) was diftant from the Cittie about the fpace of a mile. At the end of which lane, betweene the Riuer and the hill, there was a little *Moore* about two foot deepe on the right hande, and on the left hand were the mountaines, and the garrifons of *Pango*, that had befieged & befet the hill, fo that there was none other iffue for them to efcape, but onely by paffing ouer the *Moore*, which was in length as farre as the fhotte of an Arcubufe could reach, and as much in bredth, and then to come to the Riuer. *Mani-Pango* beleeuing all this, that they had related vnto him, fent prefently to ftop that paffage, with planting fharpe ftakes in the bottome of the *Moore*, which were couered with water, to the ende that if his enemies fhoulde flie in the darke of the night becaufe they would not be feene, they fhoulde be all ftaked and taken therein. All that night he with all his armie remayned in great ioy, and awaited the frefh morning, that he might giue the affault vpon the Cittie, bethinking himfelfe in the meane while, what courfe might be moft eafie and conuenient for him to attempt the fame.

A ftratagem of *Mani-Págo.*

But *Don Alfonfo* on the other fide, hauing confeffed himfelfe, and confulted with all the moft faithful and loyall frendes that hee had, expected his enemie, who affuring himfelfe of the victorie, and hauing now granted all the Cittizens goodes, and all the ftates and Gouernementes of the kingdome, to his great Lords about him, very earely in the morning with a furious violence gaue affault to the Cittie, on that fide which is towardes the *North*, where the great and wide plaine

Mani-Pango affaulteth the Cittie.

T   reftraining

reftrayning it felfe into a narrow ftraite, entreth (as it were into a rounde circle, naturally compaffed about with certaine hilles, and then maketh a large way, as broade as a man maye fhoote with a Gunne, vntill you come to the fite or place where the Cittie ftandeth, which is a little plaine of two miles compaffe, wherein (as it hath beene tolde you) the Cittie and the *Church*, and the Lordes houfes and the kings court are fituate. In this place did *Don Alfonfo*, with thofe few that he had with him, fettle himfelfe againft the *Pagans*, and againft his *Enemie-Brother*, who before hee coulde confront the Kinge, was vtterly difcomfited, difpearfed and put to flight. Wherevppon the king perceyuing that he was ouerthrowne and driuen to runne away, was wonderfully amazed, not knowing himfelfe how this matter came to paffe, feeing that he had not ioyned battel, nor fought with his enemies, and therefore muft needes thinke, that it fo fell out by fome hidden and fecreate meanes to him vnknowne. Notwithftandieg the day following *Mani-Pango* returned to the affault in the fame place, but hee was in the fame manner once again difcomfited and conftrained to flie: whereby hee knew affuredly that this his loffe and ouerthrow was not occafioned by the valour of his enemies, but onely by fome miracle. So that the people of the Cittie mocking and fcorning thofe *Idolaters*, and taking ftomacke vnto them, for thefe two victories thus happened, beganne nowe to make no reconing of them, and woulde with all violence haue runne vpon them. To whome their aduerfaries made this aunfwere, *Tufh you are not the men that haue thus vanquifhed vs, but it was a certaine faire Lady all in white*

Mani-Pango difcomfited without any fight.

Mani-Pango the feconde time difcomfited in like manner.

white, which with her admirable brightnesse had blinde-
ded vs , and a Knight riding vppon a white palfrey, that „
had a redde Crosse vppon his breast: and hee it was that „
fought against vs, and turned vs to flight. Which when „
the King vnderftoode, he fent to tell his brother, that
of thofe two, the one was a *Virgin,* the *Mother* of *Chrift,*
whofe faith he had embraced: and the other was S.
Iames, who both were fent from God to fuccour and
relieue him, and that if he alfo would become a *Chri-*
ftian, they would likewife fhew great grace and fauour
vnto him. But *Mani-Pango* would not accept of this
meffage, but all the night following did put himfelfe
in a readineffe to befiege the Cittie vpon both fides at
once, the one with one part of his Armie at the ftraite
aboue mentioned, and the other with another parte of
his people, himfelfe in his owne perfon compaffing
about by the lane that afcendeth from the riuer, and fo
in a place vtterly vnprouided of eyther watch or ward,
he thought to attempt the victorie. Thofe that were
aboue at the ftrait did firft ioyne battell, and were quite
difcomfited and ouerthrowne : and *Pango* himfelfe,
hoping to haue thruft forward on the other fide, while
his enemies were wholly occupyed in defending themfelues at the ftraite, found himfelfe greatly deceyued :
for his people were already put to flight by thofe of the
Cittie. who perceyuing the great noyfe, that *Pango*
and his troupes made in afcending the hill on the o-
ther fide, ranne with all fpeed to meete with that danger, and driuing him and all his people backe againe,
put them in difarray, and then fo vexed and molefted
them with fuch a furie of dartes and other weapons,
which they threwe among them, that *Pango* being o-

Mani-Pango
affaulteth the
Cittie on both
fides at once.

T 2   uercome

The ftrata-
gem of *Mani-
Pango* turneth
to his owne
deftruction.

uercome with feare and daunger ranne away, and fell
into the fnares and nettes which he himfelfe had layde
for the *Chriftians*. For lighting among the forefaide
ftakes, he was with one of them thruft into the bodie,
and fo being furprifed with an euill death, he finifhed
his life, as it were in a rage. For you muft vnderftand
that the fharpe ends of the faid ftakes were envenomed
with a certaine poyfon, which taking holde of the
blood, and entring fomewhat into the flefh, woulde
kill without all cure or remedy.

By this victory and death of his brother did the king
remaine in fecuritie and libertie, wiihout all contradi-
ction, and then thinking with himfelfe, that his people and fubiectes were in a great doubt and quandarie,
and durft not for feare prefent themfelues before him,
by reafon of the errour that they had committed a-
gainft him, like a good Prince hee fent to fignifie vnto
them, that he would pardon their former faultes, and
receiue them into his grace and fauour. Wherevpon
they came and yeelded themfelues vnto him with all
obedience, all fauing the *Captaine Generall*, whofe name
was *Mani-Bunda*. For hee feared greatly to appeare
before the king, for very fhame of his difloyaltie and
villanie: but yet at the laft hee obtained his pardon,
with a certaine penance enioyned him, that he fhould
go and ferue in the building of the *Church* : wherevpon he became afterwardes fo humble and deuout a
Chriftian: that when the King woulde haue eafed him
of that trauell, he would not by any meanes giue ouer
his labour, vntill fuch time as all the *Church* was wholly built and finifhed.

The Kingdome being thus pacified, and all things
well

well eftablifhed, the king *Don Alfonfo* tooke order, that they fhould prefently go in hande with the fabricke of the principall *Church*, called *S. Croffes*, which was fo named of the *Croffe* that was there planted (as wee tolde you before) and alfo becaufe vpon the feaft day of the *Holy Croffe* the firft ftone was layed in the foundation thereof. Moreouer hee commaunded that the men fhould bring ftones, and the weomen fhoulde fetch fand from the Riuer, for the furthering of this worke. The king woulde needes bee the firft *Porter* himfelfe, and vppon his owne fhoulders brought the firft basket of ftones, which he caft into the foundation, and the *Queene* her basket of fande likewife, thereby giuing an example to the Lordes and the Ladies of the Court to do the like, and to encourage and harten the people in fo holy an action. And fo this fabricke being furthered by fo good worke-maifters and workemen, in a very fhort time was fully finifhed, and therein were celebrated *Maffes*, and other diuine feruice, with great folemnitie, befides a number of Lords and others that were there baptifed and chriftened: fo that the multitude of fuch as came to bee partakers of the *Holy Baptifme* abounded fo greatly, that there were not *Prieftes* enough to execute that office.

After this the king difpatched away the *Portingall Embaffadour*, who till this time had remained at the Court, by reafon of thefe troubles: and with him hee fent alfo another *Embaffadour* of his owne, called *Don Roderico*, and diuerfe others that were of kinne both to himfelfe and to his *Embaffadour*, to the ende that they fhould learne both the doctrine of the *Chriftians* in *Portingall*, and alfo their language, and further declare vn-

The building of the Church called Saint Croffes.

K. Alfonfo difpatcheth the Portingal Embaffadour, & another of his owne into Portingall.

T 3

to the

The K. com=
mandeth all
Idolles to be
brought in, &
all other
things that are
contrary to
Chriftian Re-
ligion.

to th e King all thefe accidents that had happened.

     Moreouer hee caufed the Lordes of all his pro-
uinces to bee affembled together in a place appointed for that purpofe, and there publikely fignified vnto them, that whofoeuer had any *Idoles,* or any thing
els that was contrary to the *Chriftian* Religion, he fhould
bring them forth and deliuer them ouer to the *Licuete-
nantes* of the Countrey : Otherwife whofoeuer did
not fo, fhould be burned themfelues without remiffi-
on or pardon.   Which commandement was incontinently put in execution.   And a wonderfull thing
it is to bee noted, that within leffe then one moneth,
all the *Idolles* , and *Witcheries* and *Characters,* which they
worfhipped and accounted for *Gods,* were fent and
brought vnto the Court.   And certainely the number
of thefe toyes was infinite: for euery man adored and
reuerenced the thing that beft liked him, withour any
order, or meafure, or reafon at all, fo that there was
among them a huge multitude of *Deuilles,* in fundrie
ftraunge and terrible fhapes.   Many there were, that
carryed a deuotion to *Dragons* with winges, which
they nourifhed and fed in their owne priuate houfes,
giuing vnto them for their foode the beft and moft
coftly viandes that they had.   Others kept *Serpent s*
of horrible figures: Some worfhipped the greateft
Goates, they could get, fome *Tygres,* and other moft
monftrous Creatures, yea the more vncouth & deformed the beaftes were, the more they were honoured.
Some held in veneration certaine vncleane foules and
night-birdes, as *Backes, Owles* and *Schritche-Owles,* and
fuch like. To be briefe , they did choofe for their Gods
diuers *Snakes,* and *Adders,* and *Beaftes,* and *Birdes,* and
                                         Hearbes

Hearbes, and *Trees,* and fundry *Characters* of woode and of ſtone, & the figures of all theſe things aboue rehearſed, aſwell painted in colours, as grauen in woode and in ſtone, and in ſuch other ſtuffe. Neyther did they onely content themſelues with worſhipping the ſaide creatures when they were quick and aliue, but alſo the very skins of them when they were dead, being ſtuffed with ſtraw.

The acte of this their adoration was performed in diuers ſortes, all wholly addreſſed and directed to expreſſe their humilitie, as by kneeling on their knees, by caſting themſelues groueling vpon the earth, by defiling their faces with duſt, by making their prayers vnto their *Idoles* in wordes and in actions, and by offering vnto them the beſt parte of the ſubſtaunce which they had in their poſſeſſion. They had moreouer their *Witches,* which made the fooliſh people to belieue, that their *Idoles* could ſpeake: and ſo deceyued them: and if any man being in ſicknes or infirmitie woulde recommend himſelfe vnto them, and afterwardes that man recouered his health, the *Witches* woulde perſwade him that the *Idole* had beene angry with him, but now was appeaſed and had healed him. And this is in part that which was vſed among the *Moci-Conghi* concerning their *Religion,* before they had receiued the *Water* of *Holy Baptiſme,* and the knowledge of the liuing *God.*

Now the King hauing gathered togerher all theſe abhominable *Images,* and put them into diuers houſes within the Cittie, and commanded, that to the ſame place, where a little before hee had fought and vanquiſhed his brothers Armie, euery man ſhould bring a

T 4

burthen

Their deuout worſhipping of Idols.

Witches

The K. burned all the Idols.

burthen of woode, which grew to be a great heape, &
when they had cast into it all the said *Idoles*, & pictures,
and whatsoeuer els the people afore that time held for
a God, he caused fire to be set vnto them, and so vtterly consumed them.   When he had thus done, he as-
sembled all his people together, and in steed of their
Idoles which before they had in reuerence, hee gaue
them *Crucifixes* and *Images* of *Saintes*, which the *Portin-*
galles had brought with them, and enioyned euery
Lord, that euery one in the Cittie of his owne Gouernment and Regiment shoulde builde a *Church*, and set
vp *Crosses*, as he had already shewed vnto them by his
owne example.   And then he tolde them and the rest
of his people, that hee had dispatched an *Embassadour*
into *Portingall* to fetch *Priestes*, that should teach them
Religion, and administer the most holy and holesome
Sacraments to euery one of them, and bring with them
diuers *Images* of *Christ*, of the *Virgin Mother*, and of o-
ther *Saintes* to distribute among them.   In the meane
while hee willed them to bee of good comfort, and to
remaine constant in the faith.   But they had so liuely
imprinted the same in their hartes, that they neuer
more remembred their former beliefe in false and lying *Idoles*.

He ordayned moreouer, that there shoulde be three
Churches builded.   One in reuerence of our *Sauiour*,
to giue him thanks for the victorie which he had granted vnto him, wherein the Kinges of *Congo* doe lye buried, and whereof the *Cittie Royall* tooke the name,
(for as it was tolde you before, it is called *S. Sauiours*.)
The second *Church* was dedicated to the *Blessed Virgin*,
the *Mother* of *God*, called *Our Ladie of Helpe*, in memory
of

The king
commandeth
euery Lorde
to build a
Church in the
Cittie of his
owne gouern-
ment.

The K. build-
eth 3.Churches
One to Saint
Sauiour.

The second to
our Ladie of
Helpe.

of the fuccour which he had againſt his enemies: And
the thirde was conſecrated to *S. Iames*: in honour and The third to
S. Iames.
remembraunce of the miracle, which that *Saint* had
wrought by fighting in the fauour of the *Chriſtians*,&
ſhewing himſelfe on horſebacke in the heat of the battell.

    Not long after this, the ſhippes arriued from *Por-* The ſhips re-
turne from
tingall, with many men that were skilfull in the holy *Portingall*
ſcriptures, and diuers religious *Friers* of the orders of with *Friers*,&
S. Frauncis, and of *Saint Dominike*, and of *Saint Auſtine*, *Prieſtes.*
with ſundry other Prieſtes, who with great charitie
and feruencie of ſpirite, ſowed and diſpearſed the *Ca-*
tholike Faith ouer all the Countrey: which was preſently embraced by all the people of the kingdome,
who held the ſaid *Prieſts* in ſo high reuerence, that they
worſhipped them like *Saintes*, by kneeling vnto them,
and kiſſing their hands, and receiuing their bleſſing, as
often as they met them in the ſtreetes.   Theſe *Prieſtes*
being arriued into their ſeueral Prouinces, did inſtruct
the people in the faith of *Chriſt*, and taking vnto them
certaine of the naturalles of the Countrey, they taught
them the true heauenly doctrine, whereby they might
the better declare the ſame to their owne Countreymen in their owne proper language. So that in proceſſe of time the *Catholike Faith* was rooted ouer all
thoſe Countreyes in ſuch ſorte, as it perſeuereth and
continueth there euen till this day, although it hath
endured ſome ſmall hinderance, as in conuenient place
we ſhall ſhew vnto you.

V   Chap.

Chap. 4.

The death of the King Don Alfonso, and the succession of Don Piedro. How the Islande of Saint Thomas was first inhabited, and of the Bishop that was sent thether. Other great accidents that happened by occasion of Religion. The death of two Kings by the conspiracie of the Portingalles & the Lordes of Congo. How the Kinges linage was quite extinguished. The banishment of the Portingalles.

WHile these matters were thus in working for the seruice of God, & that *Christianitie* was nowe begun and encreased with so happy successe, it pleased God to call away to himselfe the King *Don Alfonso*, who at the time of his death yeelded great signes, which beautified and exalted his former life, For he dyed in great faith, declaring that his hower was now come, and discoursed of the Christian Religion with so great confidence and charitie, as it euidently appeered that the *Crosse* and *Passion*, & the true beliefe in our *Sauiour Iesus Christ* was imprinted in the roote of his heart. To *Don Piedro*, his sonne & successour he did especially & principally recommend the

King Alfonso dyeth.

Don Piedro succeedeth him.

the *Chriſtian doctrine*, which in deed following the example of his father, he did maintain and vphold accordingly.

In his time, there began to ſayle into theſe quarters a great number of veſſels, and the *Iſlande* of *S. Thomas* was inhabited with *Portingalles*, by the Kinges commandment.   For before thoſe dayes it was all waſte and deſert within lande, and inhabited onely vpon the ſhore by a few ſaylers that came from the countries adioyning.   But when this *Iſlande* in proceſſe of time was well peopled with *Portingalles*, and other nations that came thether by licence of the King, and became to be of great trafficke, and was tilled and ſowed, the king ſent thether a *Biſhoppe*, to gouerne the *Chriſtians* that were in that *Iſlande*, and thoſe alſo that were in *Congo*: which the ſaid *Biſhoppe* did accompliſh preſently vpon his arriuall, and afterwardes in *Congo*, where hee tooke poſſeſſion of his Paſtorall charge. When he was come into the kingdome of *Congo*, it was a thing incredible to ſee, with howe great ioy hee was entertained by the Kinge and all his people.   For from the ſea ſide euen vnto the Cittie, being the ſpace of a hundred and fiftie miles, he cauſed the ſtreetes to bee made ſmooth and trimme, and to be couered all ouer with Mattes, commanding the people, that for a certaine ſpace ſeuerally appointed vnto them, they ſhoulde prepare the wayes in ſuch ſort, that the *Biſhoppe* ſhoulde not ſet his foote vpon any part of the grounde which was not adorned.   But it was a farre greater wonder, to behold all the countrey thereaboutes, and all the trees, and all the places that were higher then the reſt, ſwarming with men and weomen that ran forth to ſee the *Biſhop*,

The Iſle of S. Thomas beginneth to be inhabited.

The King of Portingall ſendeth one to be Biſhop of the Iſle of S. Thomas, and of Congo.

The entertainment of the Biſhop in Congo.

as a man that was holy and fent from God, offering vnto him, fome of them lambes, fome kiddes, fome chickins, fome *Partriches*, fome venifon, and fome fifh, and other kindes of victuailes in fuch aboundance, that hee knew not what to do withall, but leaft it behind him; whereby he might well know the great zeale and obedience of thefe new *Chriftians*. And aboue all other thinges it is to be noted for a memorable matter, that the *Bifhoppe* going on his way, there met him an innumerable multitude of men, & weomen, and girles, and boyes, and perfons of fourefcore yeares of age, and aboue, that croffed him in the ftreetes, and with fingular tokens of true beliefe required the water of *Holy Baptifme* at his hands: neyther would they fuffer him to paffe vntill hee had giuen it them: fo that to fatiffie their defires, hee was greatly ftayed in his viage, and was faine to carry water with him in certaine veffelles, and falte, and other prouifion neceffary for that action.

But I will leaue to report vnto you all the welcome and entertainment, that was made vnto him in euery place where he came, and the liuely ioy that generally and particularly was fhewed for the comming of this *Bifhoppe*. And now I will tell you, that hee arriued at the Cittie of *Saint Sauiours*, where hee was met by the *Priefes*, and by the king, and by all the Court, and fo in proceffion entred into the Church, & after due thanks giuen to God, hee was conducted to his lodging that was affigned vnto him by the king. And then prefently he beganne to reforme & reduce to good order, the Church it felfe, and the *Frters*, and *Priefes* that dwell therein: ordayning the faide Church to bee the *Cathe-*

The *Bifhoppe* foundeth the Cathedrall Church of *S, Croffes*.

drall

drall Church of *Saint Croſſes*, which at that time had belonging vnto it twentie and eyght *Cannons*, with their
Chaplens, and a Mayſter of the *Chappell*, with *Singers*,
and *Organs*, and *Belles*, and all other furniture meete
to execute diuine ſeruice. But this *Biſhoppe*, who laboured in the *Lords Vineyard*, ſometimes in *Congo*, and
ſometimes in the *Iſle* of *Saint Thomas*, going and comming continually by ſhippe, the ſpace of twentie daies,
and ſtill leauing behinde him his *Vicars* in the place
where he himſelfe was abſent, at the laſt dyed, & was The *Biſhop*
buried in the *Iſland* of *S. Thomas.* dyeth.

After this *Biſhoppe* ſucceeded another *Biſhoppe* in
Congo, being a *Negro*, and deſcended of the blood *Roy-*
all, who before had beene ſent by *King Alfonſo* firſt into *Portingall*, and afterwardes to *Rome*, where hee learned the *Latine* tongue, and the *Chriſtian Religion*, but
being returned into *Portingall*, and landed out of
his ſhippe, to goe and enter vppon his *Biſhopricke* of The ſecond *B.*
S. Saniours, hee dyed by the way: wherevpon the king- dyeth.
dome remained without a *Paſtor* for the ſpace of diuers
yeares. *Don Piedro* alſo the *King* aforeſaide dyed like- The K. *Don*
wiſe without children, and there ſucceeded him his *Piedro* dyeth.
brother, called *Don Franceſco*, who in like manner la- *Don Franceſco*
ſted but a while: and then was created the fift *King*, ſucceedeth &
named *Don Diego*, who was next of all the race *Royall*: *Don Diego* the
A man of haughtie courage, and magnificall, and wit- fift King.
tie, of a very good diſpoſition, wiſe in counſell, and
aboue all other qualities, a maintayner of *Chriſtian*
Faith: and in briefe ſo great a warriour he was, that in
few yeares hee conquered all the countries adioyning.
He loued the *Portingals* very much, ſo that he forſooke
the vſuall garmentes of his owne naturall countrey, &

attired

attyred himselfe after the *Portingall* fashion. He was ve-

The K. *Diego* very sumptu- ons.

ry sumptuous aswell in his apparell, as also in the ornaments and furniture of his pallace: he was besides very
courteous and liberall, and woulde bestowe largely
both vpon his owne subiectes and also vpon the *Portingalles*. With great cost woulde hee prouide and buy
such stuffe as pleased him, and woulde often say, that
*Rare thinges shoulde not bee in the handes of any but onely of
Kinges.* He vsed to weare one suite of apparel but once
or twice and then he would giue it away to his followers.   Wherevpon the *Portingalles* perceyuing that he
did so greatly esteeme cloth of gold and Arras, & such
other costly houshold stuffe, they brought great store
therof out of *Portingall*, so that at that time, Arras-hang-
ings, and cloth of gold, and of silke, and such like Lord-
ly furniture beganne to bee of great estimation in that
kingdome.

　　In the time of this *King*, there was a thirde *Bishop* of
Saint Thomas, and *Congo*, by nation a *Portingall*, who

The third B.
of *S. Thomas*,
& of *Congo*.

with the vsuall ceremonies was entertayned both by
the way, and also in the Court at *Saint Sauiours*. And
nowe the *Deuill*, the common enemie of *Christian Religion*, being much grieued with the happie successe and
promoting of the *Catholike Faith*, beganne to sowe his

Dissention
betweene the
Friers and
Priests, & the
new *Bishop*.

Darnell of diuision betweene the *Friers* and *Priestes*, and
their new *Bishoppe*: which sprung vp and arose from the
long libertie, wherein they had nowe liued so many
yeares without a *Pastor*, so that euery man esteemed
himselfe not onely to be as good as the *Bishoppe*, but also to be a farre better man then he was: and therefore
would yeeld no obedience to their *Prelate*, in such sort
that there was rayfed among them so great a discord &
　　　　　　　　　　　　　　　　　　　dissention

diſſention, as it wrought a grieuous ſcandale and wicked example among the people. But the king like a
good *Catholike*, and a faithfull, did alwayes maintaine
the *Biſhops* part, and to cut of theſe troubles and ſtirres
he ſent ſome of theſe *Prieſts* to priſon into *Portingal*, and
others into the *Iſle* of *Saint Thomas*, and ſome others
went away with all their ſubſtaunce of their owne ac-
corde: and by theſe meanes, the doctrine of theſe mi-
niſters, in ſteede of encreaſing, did greatly diminiſh
through their owne default,

    Neyther was our common aduerſaries herewithal
contented, but woulde needes proceed further by ſet-
ting diſcorde betweene *Kinges* and ſubiectes. For after the death of this *King*, there ſtarted vp three *Princes*
at once to challenge the ſucceſſion. The firſt was the
Kinges ſonne, whom fewe of them fauoured, becauſe
they deſired to haue another, ſo that he was ſlaine incontinently. The two other that remayned were of
the bloud *Royall*: One of them was created *King* by
his fauourites and followers, with the good lyking of
the greater parte of the people, but vtterly againſt the
mindes of the *Portingalles* and certayne of the Lordes,
who aymed and endeauoured to ſet vp the other. Inſomuch as the foreſaide Lordes, together with the *Portingalles*, went into the *Church* to kill the *King* elected:
making this reckoning with themſelues, that if they
ſlewe him, the other muſt of neceſſitie bee made *King*.
But at that very ſelfe ſame time, thoſe of the contrary
faction had ſlaine the *King* that was already made by
the *Portingalles*, perſwading themſelues aſſuredly, that
he being dead there would bee no difficultie for them
to obtaine the ſtate for their *King*, becauſe there was

After the death of K. *Diego*, three Princes at once challenge the Kingdom, and all three ſlaine.

                                                        none

none other leaft, that by law could challenge the *Scep-*
ter Royall.   And thus in an houre and in two feuerall
places were thefe two *Kinges* murthered at once.

The *Fortin-*
galles flaine &
difpearfed.
In thefe confpiracies and flaughters, when the people faw, that there were no lawfull perfons leaft to enioy the *Royall Crowne,* they laide all the blame vpon the
*Portingals,*who were the caufers of all thefe mifchiefes :
and therevpon they turned themfelues againft them,
and flew as many of them as they could finde : Onely
they fpared the *Priests,*and would not touch them, nor
any other that dwelt in other places.

Don Henrico
created king.
Seeing therefore (as before is faide) that there was
none of the blood *Royall* leaft to be placed in the *Gouern-*
ment, they made choice of one *Don Henrico, Brother* to
Don Diego the *King* deceafed.   And this *Henrico,* going
to warre againft the *Anzichi,* leaft behinde him in his
fteede for *Gouernour,* vnder the title of *King,* one *Don*
Aluaro, a young man of twentie and fiue yeares of age,

K, Henrico di-
eth, & *Don*
Aluaro fuccee-
deth: and fo
the ftocke of
of the ancient
Kings of *Con-*
go ceafed.
fonne to his wife by another husband.   But *Don-Hen-*
rico dyed fhortly after the warre was ended, and therevpon the faide *Don Aluaro* was with the common con-
fent of them all, elected *King* of *Congo,* and generally
obeyed of euery man.   And thus fayled the *Royall*
Stocke of the auncient *Kinges* of *Congo,* in the perfon of
Don Henrico.

K. Aluaro re-
ftoreth the
Portingals.
But *Don Aluaro* was a man of good iudgement and
gouernenent, and of a milde difpofition, fo that he did
prefently appeafe all thefe tumults in his kingdome, &
caufed all the *Portingals* that by the laft warres were difpearfed ouer all the countries thereaboutes, to bee gathered together, afwell religious perfons as lay men, &
by their meanes hee was much better confirmed in the
                                                        Catholike

Catholike Faith then he was before. Moreouer he vſed
them very courteouſly, and cleared them of all faultes
that were laide to their charge, declaring vnto them by
gentle diſcourſes that they had not beene the occaſion
of the former troubles, as euery man wold conteſſe and
acknowledge: and to that effect he determined with
him ſelfe to write a large information touching al theſe
accidentes to the King of *Portingall*, and to the *Biſhoppe*
of *S. Thomas*, which he did accordingly, and diſpatched
certain *Meſſengers* vnto them with his letters. When the
Biſhoppe of *S. Thomas* vnderſtode theſe newes, he was
very glad thereof, and whereas before he durſt not ad-
uenture to go into the *Kingdome* of *Congo* in the heate of
all thoſe troubles, he did now preſently take ſhip, and
ſayled thether, where he imployed himſelfe wholly
with all his authoritie to pacifie the former diſſentions,
and to ſet downe order for all ſuch matters as concer-
ned the worſhippe of *God*, and the office of his *Prieſtes*.
And a while after hee had ſo done, hee returned to his
habitation in the *Iſle* of *Saint Thomas*, where by meanes
of ſicknes he finiſhed his dayes. And this was the third
time, that thoſe partes remayned without a *Biſhop*.

The B. of S. Thomas returneth into Congo.

The B. of S. Thomas dieth.

Nowe it came to paſſe, that for want of *Biſhoppes*, the
King and the *Lordes*, and the people likewiſe, began to
waxe cold in the *Chriſtian Religion*, euery man addicting
himſelfe licentiouſly to the libertie of the fleſh, and e-
ſpecially the *King*, who was induced therevnto by diuers yong men of his owne age, that did familiarly con-
uerſe with him. Among whom there was one principall man, that was both a *Lorde*, and his kinſman, called
Don Franceſco Bullamatare, that is to ſay, *Catche-Stone*.
This man, becauſe he was a great *Lorde*, and wholly e-

K. Aluaro liueth licentiouſly.

Franceſco Bulla Matare an ill companion & counſellour to the King.

X   ſtranged

ſtranged from all inſtructions of *Chriſtianitie*, walked inordinately after his owne pleaſure, and did not ſticke to defende openly, *That it was a very vaine thing to keepe but one wife, and therefore it were better to returne to their former auncient cuſtome.* And ſo by his meanes did the *Deuill* open a gate to the ouerthrowe and deſtruction of the *Church* of *Chriſt* in that kingdome, which vntill that time with ſo great paine and trauaile had beene there eſtabliſhed. But afterwardes the man did ſo wander and ſtray out of the way of truth, that he fell from one ſinne to another, and in the end quite relinquiſhed and abandoned all true *Religion.* Yet at the laſt the ſaid *Franceſco* dyed, and was ſolemnely buried like a noble *Lorde*, in the *Church* of *Saint Croſſes* : although he was notoriouſly ſuſpected and ſpotted for his falſe *Religion.* But it fell out (and a maruellous caſe it is, to confirme the righteous in their good belief, & to terrify the wicked) that in the night time certain *Spirits* of the *Deuill* vncouered a part of the roofe of *S. Croſſes Church*, where he was enterred, and with a great and horrible noyſe, which was heard all ouer the *Cittie*, they drew him out of his *Tombe*, and carryed him away. And in the morning the *Church* doores were found ſhut, the roofe broken, and the graue without the body of the man. By this extraordinarie ſigne the *King* was at the firſt aduertiſed of the great fault that hee had committed, and ſo were the reſt alſo that followed him in his courſe: but notwithſtanding, becauſe there was no *Biſhop* in that kingdome to giue him good counſell, and the *King* but a young man and vnmarried, although he remained ſomewhat ſound in the *Chriſtian Faith*, yet he continued ſtill in the licentiouſnes of the fleſh, vntill

Ballamatare dyeth.

ſuch

such time as God had chastized him with another se-
uere discipline, as you shall hereafter vnderstand.

Chap. 5.

*The incursions of the people called Giachas in the kingdome
of Congo. Their conditions and weapons. And
the taking of the Royall Cittie.*

 Or not long after, there came to
robbe and spoyle the Kingdome
of *Congo*, certaine nations, that
liue after the manner of the *Arabians*, and of the auncient *Noma-
des*, and are called *Giachas*. Their
habitation or dwelling is about
the first *Lake* of the *Riuer Nilus*,
in a prouince of the Empyre of *Moenemugi*. A cruell
people they are and a murderous, of a great stature,
and horrible countenance, fed with mans flesh, fierce
in battell, and valorous in courage. Their weapons are
Pauises or *Targates*, *Dartes* and *Daggers:* otherwise they
go all naked: In their fashions and dayly courfe of liuing they are very sauage and wilde: They haue no

What people
the *Giachas*
are: Their
conditions, &
weapons.

X 2   King

King to gouerne them, and they leade their life in the
forreſt vnder cabbins and cottages like ſhepheardes.

This people went wandring vp and downe, de-
ſtroying, and putting to fire and ſworde, and robbing
and ſpoiling all the countries that they paſſed through,
till they came to the Realme of *Congo*, which they entred on that ſide where the Prouince of *Batta* lyeth.
Thoſe that firſt came forth to make reſiſtance againſt
them, they ouerthrew, and then addreſſed themſelues
towards the *Cittie* of *Congo*, where the *King* remained
at that time in great perplexitie, for this victorie that
his enemies had gotten in the Countrey of *Batta*: yet
ſome comfort hee tooke to himſelfe, and went out a-
gainſt his aduerſaries with ſuch ſouldiers as he had, &
in the ſame place, where in times paſt *Mani-Pango*
fought with the *King Don Alfonſo*, he ioyned battell
with them. In which encounter the *King* being halfe
diſcomfited, retired into the *Cittie*, wherein when he
perceyued that he could not remaine in good ſafetie,
being vtterly forſaken of the grace of God by reaſon
of his ſinnes, and not hauing that confidence in him,
that *Don Alfonſo* had, he thought good to leaue it for a
pray to his aduerſaries, and to betake himſelfe io an *Iſlande* within the *Riuer Zaire*, called *Iſola del Cauallo*, that
is to ſay, the *Iſle of Horſe*, where hee continued with
certaine *Portingall Prieſtes*, and other principal *Lordes*
of his Kingdome. And thus were the *Ciachi* become
Lords and maiſters of the *Cittie Royall*, and of the whole
Realme. For the naturall inhabitants fled away, and ſaued themſelues in the mountains, & deſert places : but
the enemies burned and waſted, *Cittie*, and *Churches*, &
all, and ſpared no mans life, ſo that hauing diuided
them-

The *Giachas*
ſpoile the pro-
uince of *Batta*

The *Giachas*
come to the
Royall Cittie
of *Congo*.

R. *Aluaro* fli-
eth into the
Iſle of Horſes.

The *Giachas*
ſurpriſe the
Cittie, and
rule ouer all
the kingdom.

themſelues into ſeuerall armies, they ruled and gouerned ſometimes in one *Prouince*, and ſometimes in another ouer all the kingdome.

    With this perſecution did God generally afflict and
chaſtize all the inhabitantes of the ſaide Kingdome of
Congo, the King himſelfe, the *Lordes*, the people, the
Portingalles, and their *Clergie*, euery one in their degree,
and calling. As for the poore people, they went wandring like vagabondes ouer all the Countrey, and peri-
ſhed for hunger and want of neceſſaries: And for the
Kinge with thoſe that followed him, and had ſaued
themſelues in the *Iſlande*, they alſo becauſe the *Iſle* was
very little, and the multitude great, were oppreſſed
with ſo terrible a ſcarſitie of victuailes, that the moſt
part of them dyed by famine and peſtilence. For this
dearth ſo increaſed, and meate aroſe to ſo exceſſiue a
rate, that for a very ſmall pittance (God wot) they were
faine to giue the price of a ſlaue, whome they were
wont to ſell for tenne *Crownes* at the leaſt. So that the
Father was of neceſſitie conſtrayned to ſell his owne
ſonne, and the brother, his brother, and ſo euery man
to prouide his victuailes by all manner of wickedneſſe.
The perſons that were ſolde for the ſatisfying of other
mens hunger, were bought by the *Portingal Marchants*,
that came from *S. Thomas* with their ſhips laden with
victuailes. Thoſe that ſold them, ſaid they were ſlaues,
and thoſe that were ſolde, iuſtified and confirmed the
ſame, becauſe they were deſirous to be ridde of their
greedie torment. And by this occaſion there was no
ſmall quantity of ſlaues, that were borne in *Congo*, ſolde
vpon this neceſſitie, and ſent to the *Iſle* of *S. Thomas*, &
to *Portingall*, among whome there were ſome of the

*The King &
thoſe that fol-
lowed him,
plagued with
an extreame
famine.*

*Many of the
bloud Royall
ſold for ſlaue.
to the Portin-
galles.*

         X 3   bloud

bloud R*oyall*, and some others, principall *Lordes.*

By this affliction, the King did manifestly learne &
know, that all these great miseries and aduersities a-
bounded for his misdeedes: and although he was not

King Aluaro falleth into a Dropsie.

much punished with hunger, becaufe hee was a King,
yet he did not escape the cruel infirmitie of the *Dropsie,*
that made his legges to swell exceedingly, which dif-
ease was engendred partely by the ayre, and very ill
diet, and partely by the moystnesse of the *Islande,* and
so it accompanied him euen vntill his death. But in the
meane while, being stricken to the hart with these mif-
fortunes and calamities, he conuerted and turned to
God, requiring pardon for his offences, and doing
pennance for his sinnes: and then was counselled and
aduised by the *Portingalles* that he shoulde sende to re-

K. Aluaro sen- deth to the K. of Portin- gall for succor.

queft succours of the *King* of *Portingall,* by certayne
Embassadours, that might recount vnto him all the mifchiefes which had lighted vpon him. This *Embassage*
was accordingly performed, at the same time that the

Don Sebastian the King of Portingal sen- deth succour vnto him.

K. *Don Sebastiano* began his raign, who with great speed
and kindnesse sent him succours by a *Captaine,* called
Francesco di Gouea, a man well exercised in diuers wars,
both in *India,* and also in *Africa,* who lead with
him sixe hundred *Souldiers,* and many
Gentlemen Aduenturers, that did
accompany him.

Chap.

Chap. 6.

The King of Portingall sendeth aide, and an Embassadour to the King of Congo. The knowledge of the Mettall mines, which abound in Congo, is denyed the King of Portingall. At the same time the King of Congo dispatcheth Embassadours to the King of Spaine, to request Priestes of him, & what befell vnto them. He sendeth diuers proofes of the Mettalles. The vow of Odoardo Lopes.

His *Captayne Francesco di Gouea,* carried with him a commandement from his *Kinge,* that the *Islande of Saint Thomas* shoulde prouide him ships, and victualls, and whatsoeuer els was requisite for this enterprise. And with this prouision hee arriued at the last in the *Isle* of *Horse,* where the *King of Congo* was resident. In whose company the *Portingalles* departing from thence, & gathering together all the men of warre in that Countrey, with all speed possible, put themselues onwardes against their aduersaries, and fought with them sundry times in plaine battell, so that

Francesco di Gouea restoreth the King, and driueth the *Giachas* out of *Congo.*

X 4   at

at the ende of one yeare and a halfe, they restored the King into his former estate. Which victory they atchieued in deede by the noyse and force of their *Arcubuses* (for the *Giachi* are exceedingly afraid of that weapon) rather then by the valour and strength of their souldiers. And so they were in spight of their teeth driuen out of the Realme of *Congo*, & but few of them there were that returned home againe to see their frendes. But the *Portingall Captaine* stayed there for the space of foure yeares to settle the King in his Kingdome, and then returned into *Portingall* with letters of request to his *King*, that hee woulde sende ouer some moe *Priestes* to vpholde and maintaine the *Christian Religion*. Howbeit a number of *Portingalles*, that came by shippe with him, remained behinde him in these Countries, and are at this daye become very rich and wealthie men. And the King being thus established in his former degree, and the Kingdome all in quyet and peace, became a very good *Christian*, and married the *Ladie Catarina*, who is yet aliue: by whom he had fower daughters, and by certaine *Maide-seruants* which he kept, two sonnes and one daughter. And because in those regions the weomen doe not succeede: there remayned as heyre of his kingdome his elder sonne, called also *Don Aluaro*, who liueth at this day.

During the time, that the foresaide *Captaine* stayed in *Congo*, the *King* of *Portingall Don Sebastiano* vnderstanding, that there were in that *Kingdome* diuers *Caues* and *Mines* of *Siluer*, of *Golde*, & other *Mettalles*, sent thether two persons that were cunning and skilful in that Arte, (for therein they had serued the *Castilians* in the *West*) to make search for them, and to drawe some

Francesco di Gouea, after foure yeares returneth into Portingal with letters for mo Priestes.

The K. becommeth a good Christian, & marieth.

The K. of Portingal sendeth to make search in Congo for mettal Mines.

some profite thereof.   But the *King* of *Congo* was by a certaine *Portingall,* called *Francesco Barbuto*, that was his *Confessour* and great familiar, perswaded to the contrary, that he should not in any case suffer those *Mines* to be discouered: signifying vnto him, that thereby peraduenture the free enioying and possession of his Kingdome might by little and little be taken quite from him, and therefore aduised him that he woulde cause these skilfull Maisters to bee ledde and guided by some other wayes, where hee knewe there were no *Mettall-Mynes* to be founde, which he did accordingly.   But assuredly, it grew afterwardes to a great mischiefe, that the *King* would not suffer this Arte of digging and melting of mettalles, so greatly esteemed ouer all *Europe,* to be exercised in *Congo.* For therevpon beganne the great trade and trafficke in that Countrey to cease, and the *Portingall Marchants* did not greatly care for venturing thether, or dwelling there any more: and so consequently very few *Priestes* resorted among them. So that aswell vpon these occasions, as also for other such causes afore rehearsed, the *Christian Religion* waxed so colde in *Congo,* that it wanted verye little of being vtterly extinguished. But the *King Don Aluaro* (as it hath beene tolde you) after all these mighty afflictions laid vpon him by the hand of God, for the punishment of the sinnes which he had committed against *Religion,* had acknowledged his errour, and became a good *Christian,* cherishing the *Portingals,* whom he called his *Sonnes,* and doing them all the pleasure hee could.   Especially and aboue all thinges hee ceased not, still to sende new *Embassadours* into *Portingall,* with earnest request that he might haue moe *Priestes*, and

Francesco Barbuto disswadeth the King from making the search, & auoydeth it by pollicy.

The inconuenience of not suffering the mettall mines to be digged & melted.

The K. sendeth new Embassadours into Portingall for mo priests

Y   such

such as were skilful in the holy Scriptures to maintaine
the *Catholike Faith*, which was now almoſt vtterly for-
gotten in that Realme, onely for want of religious
perſons, that ſhoulde teach the people and adminiſter
the *Sacramentes*, and not for any fault of their good
willes: for they were meruellouſly well inclined and
affected to the *Holy Faith*.

The *Portingal*
K. delayeth to
ſend mo
Prieſtes.   After that the aforeſaid *Captaine* was arriued in *Por-*
tingall, and had preſented the requeſtes of the *King* of
Congo to his *King*, (who was alſo but a young man)
he had none other aunſwere from him but wordes and
promiſes, that he would haue a care of the matter that
was demanded: but in the meane while hee prouided
neyther *Prieſts*, nor *Diuines* to be ſent for *Congo*. Wherevpon the King of *Congo* diſpatched againe another
principall *Embaſſadour*, being his kinſeman, called *Don*

The King of
Congo ſendeth
Don Sebaſtiano
Aiuarez to en-
treat for
Prieſtes, & to
redeeme cer-
taine of his
nobilitie that
were in Saint
Thomas iſle, &
in *Portingall*. *Sebaſtiano Aluarez*, together with a *Portingall*, to beare
him company and entreate for moe *Prieſtes*, and with-
all to redeeme certaine ſlaues borne in *Congo*, that were
in the *Iſle* of *S. Thomas* and in *Portingall*, and were ſold
vpon meere neceſſitie, as wee haue tolde you before.
Some of them woulde needes remaine ſtill in volunta-
rie ſeruitude, and many were raunſomed and brought
home into their Countrey.   By whoſe good labour
and meanes, and eſpecially by the paineful induſtrie of
ſuch as were *Lords*, & borne of noble bloud, (for ſome
there were of that dignitie among them,) the King of
Congo reſtored the *Chriſtian Religion*, which was almoſt
loſt : and ſome of them he vſed for Counſellours, and
Officers of the Realme, as men that were well practiſed
and experienced in the worlde, by reaſon of this their
long captiuitie.   To this *Embaſſadour*, the *King* gaue a
gracious

gracious aunſwere, and tolde him that hee ſhould bee ſatiſſyed according to his requeſt: But yet for all that, hee was faine to returne home agayne into *Congo,* without any *Prieſtes* or Religious perſons to go with him.

Three yeares after, the King *Don Sebaſtiano* diſpatched a certaine *Biſhoppe* (called *Don Antonio de gli Oua,* being a *Caſtilian* borne) principally to the *Iſlande* of *S. Thomas:* but withall he gaue him alſo a commiſſion to viſite the kingdome of *Congo:* who being arriued at *S. Thomas,* fell at iarre with the *Captayne* there, and ſo ſayled into *Congo,* where hee was alſo perſecuted by the ſaide *Captaine* and his frendes that hee had there: For they informed the *King,* that hee was an ambitious man, of a haughtie ſpirite, and very obſtinate, & thereby did vtterly diſcredite him with the King and all his Court: Wherevpon being induced therevnto by theſe accuſations, the King forbad him at the firſt to enter within his Realme, but afterwardes he receyued him with great honour, and ſent his ſonne to entertain him, and to accompany him to the Cittie. There he ſtayed about eyght monethes, and then departed againe, ſomewhat before the King of *Portingall* paſſed into *Africa,* and leaſt behinde him in *Congo,* two *Friars,* and fower *Prieſtes.* The *Biſhoppe* being thus gone, & the King ouerthrowen in *Africa,* there was exalted to the Crowne of *Portingall, Don Henrico* the *Cardinall,* to whome the King of *Congo* did write, with great inſtaunce, and earneſt requeſt; that he would ſend him ſome religious perſonnes, and Preachers: but he could obtaine nothing at his handes, becauſe the *Cardinall* liued but a ſhort time in that *Gouernement.*

After

Philip K. of
Spaine fuccee-
deth the
Cardinall.
K. Philip fen-
deth Sebastia-
no di Costa to
Congo to figni-
fie his arriuall
to the Crowne
of Portingall.

After *Don Henrico* fucceeded *Phillip* King of *Caſtile*, who fent aduertifementes to the Captain of *Saint Thomas*, that he was inueſted in the Crowne of *Portingall*, and letters alfo to the King of *Congo*, to the fame effect. Wherevpon the Captaine did prefently difpatch one *Sebaſtiano di Coſta*, that with the title of *Embaſſadour*, fhoulde carry thefe newes and letters vnto the faide King.   When thefe letters were prefented, and all

The King of
Congo offereth
K. Philip of
Spaine the dif-
couery of the
Mettall mines
in Congo, with
requeſt for
Prieſtes.

complementes performed, the king of *Congo* returned him againe to the Court to king *Phillip*, with anfwere of his letters, and therein proffered to difcouer vnto him the mettall mines, which heretofore had beene concealed from all the other kinges his predeceſſors, and withal fent him diuers trialles of them: Befeeching him efpecially with all affectionate entreatie, that (as foone as poſſiblie he could) hee woulde furnifh him with fome ſtore of Prieſtes: declaring alfo vnto him the miferable ſtate and condition, whereinto his peo-

Coſta dyeth by
the way, and
his meſſage
knowen by let-
ters that were
found.

ple were fallen, by reafon of the troubles that had happened about the *Chriſtian Religion.*   But *Coſta* died by the way, the veſſell wherein he fayled being caſt away vpon the fhore of *Portingall*, and euery man drowned that was in it: and the naughtie newes were knowen by the contentes of the Letters, that were found in a little cheſt, which was driuen on land by the waues of the fea: & by a briefe note of fuch Commiſſions, as he

The King of
Congo fendeth
Odoardo Lopez
to the King of
Spaine, & to
the Pope with
letters of cre-
dence, and
inſtructions.

had in charge to deliuer to the king.   When the king of *Congo* hearde of this accident, hee did not ceafe, but ſtill continued and perfeuered in his godly purpofe, & woulde not fuffer Chriſtianitie to bee vtterly extingui-fhed in his Kingdome, as it was very likely to be. And therefore he determined yet once again to fend a new

Embaſſa-

Embaſſadour of his owne to the *King* of *Spaine*. But foraſmuch as there aroſe ſome difficulties and differences among ſome *Lordes* of the *Court*, that deſired this honour, the king becauſe he woulde not diſpleaſe any of them, by preferring one of them before another, made choice of one *Odoardo Lopez* a *Portingall* borne, from whoſe mouth *Pigáfetta* tooke this preſent report, and put it in writing. This man had dwelt now a good time in thoſe Regions, and was well experienced in the affaires of the worlde, and being by good chaunce at that time in the Court, he was thus emploied with the good fauour and countenance of the king: who deliuered vnto him in writing very ample inſtructions, for all matters whereof hee was to treate, as well with his *Catholike Maieſtie* in *Spaine*, as alſo with his *Holineſſe* at *Rome*: together with very earneſt letters of credence, and authoritie, and commoditie to them both, and ſafe conductes, and exemptions in all liberties, both within and without, beſides his effectuall recommendations of him to all other *Chriſtian Princes*, with all ſuch other priuileges and declarations, that might ſhew how dearly the king eſteemed his perſon, as to an *Embaſſadour* in ſuch cauſes appertaineth.

The ſumme of his *Embaſſage* was this : *That he ſhould preſent his Letters to the King* Don Phillip, *and at large diſcourſe vnto him the ſtate, wherein the kingdome of* Congo *ſtoode touching matter of Religion, by the reaſon of the former warres, and ſcarcitie of* Prieſtes, *and thereupon requeſt his Maieſtie to prouide him a competent number of Confeſſors, and Preachers, that might bee ſufficient to maintaine the Goſpell in thoſe remote Countries, being but lately*

The Embaſſage of Odoardo Lopez to the K. of Spain

Y 3   *conuerted*

conuerted to Christianitie. *Moreouer that he should shew vnto him the sundrie trialles of Mettalles, which hee had made, and many other matters, which were worthie to bee knowen: and withall that he should proffer vnto him in his name, free & liberal trafficke of them, which heretofore was euer denyed to his Predecessors. Touching the* Pope, *That he should likewise on his behalfe kisse his feete, deliuer vnto him his letters, and recount the miserable trouble and detriment that his people had suffered for the* Christian Faith. *That he shold recōmend those poor soules to his* Holines, *& beseech him as the Vniuersal Father of all* Christians, *to haue compassion vpon so many faithful persons, who because they had no Priestes to deliuer the holy Faith vnto them, and to administer the wholesome* Sacramentes, *were by little and little falling into euerlasting perdition.* And being thus dispatched, he departed from the Court, and went about certaine seruices for the King, wherein he spent about eyght Monethes: So that in *Ianuary*, being then *Sommer* time in *Congo*, he embarked himselfe in a vessell of a hundred Tunne burthen, which was bound with her lading for *Lisbone.*

His Embassage to the *Pope.*

Now as he sayled, he came to the sea of the *Islands* of *Cape Verde*, where the vessell being somewhat olde, began to take in much water, at a leake that was open in the foreship. So that the wind blowing very lustely and strongely before, and the Saylers being not able eyther to reach the *Islandes* aforesaid, or to gayne the firme lande of *Africa*, much lesse (though they woulde neuer so fayne) to follow on their voyage, by sayling on with the halfe ship, and to straine the vessel that leaked so much, the *Pilot* thought it better to turne

Odoardo Lopez at the Islandes of *Cape Verde.*

his

his courfe, and taking the wind in the poope, to goe &
faue themfelues in the *Iflandes* of *Noua Hifpania*. And
fo after terrible ftormes, and extreame dangers of
drowning, and of perifhing with hunger for want of
all kinde of meate, they arriued with much adoo at a **The *Iſle of***
little *Iflande*, called *Cubagoa*, and fituate ouer againft the **Cubagoa,**
Ifle of *Saynt Margarete*, where they fifh for *Pearles*. From **Margarete.**
thence, when they had in fome hafte amended their
fhippe, and fomewhat refrefhed themfelues, they fayled with a fhort cut to the firme lande, and tooke hauen in a Porte called *Cumana*, or (as it is called by another name) *The new kingdome of Granado in the Weft In-* **Cumana or the**
dies. This battered and wetherbeaten veffell was no **new kingdom**
fooner arriued in this fafe harbour, but it funke prefent- **the *Weſt Indies***
ly to the bottome, but the perfons that were in her **The ſhip ſunk**
were all faued, although afterwardes they fell ficke to **in the hauen.**
the death by reafon of the great griefe, which they
had endured in hunger, in thirft, and in want of all o-
ther fuftenance, and chiefly by the horrible ftormes of
that tempeftuous *Ocean*.

While the forefaide *Embaffadour* endeauoured in **Odoardo Lopez**
this place to recouer his former health, the company **ſtayeth in Cu-**
of fhippes which is called *La Flotta*, that is to fay, the **and a halfe.**
Fleete, and vfeth euery yeare to fayle from that coaft
for *Caftile*, departed from thence, fo that he was conftrayned to ftay for a new Nauie, and fo confumed a
whole yeare and a halfe without doing any good. In
this meane time the King of *Congo*, hauing neuer receyued any tydinges of this his *Embaffadour Odoardo*,
but accounting him for dead, and not knowing that he
was driuen by tempeft into the *Weſt Indies*, continued

ftill

ftill conftant in his former purpofe, to procure fome re-

medy for Chriftianitie in his kingdome.   And therefore hee fent another *Embaffadour*, with the felfe fame
commandements, called *Don Piedro Antonio* the feconde perfon in all his Realme, and with him one *Gafparo Diaz*, a *Portingall* borne, a principall man and very
rich, and an auncient inhabitant in that Countrey, to
the ende that hee fhoulde accompany the faide *Don
Piedro*, and fuffer him to want nothing, and in any cafe
ioyne his good help to procure, that the requeft, which
he hoped to obtain of the king of *Spaine*, might be fully
effected : with a further expreffe commandement, that
if they did meete with the faide *Signor Odoardo*, they
fhould deale in their bufineffe with his aduife & coun-
fell.   But an infortunate end had this *Embaffadour*, for

he was taken at fea by *Englifhmen*, and his fhippe alfo,
which being drawen towardes *Englande*, when it was
neere vnto the Coaft, by great miffortune it ranne a-
thwart the fhoare, ane there *Don Piedro Antonio* & his
fonne were both drowned: but the *Portingal* and fome

fewe others with him efcaped, and arriued in *Spaine*, at
fuch time as the faid *Odoardo* was come to the Court, &
had entred vppon the charge of his *Embaffage*.   And
therefore this *Gafparo* wrote to *Odoardo*,   that hee was
minded to returne home into *Congo*, and not to goe to
the Court at all: whether it were for the death of the
Cardinall, or for any other refpect, I cannot tell, but
home he returned in deed, as he faid he would.

In the time that our *Signor Odoardo* remained in the
Weft India, which is fituate vnder the fame skie, and
vnder the fame climate, and of the fame temperature

of

ofayre, that *Congo* is fubiect vnto: hee noted that the colour of the skinnes of the inhabitants in both coun- The blacknes of a mans skinne, is not caufed by the heat of the funne. tries was farre different: For in *Congo,* they are general- ly and for the moft parte blacke, and in *India* almoft white, that is to fay, of a middle colour, betweene white and blacke, which the *Spaniardes* call *Mulato, Browne,*or *Darke-Tawney.* Whereby he would fignifie, thar it is not caufed by the Sunne, as it hath beene recorded of long time, but that it commeth of nature it felfe, who worketh it by fome fecreat reafon, which neuer yet to this day, eyther by auncient *Philofopher,* or new writer, hath beene fully fet downe or vnderftoode.

When he had recouered his health, he fayled to *Odoardo Lopez* fayleth to *San Domingo.* the Porte of the Cittie of *San Domingo* in the *Ifland* of *Hifpaniola,* that there at the firft paffage he might take fome fhippe that went towardes *Caftilia:* and by good chaunce he found a *Portingall* veffell, among the reft of the Nauie, which was minded to ioyne with the *Fleete* of fhippes, that paffed from the firme lande to *Caftilia,* and fo to goe in good companie and better fafetie. All thefe fhippes being thus vnited together, *Lopez* in a *Portingal* fhip commeth with the fleete to *Terzera,* to *S. Lucar,* to *Siuile,* & fo into *Portingal.* they arriued by the helpe of a very good winde, at *Terzera,* which is one of the *Iflandes* called *Azores,*that is to fay, the *Sparre-Haukes.* and from thence to *San Lucar di Barameda,* which is a hauen in the mouth of the Riuer *Guadalchibir,* and fo to *Siuile:* from whence he tooke his iourney into *Portingall* to fee his frendes, and to furnifh himfelfe with all thinges neceffarie for his bufineffe, and at the laft hee rode to the Court, *Lopez* goeth to the Spanifh Court in *Madrill.* which was at that time in *Madrill.* There hee was courteoufly entertained by his *Catholike Maieftie,* to

Z whom

whom he propounded the contents of his Commissions.   But diuers great accidentes there happened, & many difficulties that crossed him, and altogether hindered the course of those affaires, which hee had to accomplish in the name of the King of *Congo*.   For first hee hearde the dolorous newes of the Kinges death, that sent him on this message: and then the *King Don Philip* was wholly busied about the conquest of *England*, so that his busines went nothing forwardes, but was delayed from time to time: neyther did he see any meanes of dispatch, but rather hee was giuen to vnderstand, that for that time they could not intende to harken vnto him.

Alaro King of Congo dieth

K. Philip busied about the conquest of England.

Now the foresaide *Odoardo*, being afflicted with so many aduersities, began to call to mind the innumerable perilles that he had passed, and the deadly infirmitie wherewith he was plagued, after that long, & horrible nauigation.   He saw that he was sometimes cast downe, and sometimes exalted: and knew that in this worlde there was none other rest or quiet, but in God Almightie. He was greatly oppressed with hart griefe, which he did dayly and continually endure, becaufe he could not relieue the necessities wherewith the people of *Congo* were vexed and troubled, and manifestly perceyued, that those poore soules incurred the extreame daunger of falling into the vtter darkenesse of hell.   He considered the great expenses, that euery day must be defrayed at the Court for the maintenance of himselfe and his familie.   Lastly, he was wholly depriued of all hope, that he should euer be able to bring that matter to effect, which the king of *Congo* had imposed vpon him.   And therefore he made choice of

Odoardo Lopez chaungeth his kind of profession.

another

another courſe, that was not onely profitable for him,
but alſo moſt wholeſome for his ſoule. For the good
Angell had touched his harte, and cauſed him with a
manly courage to abandon the *Sword*, and to take the
Croſſe vpon him: and thereupon hee renounced the
worlde with all the deceitfull pompe and glorie
thereof, and in *Madrill* apparelled himſelfe in a graye
courſe habite, and ſo went to *Rome*, to declare to *Six-* *Lopez* goeth
tus Quintus the *Pope* the tenor and Commiſſion of his to *Rome*,
where he was
Embaſſage, becauſe he would not altogether neglect kindly enter-
the good intent and meaning of the King, that had ſent tayned by the
him, although he were now deſcended into a better *Pope.*
life.   He was kindly welcomed and receiued by his
Holines, to whom hee diſcourſed the miſerable eſtate,
wherein the Chriſtian people of the Realme of *Congo*
did ſtand, for want of the worſhip and ſeruice of God,
and alſo the ſmall number of Prieſtes, that were there
to inſtruct them in the doctrine of the *Goſpel*, and to deliuer vnto them the *Sacraments* of the *Church*, eſpecially the multitude in that countrey being (as it were)
innumerable, that euery day reſorted together, to bee
baptiſed, inſtructed, confeſſed and communicated.
Moreouer he made a vowe and reſolued in his minde, The vow of
that with ſuch ſtore of wealth, as God had bleſſed him *Odoardo Lopez*
withall in *Congo* (which was not very ſmall) he would to erect a Se-
minary, & an
builde a houſe, wherein for the ſeruice of God, there Hoſpitall in
ſhould dwell certaine learned men, and ſundrie *Prieſts*, *Congo.*
to inſtruct the youth of thoſe Countries in all good
languages, and in the arts liberal, and in the doctrine of
the *Goſpell*, and in the miſteries of our ſaluation.   Out
of which houſe, as it were out of a holy Schoole, there
might come forth from time to time, many learned
                              Z 2   men

men and well ſtudied in the law of God, that ſhoulde
be able in their owne naturall Countrey tongue, to a-
waken and raiſe againe the Faith of *Chriſt*, which was
now aſleepe, and dried vp in thoſe Regions: and thereby in proceſſe of time there woulde ſpring vp many
fruits of bleſſing, & vigilant ſoules in the *Chriſtian Faith*.
Herevnto he ment alſo to adde an *Hoſpitall*, that might
be a recourſe and harbor for *Gods* poore, which com-
ing and ſayling out of ſtrange *Countries* ſhould haue reliefe and entertainment in that *Hoſtelry*, and there be
cured and reſtored of their infirmities and neceſſities.
With this purpoſe therefore he went to *Rome*, to ob-
teyne of his holynes a licence to erect this *Seminary* and
Hoſpitall, and to beſeech him alſo that he would graunt
him *Iubilies*, *Indulgences*, and other *Diſpenſations*, that for
ſuch *Chriſtian* and wholſom works are requiſite, eſpecially to the vſe & benefit of thoſe *Countries*, which are
ſo remote from *Chriſtendome*. He preſented himſelfe to
the *Pope*, & deliuered vnto him his letters of credence,
and then declared vnto him at large the tenor of his
Commiſſions, wherein he had a gracious audience.

The *Pope* re-
mitteth the
whole matter
to the K. of
Spaine.

But when the *Pope* did vnderſtand that the kingdome of *Congo* belonged to the king of
Spaine, he remitted that matter
wholly vnto him.

Chap.

Chap. 7.

Of the Court of the King of Congo. *Of the apparell of that people before they became Chriſtians and after. Of the Kinges table, and manner of his Court.*

Etherto we haue manifeſtly diſcouered the beginning of *Chriſtian Religion* in *Congo*,& conſequently the ſtrange accidents that happened therein.And now it is time to diſcourſe & lay open the manners and faſhions of that Court,& other cuſtomes and conditions appertayning to that Realme.   In auncient time this King and his Courtiers were apparelled with certaine cloath made of the *Palme-Tree,* (as we haue tolde you before) wherewith they couered themſelues from the girdleſteed downewardes, and girded the ſame ſtreyght vnto them with certaine girdles made of the ſame ſtuffe, very faire and well wrought. They vſed alſo to hang before them, like an apron, certaine delicate and dainty skinnes, of

The auncient apparell of the King of Congo and his Courtiers.

little *Tygres*, of *Ciuet-Cattes*, of *Sabelles*, of *Marternes*, and of such like creatures for an ornament: and for a more glorious pompe and shew, they did weare vpon their shoulders a certaine cape like a Whoode. Vpon their bare skinne they had a certaine rounde garment like a *Rotchet*, which they call *Incutto*, reaching downe to their knees, made after the manner of a net, but the stuffe of it was very fine cloth of the said *Palme-Tree*, & at the skirtes there hung a number of threede-taffelles, that made a very gallant shew. These *Rotchets* were turned vp againe, & tucked vpon their right shoulder, that they might be the more at libertie on that hande. Vpon that shoulder also they had the taile of a *Zebra*, faftned with a handle, which they vsed for a kinde of brauery, according to the most auncient custome of those partes. On their heades they wore cappes of yellow and redde colour, square aboue and very little, so that they scarcely couered the toppes of their heads, and worne rather for a pompe and a vanitie, then to keepe them eyther from the ayre or from the Sunne. The most part of them went vnshodde: but the King and fome of the great *Lords* did weare certaine shooes of the olde fashion, such as are to be seene in the ancient *Images* of the *Romanes*, and these were made also of the woode of the *Palme-Tree*. The poorer forte and the common people were apparelled from their middle downewardes, after the same manner, but the cloath was courfer: and the rest of their bodie all naked. The women vsed three kindes of trauerfes, or (as it were) aprons: beneath their girdlefteed. One was very long and reached to their heels: the fecond shorter then that, and the thirde shorter then both the other

The auncient apparell of the meaner fort.

ther

ther, with fringes about them, and euery one of thefe three was faftened about their middle, and open before. From their breaftes downewardes, they had another garment, like a kinde of dublet or iacket, that reached but to their girdle: and ouer their fhoulders a certaine cloake. All thefe feuerall garmentes were made of the fame cloth of the *Palme-Tree*. They were accuftomed to goe with their faces vncouered, and a little cappe on the head, like a mans cappe. The meaner forte of weomen were apparelled after the fame manner, but their cloth was courfer: Their Maid-feruantes and the bafeft kind of women were likewife attyred from the girdle downeward, and all the reft of the bodie naked.

But after that this kingdome had receyued the *Chriftian Faith*, the great *Lords* of the *Court* beganne to apparell themfelues after the manner of the *Portingalles*, in wearing cloakes, *Spanifh Capes*, and *Tabards* or wide Iackets of *Scarlet*, and cloth of *Silke*, euery man according to his wealth and abilitie. Vpon their heads they had hats, or caps, and vpon their feet Moyls or Pantoffles, of *Veluet* and of *Leather*, and buskins after the *Portingall* fafhion, and long *Rapiers* by their fides. The common people, that are not able to make their apparell after that manner doe keepe their olde cuftome. The women alfo go after the *Portingall* fafhion, fauing that they weare no cloakes, but vpon their heads they haue certaine veyles, and vpon their veyles blacke veluet cappes, garnifhed with iewelles, and chaines of golde about their neckes. But the poorer forte keep the old fafhion: for onely the *Ladies* of the Court doo bedecke themfelues in fuch manner as wee haue

Their new kind of apparell.

Z 4 tolde

tolde you.

The Court of Congo now imitateth the Court of Portingall.

After the King himfelfe was conuerted to the *Chriftian Religion*, hee conformed his Court in a certaine forte after the manner of the King of *Portingall*. And firft for his feruice at the table when he dyneth or fup-peth openly in publike, there is a *Throne* of *Eftate* erected with three fteppes, couered all ouer with *Indian Tapiftrie*, and therevpon is placed a Table, with a chaire of *Crimʒen Veluet*, adorned with boffes and nailes of Golde. Hee alwaies feedeth alone by him-felfe, neyther doth any man euer fit at his table, but the Princes ftand about him with their heads couered. He hath a *Cupborde* of Plate of *Gold* and *Siluer*, and one that taketh affay of his meat and drinke. He maintaineth a guarde of the *Anzichi*, and of other nations, that keep about his pallace, furnifhed with fuch weapons as are aboue mentioned: and when it pleafeth him to goe a-broade, they founde their great inftrumentes, which may bee hearde about fiue or fixe miles, and fo fignifie that the King is going forth. All his Lords do accom-pany him, and likewife the *Portingalles*, in whom hee repofeth a fingular truft: but very feldome it is that he goeth out of his pallace.

The cuftomes and lawes of Congo.

Twice in a weeke hee giueth audience publikely, yet no man fpeaketh vnto him but his *Lordes*. And becaufe there are none, that haue any goods or lands of their owne, but all belongeth to the *Crowne*, there are but few fuites or quarelles among them, fauing peraduenture about fome words. They vfe no writing at all in the *Congo* tongue. In cafes criminall they pro-ceede but flenderly, for they doo very hardely and feldome condemne any man to death. If there be a-

ny

ny ryot or enormitie committed againſt the *Portingals*
by the *Moci-Conghi*,(for ſo are the inhabitants of the
Realme of *Congo* called in their owne language,) they
are iudged by the lawes of *Portingall*. And if any miſ-
chiefe bee founde in any of them, the king confineth
the malefactor into ſome deſert *Iſland*: for he thinketh
it to bee a greater puniſhmente to baniſh him in this
ſorte, to the end he may doe pennance for his ſinnes,
then at one blow to execute him. And if it ſo happen
that thoſe which are thus chaſtized, doe liue tenne or
twelue yeares, the King vſeth to pardon them, if they
be of any conſideration at all, and doeth imploy them
in the ſeruice of the State, as perſons that haue beene
tamed and well ſchooled, and accuſtomed to ſuffer
any hardeneſſe. In Ciuill diſagreements there is an
order, that if a *Portingall* haue any ſuite againſt a *Moci-*
Congo, he goeth to the Iudge of *Congo*: but if a *Moci-*
Congo doe impleade a *Portingall*, hee citeth him before
the *Conſul* or Iudge of the *Portingalles*: for the King
hath graunted vnto them one of their owne nation to
be Iudge in that countrey. In their bargains between
them and the *Portingalles*, they vſe no writinges nor
other inſtrumentes of billes or bondes, but diſpatch
their buſineſſe onely by word and witneſſe.

They keepe no hiſtories of their auncient Kinges
nor any memoriall of the ages paſt, becauſe they cannot write. They meaſure their times generally by
the Moones. They knowe not the houres of the day
nor of the night: but they vſe to ſay, *In the time of ſuch*
a man ſuch a thing happened. They reckon the diſtan-
ces of countries not by miles or by any ſuch meaſure,

A a   but

but by the iourneyes and trauell of men, that goe from one place to another, eyther loaden or vnloaden.

Touching their affembling together at feaftes, or other meetinges of ioy, as for example, when they are marryed, they fing *Verfes* and *Ballades* of *Loue*, and play vppon certaine Lutes that are made after a ftrange fafhion. For in the hollowe parte and in the necke they are fomwhat like vnto our *Lutes*, but for the flat fide, (where wee vfe to carue a *Rofe*, or a *Rundell* to let the founde goe inwarde) that is made not of wood, but of a skinne, as thinne as a bladder, and the ftringes are made of hayres, which they draw out of the *Elephantes* tayle, and are very ftrong and bright : and of certaine threedes made of the woode of *Palme-Tree*, which from the bottome of the inftrument doe reach and afcende to the toppe of the handle, and are tyed euery one of them to his feuerall ringe. For towardes the necke or handle of this *Lute*, there are certaine rings placed fome higher and fome lower, whereat there hange diuers plates of *Iron* and *Siluer*, which are very thinne, and in bigneffe different one from another, according to the proportion of the inftrument. Thefe ringes doo make a founde of fundrie tunes, according to the ftriking of the ftringes. For the ftringes when they are ftriken, doo caufe the rings to fhake, and then doo the plates that hang at them, helpe them to vtter a certayne mingled and confufed noyfe. Thofe that play vppon this Inftrument, doo tune the ftrings in good proportion, and ftrike them with their fingers, like a *Harpe*, but without any quill very cunningly : fo that they make thereby (I cannot
                                                                    tell

tell whether I ſhoulde call it a melodie or no, but) ſuch
a ſounde as pleaſeth and delighteth their ſences well
enough. Beſides all this (which is a thing very admirable) by this inſtrument they doo vtter they con-
ceites of their mindes, and doo vnderſtande one another ſo plainely, that euery thing almoſt which may
be explaned with the tongue, they can declare with
their hande in touching and ſtriking this inſtrument.
To the ſounde thereof they do dance in good meaſure
with their feet, and follow the iuſt time of that muſicke
with clapping the palmes of their handes one againſt
the other. They haue alſo in the *Court, Flutes* and
Pipes, which they ſound very artificially, and according to the ſounde they daunce and moue their feet,
as it were in a *Moreſco*, with great grauity and ſobrietie.
The common people doe vſe little *Rattles*, and *Pipes*, &
other inſtrumentes, that make a more harſh and rude
ſound, then the Court-inſtruments do.

In this kingdome, when any are ſicke, they take Their Phiſick.
nothing but naturall phiſicke, as *Hearbes*, and *Trees*,
and the barkes of *Trees*, and *Oyles*, and *Waters* and
Stones, ſuch as *Mother Nature* hath taught them. The
Ague is the moſt common diſeaſe that raigneth among
them: and plagueth them in Winter by reaſon of
the continuall raine, that bringeth heat and moyſture
with it more then in Sommer, and beſides that the ſicknes which here we cal the *French diſeaſe*, & *Chitangas* in
the *Congo* tongue, is not there ſo daungerous and ſo
harde to be cured, as it is in our Countries.

They heale the Ague with the poulder of a wood, Their medi-
called *Sandale*, or *Saunders*, whereof there is both redde Ague.

A a 2 and

and gray, which is the woode of *Aguila.* This poulder being mingled with the oyle of the *Palme-Tree,*
and hauing annointed the bodie of the ficke-perfon
two or three times withall from the head to the foote,
the partie recouereth.   When their head aketh, they
let bloude in the temples, with certaine little boxing
hornes: firft by cutting the skinne a little, and then
applying the *Cornets* therevnto , which with a fucke
of the mouth, will be filled with bloud: and this manner of letting bloude is vfed alfo in *Ægipt.*   And fo in
any other parte of a mans body, where there is any
griefe, they drawe bloude in this fafhion and heale it.
Likewife they cure the infirmitie called *Chitangas,* with
the fame vnction of *Saunders:* whereof there are two
forts, one redde (as we tolde you) and that is called
Tauila: the other gray, and is called *Chicongo:* and
this is beft efteemed, for they will not fticke to giue or
fell a flaue for a peece of it.   They purge themfelues
with certaine barkes of trees, made into powder, and
taken in fome drinke: and they will worke mightely
and ftrongly.   When they take thefe purgations,
they make no great account for going abroad into
the ayre.   Their woundes alfo they commonly cure
with the iuyce of certaine hearbs, and with the hearbs
themfelues.   And the fayde *Signor Odoardo* hath affirmed vnto me, that he fawe a flaue, which was ftab-
bed through with feauen mortall woundes of an Arrow, and was recouered whole and found, onely with
the iuyce of certaine hearbes, well knowen vnto them
by experience.   So that this people is not encumbred
with a number of *Phificians,* for *Surgery,* for *Drugges,*
for

Their medi-
cine for the
head-ache, &
other griefes
of the body, is
letting of
blood.

Their medi-
cine for the
French pocks.

Their Purga-
tions.

Curing of
wouudes,

for *Sirruppes*, for *Electuaries*, for *Playsters*, and such
like Medicines, but simply doe heale and cure themselues with such naturall Plantes as grow in their owne
Countrey.   Whereof they haue no great neede neither; for liuing (as they doo) vnder a temperate clymate, and not ingorging themselues with much varietie of meates to pleafe their appetites, nor furchar-
ging their ftomackes with wine, they are not greatly
troubled with thofe difeafes, that commonly
are engendred of meates and drinkes
that remaine vndigefted.

Aa 3   Chap.

Chap. 8.

Of the Countries, that are beyonde the Kingdome of Congo
towardes the Cape of Good-Hope : and of
the Riuer Nilus.

Ow that we haue feene the King-
dome of *Congo,* and the conditi-
ons both of the Countrey and
people that dwell therein, and alfo of the nations therevnto adioyning, it remayneth that wee
difcourfe a little further, and that
with all breuitie, of the reft of *A-*
frica, towardes the *Cape* of *Good-Hope,* all along the
Ocean, whereby they vfe to fayle into *India* euen as
farre as the redde fea: and then we will returne backe
againe into the *Inlande,* and treate of the Riuer *Nilus,*
and of *Preti-Gianni,* and of all his kingdomes: to the
ende, that fo farre, as our matter will beare, we may
make a perfecte relation of thofe Regions, which hitherto haue not fo well and fo rightly been conceaued
of euery man.   Beyond the Kingdome of *Congo,* we
haue fignified vnto you, that there are other countries
belonging

belonging to the King of *Angola*, and beyond that towardes the *Cape* of *Good-Hope*, a King called *Matama*,
who ruleth ouer diuers Prouinces, which are called
Quimbebe. This Realme (as we tolde you) from the
firſt *Lake* and the confines of *Angola*, contayneth all the
reſt of the countrey *Southwardes*, till you come to the
Riuer of *Brauagul*, which ſpringeth out of the mountaines of the *Moone*, aud ioyneth with the Riuer *Mag-*
nice, and that ſpringeth out of the foreſaide firſt *Lake* :
Theſe mountaines are diuided by the *Tropicke* of *Ca-*
pricorne, towardes the *Pole Antarctike*, and beyonde
this *Tropike* lyeth all the Countrey and borders of the
Cape of *Good-Hope*, which are not ruled and gouerned
by any one Kinge, but by diuers and ſundry ſeuerall
Princes. In the middeſt betweene that *Cape* and the
Tropike, are the ſaide Mountaines of the *Moone*, ſo famous and ſo greatly renowned among the auncient
writers, who do aſſigne them to be the originall head
and ſpring of the *Riuer Nilus*: which is very falſe and
vntrue, as the ſituation of the countrey doth plainely
ſhewe, and as wee a little hereafter will diſcouer vnto
you. This Countrey is full of high and rough mountaines: it is very coulde, and not habitable: It is frequented and haunted with a few perſons that liue after
the manner of the *Arabians*, vnder little cabbins in the
open fieldes, and apparelled with the skinnes of certaine beaſtes. It is a ſauage and a ruſticall nation, with-
outall faith and credite, neyther will they ſuffer any
ſtraungers among them. Their furniture is Bowes
and Arrowes. They feede vpon ſuch fruites, as the
lande breedeth, and alſo vpon the fleſh of beaſtes.

A a 4   Among

Among thefe *Mountains* of the *Moone*, there is a *Lake*
called *Gale*: a very little one it is, and lyeth fomewhat
towardes the *Weſt*.   Out of this *Lake* there iſſueth a
Riuer called *Camiſſa*, and by the *Portingalles* named *The*
ſweete Riuer, which at the point of the *Cape of Good-Hope*
voydeth it ſelfe into the fea, in that very place that is
termed *The Falſe Cape*.   For the ſhippes of the *Indies*
fayling that way, doo firſt diſcouer another greater
Cape, which is called *The Cape of the Needles*, and then
afterwardes this leſſer *Cape*: Wherevpon they call it
The Falſe Cape, becauſe it is hidde and couered with
the true and great *Cape*.   Betweene theſe two *Capes* or
Promontories, there is the diſtance of an hundred miles,
contayning the largeneſſe and breadth of this famous
Cape: which being deuided into two points, as it were
into two hornes, it maketh a *Gulfe*, where ſometimes
the *Portingall* ſhippes doe take freſh water, in the Riuer
that they call the *Sweet Riuer*.

The inhabitantes of this coaſt, which dwell betweene theſe two points, are of colour blacke, although
the *Pole Antarctike* in that place be in the eleuation of
thirtie and fiue degrees, which is a very ſtrange thing:
yea the rude people that liue among the moſt colde
mountains of the *Moone* are blacke alſo.   This I write
of purpoſe, to aduiſe and moue the *Philoſophers* and
ſuch as ſearch the effectes of nature, that they would
fall into their deepe contemplation and ſpeculation, &
therevpon teach vs, whether this blacke colour be oc-
caſioned by the *Sunne*, or by any other ſecrete and vnknowne cauſe : Which queſtion I for this time doe
meane to leaue vndecided.

Now

The Lake
Gale,

Camiſſa i .The
ſweet *Riuer*.

The *Falſe*
Cape.

The *Cape* of
the *Needles*.

Another note,
That the co-
lour of blacke
in mens skins
doeth not pro-
ceed from the
heat of the
Sunne.

Now forafmuch as this *Promontory* of *Good-Hope,* is the greateft *Cape* of all, and ftretcheth out into the Sea farther then any other in the whole vniuerfall worlde, and is very daungerous to paffe (as all *Promontories* are:) and for that alfo the fea is there moft terrible, and from the lande there blow moft horrible winds, which caufe that *Ocean* to be exceedingly tempeftuous and ftormie, fo that many *Portingall* fhippes of admirable burthens, haue beene caft away therein: and laftly, becaufe the auncient *Hiftoriographers* did neuer knowe it, no not fo much as by hearefay, and it is not long ago fince the King of *Portingalles* Fleetes did firft difcouer the fame: It fhal not be impertinent, but rather a matter of great conuenience in this place to decipher the meafure thereof, & to make fo manifeft a declaration of it, as may ferue alfo to vnderftande, how great the nauigation is from *Portingall* into *India,* by compaffing the Coaft of the *Cape* of *Good-Hope* onely, almoft the fpace of fixe thoufande miles, as a little hereafter it fhall be fhewed vnto you,

For from the Riuer of *Ferdinando Poo,* where the faid *Cape* beginneth to iut-out into the fea, as farre as to the *Poynt,* which we call the *Point of Needles,* there is contayned vpon the fhoare more then two thoufande and 200. myles from the *North,* to the *South,* and on the contrary fide, from the faid *Point* to the *Cape* of *Guarda-Fuy,* right ouer againft the *Iflande* of *Socotora,* they reckon more then three thoufande and three hundred miles by the coaft from the *South* to the *North.* So that from *Lisbone,* compaffing about the fhoares of *Africa,* and all the *Cape* of *Good-Hope,* vnto the kingdome of

The Cape of Good-Hope very dangerous.

This is a Point of the Cape of Good-Hope.

B b *Goa*

Goa, there are moe then fifteene thoufand miles. And from thence afterwardes to *Malaca*, and to *China*, and fo forwardes, there remayneth fo long a iourney, that neuer yet in any time hetherto hath there beene fo great and fo daungerous a nauigation vndertaken and performed, as this of the *Portingalles*, neyther with great veffelles nor with fmall.   It is called the *Cape* of *Good-Hope*, becaufe all fuch as faile that way, afwell in going forth, as in returning home, doo efpecially & principally ayme at this marke, that they may paffe and get beyonde this *Promontorie*; which when they haue doone, they account themfelues to bee out of all daunger, and as it were to haue performed their iourney.   And vpon this their generall defire, they gaue it the name of the *Cape* of *Good-Hope*.

Why it is cal-led the *Cape* of *Good-Hope*.

Nowe to returne to our purpofe, and to talke further of the Coaft of *Africa*, beyonde the *Cape* or *Poynt* of the *Needelles*, there are many competent har-boroughes and hauens, the principall whereof is *Seno Formofo*, *The faire Bay*: and *Seno del Lago*, *The Bay of the Lake*: For there the fea maketh a certaine *Gulfe*, where-in are fundry *Iflandes* and *Portes*: and fomewhat be-yonde there runneth into the fea the Riuer of *S. Chri-ftopher*, and at the mouth thereof there lye three pret-tie *Iflettes*.   A little further forwardes, the Coaft run-neth all along by a Countrey, which the *Portingalles* call *Terra do Natal*, the Land of the *Natiuitie*, becaufe it was firft difcouered at *Chriftmaffe*: and fo reacheth to the *Cape* called *Della Pefcheria*.   Betweene which *Cape* and the Riuer *Magnice*, within the Land is the Kingdome of *Buttua*. whofe Territories are from the

Seno Formofo.
Seno del Lago.

Riuer of Saint Chriftopher.

Terra do Nadal.
Capo della Pef-cheria.

R. Magnice.
The King-dome of *But-tua.*

rootes

rootes or bottome of the mountaines of the *Moone*, vntill you come to the riuer *Magnice* towards the *North*, The Kingdom
where the countrey of *Monomotapa* ſtandeth, and weſt- of *Monomotapa*
wardes from the Riuer *Brauagul* towardes the ſea all a- *R. Brauagul.*
long the bankes of the Riuer *Magnice*.   In this king- Store of *Gold*
dome there are many mynes of *Golde*, and a people *Mines.*
that is of the ſame qualities and conditions, that the
people of *Monomotapa* is, as hereafter ſhall bee ſhewed
vnto you.   And ſo going along the ſhores of the *Oce-*
an, you come to the Riuer *Magnice*, which lyeth
in the very entraunce of the Kingdome
of *Sofala*, and the Empire of
Monomotapa.

Bb 2   Chap.

Chap. 9.

Of the Kingdome of Sofala.

His Kingdome beginneth at the Riuer *Magnice*, which springeth out of the first *Lake* of *Nilus*, and conueyeth it selfe into the sea in the middest of the *Bay*, betweene the point *Pescheria* and the *Cape* called *Capo delle Correnti*, situate in twentie and three degrees & a halfe of the *Pole Antarctik* vnder the *Tropike* of *Capricorne*. With this Riuer neere vnto the sea, there ioyne three other notable riuers, the principall whereof is by the *Portingalles* called *Saynt Christophers*, because vpon the day of that *Saintes* feast it was first discouered, but by the inhabitantes it is named *Nagoa*. The second tooke the name of one *Lorenzo Margues*, that first found it. These two Riuers do spring originally from the mountains of the *Moone*, so greatly renowned among the auncient writers, but by the people of the country they are called *Toroa*: out of which Mountains they did thinke that famous *Nilus*
ke

The originall of the Riuer Magnice.

Three Riuers runne into Magnice.

1. R. Nagoa,
2. R. Margues.

tooke alfo his beginning: but they were vtterly deceyued. For (as we haue already tolde you) the firft
Lake arifeth not out of thofe Mountaines, but lyeth a
great way diftant from it: and betweene it and them
is there a very great and a huge low plaine. Befides
that, the ftreames that flow from the faid mountaines
do runne towardes the *Eaft*, and beftow their waters
vpon other great Riuers, fo that it is not poffible for
them to paffe into the forefaide *Lake*, much leffe into
Nilus, confidering efpecially that the *Riuer Magnice*
fpringeth out of that firft *Lake*, and by a farre different
courfe from the courfe of *Nilus*, runneth towards the
Eaft, and fo ioyneth it felfe with the two Riuers aforefaide. The thirde is called *Arroe*, and arifeth on
another fide out of the Mountaines of the *Gold-Mines*
of *Monomotapa*: and in fome places of this Riuer there
are founde fome fmall peeces of *Golde* among the fand.
Thefe three Riuers enter into the great *Magnice* neere
vnto the fea, and all fower together doo make there a
great water, in a very large channell, and fo difchar-
geth it felfe into the *Ocean*. From the mouth of this
riuer all along the fea coaft, ftretcheth the kingdome
of *Sofala* vnto the Riuer *Cuama*, which is fo called of a
certaine caftel or fortreffe that carryeth the fame name,
and is poffeffed by *Mahometans* and *Pagans*: but the
Portingalles call it, *The mouthes of Cuama*: becaufe at the
entry into the fea, this riuer diuideth it felf into feauen
mouthes, where there are fiue fpeciall *Iflandes*, befides
diuerfe others that lie vp the riuer, all very full and wel
peopled with *Pagans*. This *Cuama* commeth out of
the fame *Lake*, and from the fame fprings from whence
Nilus floweth. And thus the Kingdome of *Sofala* is
B b 3   comprifed

comprifed within the faide two Riuers, *Magnice* and

Cuama vpon the fea coaft. It is but a fmal Kingdome,
and hath but few howfes or townes in it : The chiefe
and principall head whereof, is an *Iflande* that lyeth in
the riuer called *Sofala*, which giueth the name to all
the whole Countrey.   It is inhabited by *Mahometans*,
and the King himfelfe is of the fame fecte,and yeeldeth
obedience to the *Crowne* of *Portingall*, becaufe he will
not bee fubiecte to the Empire of *Monomotapa*. And
therevpon the *Portingalles* there doo keepe a Forte in
the mouth of the riuer *Cuama*, and doo trade in thofe
Countryes for *Golde*, and *Iuory*, and *Amber*, which is

founde vppon that Coaft, and good ftore of flaues,
and in fteede thereof they leaue behinde them *Cotton-
Cloth*, and *Silkes* that are brought from *Cambaia*, and is
the common apparell of thofe people.   The *Maho-*

metans that at this prefent do inhabite thofe Countries
are not naturally borne there,but before the *Portingals*
came into thofe quarters, they trafficked thether in
fmall barkes from the Coaft of *Arabia Fœlix*.   And
when the *Portingalles* had conquered that Realme,
the *Mahometans* ftayed there ftill, and nowe they are
become neyther vtter *Pagans*, nor holding of the fecte
of *Mahomet*.

From the fhoars and Coaft,that lyeth betweene the

two forefaide riuers of *Magnice* and *Cuama*, within the
land fpreadeth the Empire of *Monomotapa*,where there
is verye great ftore of *Mines* of *Golde*, which is carryed
from thence into all the regions thereaboutes,and into
Sofala, and into the other partes of *Africa*. And fome
there be that wil fay, that *Salomons Golde*,which he had

for the Temple of *Ierufalem*, was brought by fea out of
thefe

thefe Countreyes. A thing in truth not very vnlikely:
For in the Countries of *Monomotapa*, there doe remain
to this day many ancient buildings of great worke and
fingular *Architecture*, of *Stone*, of *Lime*, and of *Timber*,
the like whereof are not to be feene in all the *Prouinces*
adioyning.

The Empire of *Monomotapa* is very great, and for
people infinite.   They are *Gentiles* and *Pagans*, of co- *The people of*
lour blacke, very couragious in warre, of a middle fta- *Monomotapa.*
ture, and fwift of foote.   There are many Kinges, that
are vaffalles and fubieƈtes to *Monomotapa*, who doe oftentimes rebell and make warre againft him.   Their
weapons are bowes and arrowes, and light dartes.
This Emperour maintayneth many Armies in feuerall *The K. of*
Prouinces, deuided into *Legions*, according to the vfe *Monomotapa maintaineth*
and cuftome of the *Romanes*. For being fo great a *Lord* *many Armies.*
as he is, he muft of neceffitie be in continuall warre, for
the maintenance of his eftate.   And among all the
reft of his fouldiers, the moft valorous in name are his
Legions of women, whom he efteemeth very highly,
and accounteth them as the very finewes and ftrength
of his military forces.   Thefe women do burne their
leaft pappes with fire, becaufe they fhould bee no hin- *Left-handed*
derauncevnto them in their fhooting, after the vfe and *Amazons.*
manner of the auncient *Amazones*, that are fo greatly
celebrated by the *Hiftoriographers* of former prophane
memories.   For their weapons they praƈtife bowes
and arrowes :   They are very quicke and fwift, liuely
and couragious, very cunning in fhooting, but efpecially and aboue all venturous and conftant in fight.   In
their battelles they vfe a warlike kind of craft and fub-
tiltie :   For they haue a cuftome to make a fhew that

they

they would flie and runne away, as though they were
vanquiſhed and diſcomfited, but they wil diuers times
turne themſelues backe, and vexe their enemies mightely with the ſhot of their arrowes.   And when they
ſee their aduerſaries ſo greedie of the victory, that they
beginne to diſpearſe and ſcatter themſelues, then will
they ſuddenly turne againe vpon them,and with great
courage and fiercenes make a cruell ſlaughter of them.
So that partely with their ſwiftnes, and partely with
their deceitful wiles and other cunning ſhifts of warre,
they are greatly feared in all thoſe partes.   They doo
inioy by the Kinges good fauour certayne Countries
where they dwell alone by themſelues: and ſometimes
they chooſe certaine men at their owne pleaſure, with
whom they doo keepe company for generations ſake :
So that if they doo bring forth Male-children , they
ſende them home to their fathers houſen · but if they
be female,they reſerue them to themſelues,and breed
them in the exerciſe of warfare.

The ſituation
of the Empire
of *Monomo-*
tapa.   The Empire of this *Monomotapa* lyeth (as it were) in
an *Iſlande*, which is made by the Sea-coaſt,by the Riuer *Magnice*, by a peece of the *Lake* from whence *Mag-*
nice floweth , and by the Riuer *Cuama*.   It bordereth
towardes the *South* vpon the *Lordes* of the *Cape* of *Good-*
Hope before mentioned,   and *Northwarde* vpon the
Empire of *Moenemugi,*as by and by ſhall be ſhewed vnto you.

The kingdom
of *Angoſcia.*   But now returning to our former purpoſe, that is to
ſay, to runne forwardes vpon the ſea-coaſt, after you
haue paſſed ouer ſome parte of the Riuer *Cuama*, there
is a certain little Kingdom vpon the ſea called *Angoſcia*,
which taketh the name of certaine *Iſlandes* there ſo called

led, and lie directly againft it. It is inhabited with the like people, both *Mahometans* and *Gentiles*, as the Kingdome of *Sofala* is. Marchaunts they are, and in fmall veffelles doo trafficke along that coaft, with the fame wares and commodities, wherewith the people of *Sofala* doo trade.

A little beyonde, fuddenly ftarteth vp in fight the Kingdome of *Mozambique*,fituate in fourteene degrees and a halfe towardes the *South*, and taketh his name of three *Iflands*,that lie in the mouth of the Riuer *Meghincate*, where there is a great hauen and a fafe, and able to receiue all manner of fhippes. The Realme is but fmall, and yet aboundeth in all kind of victuailes. It is the common landing place for all veffelles that fayle from *Portingall*, and from *India* into that Countrey. In one of thefe *Ifles*, which is the chiefe and principall, called *Mozambique*, and giueth name to all the reft, as alfo to the whole kingdome, and the hauen aforefaide, wherein there is erected a Fortreffe, guarded with a garrifon of *Portingalles*, wherevpon all the other Fortreffes that are on that Coaft doo depende, and from whence they fetch all their prouifion : all the *Armadas* and Fleetes that fayle from *Portingall* to the *Indies*, if they cannot finifh and performe their voyage, will go and winter (I fay) in this *Ifland* of *Mozambique :* and thofe that trauell out of *India* to *Europe*,are conftrained of neceffitie to touch at *Mozambique*, to furnifh themfelues with victuailes. This *Ifland*, when the *Portingalles* difcouered *India*, was the firft place, where they learned the language of the *Indians*, & prouided themfelues of Pilots to direct them in their courfe. The people of this kingdome are *Gentiles:* Rufticall and

The kingdom of Mozambique.

R.Meghincate

The Ifland of Mozambique.

The inhabitants of Mozambique.

rude

rude they be & of colour blacke.   They go all naked. They are valiaunt and ftronge Archers, and cunning Fifhers with all kinde of hookes.

As you go on forwardes vpon the forefaide coaft,

The kingdom of *Quiloa*. there is another *Iflande* called *Quiloa*, in quantitie not great, but in excellency fingular : For it is fituate in a very coole and frefh ayre : It is repleniſhed with trees that are alwaies greene, and affordeth all varietie of victuailes.   It lyeth at the mouth of the Riuer *Coauo*, which fpringeth out of the fame *Lake* from whence *Nilus* floweth, and fo runneth about fixtie miles in length, till it commeth neere to the fea, and there it hath a mightie ftreame, and in the very mouth of it maketh a great *Iflande*, which is peopled with *Mahometans* and *Idolaters*, and a little beyonde that towardes the Coaft on the *Weſt* you may fee the faid *Ifland* of *Quiloa*. This

The Ifland of *Quiloa*, & the inhabitants thereof. *Iflande* is inhabited with *Mahometans* alfo, which are of colour fomething whitiſh.   They are well apparelled, & trimly adorned with cloth of filke and Cotton : Their women do vfe ornaments of *Gold*, and *Iewelles* about their handes and their neckes, and haue good ftore of houfhold ftuffe made of filuer.   They are not altogether fo black as the men are: and in their limmes they are very well proportioned.   Their houfes are made of *Stone*, and *Lime*, & *Timber*, very well wrought and of good architecture, with gardens and orchardes full of hearbes and fundry fruites.   Of this *Iflande* the whole Kingdome tooke the name, which vppon the Coaft extendeth it felfe from *Capo Delgado*, (the *Cape Delicate*, that bordereth *Mozambique* & *Quiloa*,) & is fituate in nine degrees towards the *South*, & from thence it runneth out vnto the aforefaide Riuer of *Coauo*.

In

In olde time the Kingdome of *Quiloa* was the chiefest of all the *Principalities* there adioyning, and stoode neere to the sea: but when the *Portingalles* arriued in those countries, the King trusted so much to himselfe, that he thought he was able with his owne forces not onely to defend himselfe against them, but also to driue them from those places which they had already surprised. Howbeit the matter fell out quite contrary. For when it came to weapons, hee was vtterly ouerthrowen and discomfited by the *Portingals*, and so fled away. But they tooke and possessed the *Island*, and enriched themselues with the great spoyles and booties that they found therein. They erected there also a Fortresse, which was afterwarde pulled downe by the commandement of the King of *Portingall*, because hee thought it not necessary, considering that there were others sufficient enough for that Coast.

The King of Quiloa ouerthrowen by the Portingals, and driuen out of the Island.

And here we may not leaue behinde vs the *Isle* of *S. Laurence*, so called by the *Portingalles*, because they did first discouer it vpon that *Martyrs* feast day. It is so great, that it contayneth in length almost a thousande miles, and standeth right ouer against the coast which we haue described, beginning directly at the mouthes of the Riuer *Magnice*, which are in twenty and sixe degrees of the *South*, and so going forwardes to the *North*, it endeth right against the mouthes of *Cuama* in the kingdome of *Quiloa*. Between this *Island* and the firme lande there is (as it were) a channell,

The commendation of the Isle of S. Laurence. Historia della China. Part. 3. Cap. Vltimo. La grand'Isola di S. Lorenzo lunga 275. leghe & larga 90. id est, The great Island of S. Laurence is in length 275. leagues, and in

Cc 2   which

breadth 90. leagues. The last Chapter of the historie of the Kingdome of *China*, printed in *Macao*, the first *Latine* booke that euer was printed in *China* maketh mention of this Island by the name of *Madagascar*, in these words *Madagascar trecentas fere leucas comprehendit*, *id ist*, *Madagascar* containeth almost 300. leagues.

which at the entrie *Weſtwarde* is three hundred and fortie miles broade, in the middeſt where it is narroweſt
ouer againſt the *Iſlande* of *Mozambiche* an hundred and
ſeuentie miles, and for the reſt it enlargeth it ſelfe very
much towards *India*,and contayneth many *Iſles* within
it. The ſhips that go from *Spaine* into *India*, or returne
from *India* to *Spaine*, doo alwayes for the moſt parte
paſſe and ſaile in and through this channell, if by time
or weather they be not forced to the contrary.   And
ſurely this *Iſlande* deſerueth to be inhabited with a better people, becauſe it is furniſhed with ſingular commodities. For it hath many ſafe & ſure hauens. It is wa-
tred with ſundry Riuers that cauſe the earth to bring
forth fruits of diuers kinds, as *Pulſe*,and *Ryce*, and other
graine, *Oranges*, *Limons*, *Citrons*, and ſuch like fruite.
Fleſh of all ſorts, as *Hennes* &c. and veniſon, as wilde
Boare and *Deere*, and ſuch like,& all this of a very good

The inhabi-
tants of the
Iſle of *Saint*
Laurence.
Their wea-
pons

taſt and reliſh, becauſe the ſoyle is very fat: their fiſh alſo is exceeding good.   The inhabitants are *Pagans*,
with ſome of the ſect of *Mahomet* among them.   They
are of the colour which the *Spaniardes* call *Mulato*, betweene blacke and white.   Very warlicke they are &
giuen to their weapons, which are bowes and arrows,
and dartes of very light wood, ſtrengthned with *Iron*,
whereof they make the heads of their dartes,which are
crooked like hookes: and theſe they wil caſt and throw
moſt ſlightly and cunningly.   They vſe alſo *Targattes*
and *Iackes* that are made of certain beaſts-skins, wherewith they ſaue themſelues in fight from the blowes of
their enemies.   This *Iſlande* is deuided among ſeueral
Princes, that are at enmitie one with another: for they
are in continuall warres, and perſecute one another
                                                                        with

Kingdome of Congo. 201

with Armes. There are diuers mynes of *Gold*, of *Sil-uer*, of *Copper*, of *Iron*, and of other Mettalles, The sauage people doo not vse to saile out of the *Island*, but onely from one side to the other they goe coasting a-long the shoares, with certaine barks that are made but of one stocke of a tree, which they hollowe for that purpose. The most part of them doo not willingly entertaine straungers, neyther will they consent that they shoulde trafficke or conuerse with them. Not-withstanding in certaine portes, the *Portingalles* do vse to trade with the *Islanders* for *Amber*, *Waxe*, *Siluer*, *Cop-per*, *Ryse*, and such other thinges, but they neuer come vpon the lande. In the channell before mentioned there are diuers *Islandes*, some greater, and some lesse, inhabited with *Mahometans*. The chiefe of them is the *Isle* of *Saint Christopher*, and then of *Santo Spirito*: & another called *Magliaglie*, and so the rest, as the *Isles* of *Comoro*, *Anzoame*, *Maiotto*, and some other.

Sundry Islands in the channel

But let vs returne to the sea side, and prosecute the Coast of the kingdome of *Quiloa* where we leaft. Next vnto it, is the kingdome of *Mombaza*, in the height of three degrees and a halfe towardes the *South*, which taketh the name from an *Islande* inhabited with *Maho-metans*, which is also called *Mombaza*, where there is a fayre Cittie, with houses that haue many Sollers, fur-nished with pictures both grauen and painted. The king thereof is a *Mahometan*, who taking vpon him to resist the *Portingalles*, receyued the same successe that happened to the king of *Quiloa*, so that the city was ran-sacked & spoyled by his enemies, who found therein good store of *Gold*, and *Siluer*, and *Pearle*, and *Cloth* of *Cotton*, and of *Silke*, and of *Golde*, and such other com-

The kingdom of Mombaza rich in Gold & Siluer, and Pearle.

The cittie of Mombaza spoyled as Quiloa was.

C c 3   modities

modities.   This kingdome lyeth betweene the borders of *Quiloa*, and *Melinde*, and is inhabited with *Pagans* and *Mahometans*, and yeeldeth obedience to the Empire of *Mohenemugi*.

A little beyond, is the Kingdome of *Melinde*, which being likewise but a little one, extendeth it selfe vpon the sea coast as farre as the Riuer *Chimanchi*, and lyeth in the height of two degrees and a halfe: and vp the streame of that riuer it reacheth to the Lake *Calice*, the space of an hundred miles within lande.   Neere vnto the sea along the bankes of this riuer, there is a great deale of Countrey inhabited by *Pagans* and *Mahometans*, of colour almost white.   Their houses are built after our fashion.   But there is one particularitie to be admired, that their Muttons or *Sheep* are twice as great as the *Sheepe* of our countrey: for they deuide them into fiue quarters, (if a man may so call them) & reckon the tayle for one, which commonly wayeth some twentie and fiue, or thirtie pounde.   The women are white and sumptuously dressed after the *Arabian* fashion, with cloth of *Silke*.   About their neckes and handes, and armes, and feete, they vse to weare iewelles of *Gold*, and *Siluer*:   When they go abroade out of their houses, they couer themselues with *Taffata*, so that they are not knowen but when they list themselues.   In this Countrey there is a very good hauen, which is a landing place for the vessel!es that saile through those seas.   Generally, the people are very kinde, true and trustie, and conuerse with strangers. They haue alwayes entertained and welcomed the *Portingals*, and haue reposed great confidence in them, neyther haue they euer offered them any wrong in a-

The tayle of a sheepe in *Melinde* wayeth commonly 25. or 30. pound.
Leo Afer affirmeth that he hath seene tayles of *Egyptian Sheepe*, that weighed 50. l. a peece, and sometimes 120. l. a peece.
The women & inhabitants of *Melinde*.

ny

ny refpect.

In the fea betweene thefe two *Capes* of *Mombaza*, Three *Ifles* and *Melinde* there are three *Ifles* : The firft is called 1. *Monfie.* *Monfie*, the fecond *Zanzibar*, and the thirde *Pemba*, all 2. *Zanzibar.* 3. *Pemba*, inhabited onely with *Mahometans* , that are of colour white. Thefe *Ifles* abound in all things as the others doo, whereof we made mention before. Thefe peo-ple are fomewhat enclyned to armes: but they are in deed more addicted to dreffe & manure their ground : For there groweth much *Sugar*, which in fmall barkes they carry away to fell into the firme lande with other fruites of that Countrey.

Befides thefe three realmes laft defcribed, *Quiloa*, *Melinde*, and *Mombaza*, within the Lande is the great Empire of *Moenemugi*, towards the *Weft*. It bordereth The Empire vpon the *South*, with the kingdome of *Mozambique*, of *Mohenemu-* and with the Empire of *Monomotapa* to the riuer *Coaue*, *gi.* vpon the *Weft* with the riuer *Nilus*, betweene the two *Lakes*; and vpon the *North* it ioyneth with the Empire of *Prete Gianni*. Towardes the fea, this Emperour ftandeth in good termes of peace with the forefaide kings of *Quiloa*, *Melinde*, and *Mombaza*, by reafon of their trafficke together, and the better to fecure the en-tercourfe and trade by fea : by meanes whereof they haue brought vnto them much cloth of *Cotton*, and cloth of *Silke* from diuers Countries, and other mar-chandifes that are well efteemed in thefe partes : and particularly certaine little balles, that are made in the kingdome of *Cambaia*, of a kind of *Bitumen* or clammie *Clay*, like vnto glaffe, but that it is (as it were) of a red colour, which they vfe to weare about their neckes,

like

like a payre of beades in fteed of necklaces. It ferueth
them alfo in fteede of Money, for of *Gold* they make
none account. Likewife with the filks that are brought
vnto them, they doo apparell themfelues from the girdle downewardes. In exchaunge and barter of all
thefe commodities, they giue *Gold*, *Siluer*, *Copper* and
Iuorie.

But on the other fide towardes *Monomotapa*, there
are continuall warres, yea and fometimes fo blooddy,
that it is hardely difcerned who hath gotten the victorie. For in that border there meet together two of the
greateft and moft warlike powers and forces that are
in all thofe regions: that is to fay, on the party of *Monomotapa* there came forth into the field the *Amazones*,
of whom wee tolde you before, and on the partie of
Mohenemugi are the *Giacchi*, (as the *Moci-Conghi* do
call them) but in their owne tongue they are called
Agagi, who did fometime fo greatly afflict the kingdome of *Congo*, as you may remember. Neyther are
thefe people leffe couragious or ftrong then the *Amazones*, but are of a blacke complexion, and prefump-
tuous countenances. They doo vfe to marke themfelues aboue the lippe vpon their cheekes with certain
lines which they make with *Iron* inftruments and with
fire. Moreouer, they haue a cuftome to turne their
eye liddes backewardes: fo that their skinne being all
blacke, and in that blacknes fhewing the white of their
eyes, and thofe marks in their faces, it is a ftrange thing
to behold them. For it is in deede a very dreadfull &
diuelifh fight. They are of bodie great, but deformed
and liue like beaftes in the fielde, and feede vpon mans
flefh

The Giacchas, or Agagi.

flesh. In fight they shew themselues exceedingly couragious, and doo vtter most horrible shouting and
crying, of purpose to daunte and affray their enemies.
Their weapons are Dartes, and Pauises of *Leather* that
couer all their whole bodie, and so defend themselues
therewith.   Sometimes they will encampe together,
and sticke their *Pauises* in the grounde, which are vnto
them in steed of a trench: Sometimes they wil go forwardes in the battell, and shrowde themselues vnder
them, and yet annoy their aduersaries with the shot of
their dartes.   And thus by warlike pollicie they doo
ordinarily plague their enemies, by endeauouring
with all subtiltie to make them spende their shotte in
vaine vpon their Targettes: and when they see that
they haue made an ende of shooting, then doo they
renew the battell a fresh, and driuing them to flight,
make a cruell slaughter of them without all mercie.
And this is the manner which they vse against their e-
nemies, and the *Amazones.*   But the *Amazones* on the The *Amazones*
other side, which are very well acquainted herewith-
all, doo fight against them with other militarie strata-
gems (as we haue aboue declared) and doo ouercome
the forces of their aduersaries with their swiftnes and
great skill in matters of warre.   For they doo assure
themselues, that if they be taken they shalbe deuoured:
and therefore with doubled courage they fight for
life, that they might ouercome, and in any case saue
their liues from that fierce and cruell nation.   And
in this sorte doo they maintaine continuall warre, alwayes with great mortalitie on both sides. These *Agags*
dwell at the beginning of the Riuer *Nilus,* (where it

D d   runneth

runneth *Northwardes* out of the *Lake,*) vpon both the
bankes of the Riuer, till it come to a certaine limite,
wherein they are bounded, and then *Weſtwardes* all o-
uer the banks of the ſaid *Nilus,* euen to the ſecond *Lake,*
& to the borders of the empire of *Prete-Gianni.* Touching theſe *Agags,* I thought it conuenient in this place to
adde all this, which before I had omitted.   Between
the confines of this *Moenemugi,* and *Prete-Gianni,* there
are ſundry other pettie *Lordes,* and people that are of a
white colour, and yeeld obedience ſometimes to one
of theſe two *Princes,* and ſometimes to the other.
They are men of a farre greater ſtature then
all the reſt of the people in thoſe
Countries.

Chap.

Chap. 10.

*The reſt of the Coaſt of the Ocean to the redde Sea.   Of the
Empire of Prete Gianni, and the Confines thereof.
Of the famous Riuer Nilus, and the origi-
nall ſpring thereof.*

Nd now to returne to our
former treatiſe of the coaſt,
beyond the Realme of *Me-
linde,* towardes the *Cape* of
Guarda-Fuy, there are many
places inhabited with *Mahometans,* all along the ſea
ſide, of colour being white.
Vpon this ſhoare there are
diuers good hauens, where Many good
the ſhippes of ſundry countries doo trafficke with the hauens.
foreſaide marchaundiſes.   The firſt of theſe places is
called *Patee,* the ſeconde *Braua,* the third *Magadoxo,*
the fourth *Affion,* and the laſt is the famous *Promontory* The Cape of
and *Cape* of *Guarda-Fuy:* which becauſe it is very great, Guarda Fuy.
and iutteth out a good way into the ſea, is wel knowen
to all ſaylers that come from *India,* and from *Ormuz,* &
D d 2   from

from *Arabia Fœlix*.   It is the place and harborough where the *Portingalles* are wont to attend, and yearely with their nauies to watch for the veſſelles of the *Ma-hometans*, that being laden with precious marchaundi-ſes, doo ſaile into thoſe partes without their licence, they being the Lordes of the trafficke and trade for ſpicery and all other commodities that are brought from *India*.   So that euery yeare the *Portingall Fleete* doth take great priſes of Marchauntes ſhippes in that place, as the *Engliſh* and the *French* doo at *Cape Saint Vincent*.

Diuers Ports on the ſea coaſt towards the Red Sea.

After you haue compaſſed about the foreſaid *Cape* of *Guarda-Fuy*, towarde the redde ſea, you ſhall come to other Townes and hauens of the *Mahometans*. The firſt of them is called *Methe*, and another beyond that called *Barbora*. And this is the furtheſt place, wherein you ſhall finde any people with white ſkinnes : for here the men beginne to bee all blacke.   Then there is *Ceila*, & *Dalaca*, and *Malaca*, and *Carachin*: and all this Coaſt is called in that Countrey language *Baragiam*. The people that inhabite therein are all blacke, valiant in armes, and apparelled from the girdle downewards with cloth of *Cotton*: but thoſe that are of the beſt ac-count among them doo weare vppon their ſhoulders certaine cloakes with whoodes, called *Bernuſſi*, ſuch as the olde *Romanes* vſed, and were termed *Saga Romana*. It aboundeth in *Gold*, and in *Iuory*, and in Mettalles, & in victuailes of all ſortes.

The Red Sea.

Then follow the mouthes or entrances into the red *Gulfe*, otherwiſe called the *Redde Sea*, well knowen to euery man.   In number they are two, cauſed by an *Iſlande* that lyeth betweene them, and is called *Babel-mandel*

mandel. The one of them towards the *Weſt* is fifteene miles broade, and hath a deep channell, and through this doo all the great ſhippes enter: the other is a little one, and contayneth in breadth but fiue miles, and yet is full of ſhallowes and ſhelfes of ſande, and ſome Rockes: ſo that the whole mouth is but thirtie myles in all. The one *Cape* on the ſide of *Africa* is called *Rosbel,* and the other towardes *Arabia Fœlix,* is *Ara.* From this place all the *Weſterne* Coaſt of the ſaid *Gulfe* runneth vp to *Suez,* which is the fartheſt towne there-of *Northwardes,* and is diſtant from theſe mouthes twelue hundred miles. All this *Gulfe,* both on the one ſide and on the other neere to the bankes, is much peſtered with *Iſlettes* and ſhelfes that are very ſhallow, and affordeth free and ſafe nauigation but onely in the middeſt. For the ſea following the motion & ſtreame of the *Ocean,* with great ſwiftnes doth keepe the chan-nell and the bottome in the middle, very cleane and neat, by caſting vp the filth and ſande vpon the bankes on both ſides.

The two entrances into the redde ſea.

The length of the red ſea, 1200. miles.

And now foraſmuch as we are to ſpeake of the Em-pire of *Prete Gianni,* who is the greatteſt and the rich-eſt Prince in all *Africa,* let vs tell you in briefe, that his *State* and *Gouernement* at this day reacheth from the two mouthes of the redde ſea, vnto the *Iſland* of *Syene,* which is vnder the *Tropike* of *Cancer,* excepting the Coaſtes of the ſaid ſea. For about fiftie yeares ago he loſt them by negligence, and ſuffered the *Turke* to take them from him. So that the Confines of his eſtate are theſe,viz. towards the *North-Eaſt,* and the *Eaſt,*the greater parte of the *Red Sea:* towards the *North,* Ægypt:

The Empire of *Prete Gian-ni.*

D d 3   towards

towardes the *Weſt*, the Deſertes of *Nubia*, and towards
the *South* the countrey of *Mohenemugi*: & ſo in a groſſe
and generall account, the Empire of this *Chriſtian King*
may happely bee in compaſſe ſome foure thouſand
miles.   The principall Cittie, where hee moſt remayneth and keepeth his Court, is called *Bel-Malechi*. He
ruleth ouer many Prouinces that haue their ſeuerall
Kinges.   His eſtate is very rich, and aboundeth in
Golde, in *Siluer*, in precious ſtones, and in all ſortes of
mettalles.   His people are of diuers colours, as white,
blacke, and a middle colour betweene both: they are
of a very good ſtature, and haue good countenances.
His Courtiers and Lordes are apparelled with cloth
of *Silke*, and adorned with *Golde* and ſundry Iewelles.
There is among them a lawe for apparell, according
to the ſeuerall degrees of men.   For certaine perſons
there are, for whome it is not lawfull to weare any o-
ther garment, but ſuch as are made of dreſſed skins.

        Theſe people are in a manner *Chriſtians*.   For
they doo obſerue certaine ceremonies of the Lawe
of the *Hebrewes*.   Vpon the Feaſt day of our *Ladie* in
Auguſt, all the Kinges and principall Lordes aſſemble
themſelues together in the Cittie aforeſaid, to celebrate
that feaſt, euery man bringing with him his tribute
that he oweth to the King, and the people comming
from all partes in pilgrimage to performe this their deuotion.   They haue a very ſolemne proceſſion, and
out of the *Church*, from whence they walke, they carry
with them an *Image* of the Bleſſed *Virgin* the *Mother* of
God, which is as bigge as any common perſon, and all
of *Gold*.   This *Image* hath for the eyes two very rich
                                                                and

Bel-Malechi his chiefe Cittie. He is very rich

A law for apparell.

His people are Chriſtians. A great ſolem-nitie vpon the feaſt of the Aſſumption of our Ladie.

and great *Rubies*, all the reft of the bodie is garnifhed &
adorned with iewels and curious workes: and it is carryed vpon a frame made of *Golde*, of a wonderfull and
admirable workmanfhippe.   In this proceffion alfo,
there commeth abroade in publike fhew *Prete Gianni*,
himfelfe, eyther vpon a Charriot of *Gold*, or els vpon
an *Elephant*, all garnifhed and trimmed with iewelles,
and fuch rare and precious thinges, and couered all
ouer with cloth of *Golde*.   The multitude of people
that runneth to fee this *Image*, is fo great, that many
are ftiffled in the preffe and die therevpon.

This King is called by a corrupt terme *Prete Iani*, The right
for the right namo is *Bel-Gian*.   Now *Bel* fignifieth name of *Prete*
Gianni. that which is chiefeft, perfecteft, and excellenteft in a-
ny thing, and *Gian* is a *Prince*, or a *Lorde*, and is applyed
to euery man that hath a *Gouernement* and iurifdiction,
and therefore *Belgian* is afmuch to fay,   as *The Chiefeft*
Prince : and being fo ioyned together in one worde,
it appertayneth to the King alone, and to no man elfe.
He beareth alfo the furname of *Dauid*, as the *Emperours*
of *Rome* doo vfe the name of *Cefars*.

Now it remayneth that we doo difcourfe of the ri- The Riuer
uer *Nilus*, which doth not fpring in the Countrye of *Nilus.*
Bel-Gian, much leffe out of the mountains of the *Moone*,
nor (as *Ptolomie* writeth) out of the two *Lakes*, which he *Ptolemie difa-*
fetteth down in *Parallele*, from the *Eaft* to the *Weft*, with *proued.*
a diftaunce of about foure hundred and fiftie miles betweene them.   For in the altitude of the fame *Pole*,
wherein the faid Authour placeth thofe two *Lakes*, lyeth alfo the kingdome of *Congo* and of *Angola* towards
the *Weft*, and and on the other fide *Eaftward* is the Empire of *Monomotapa*, and the Kingdome of *Sofala*, with

a diftaunce from fea to fea of twelue hundred miles.
Now within all this fpace, as *Signor Odoardo* affirmed
vnto me, there is but one onely *Lake* to bee founde,
which lyeth in the confines of *Angola* and *Monomotapa*,
and contayneth in *Diameter* an hundred ninetie and
fiue miles.   Of the *Wefterne* fide of this *Lake*, the people of *Angola* do giue fufficient information, and of
the other fide *Eaftwarde*, thofe of *Sofala* and *Monomotapa*. So that there is a ful and perfect knowledge of this
one *Lake*, but of any other thereabouts, there is no
mention at all made :   And therefore it may well bee
concluded, that there are none other to be founde in
that altitude of degrees, True it is in deede, that there
are two *Lakes*, but they are fituate in places quite contrary to that which *Ptolemie* writeth. For he (as it hath
beene told you) placeth his *Paralleles* from *Weft* to *Eaft*:
but thefe are fituate from the *South* to the *North*, as it
were in a direct line, with the diftance of about foure
thoufand miles betweene them.   Some that dwell in

Nilus doth
not hide him
felfe vnder the
ground, and
then arife a-
gaine, as fome
fay.

thofe countries do holde an opinion, that *Nilus* after it
is iffued out of the firft *Lake*, hideth it felfe vnder the
grounde, and afterwardes rifeth againe : but others
doo deny that it is fo.   *Signor Odoardo* did iuftifie it to
me, that the true hiftory and certainty of this matter,
is that *Nilus* doth not hide it felfe vnder the grounde,
but that it runneth through monftrous and defert valleyes without any fetled channell, and where no

The true
fpring of *Ni-
lus* is out of
the firft *Lake*

people inhabiteth, and fo (they fay) it finketh into the
bottome of the earth.

    From this firft *Lake* in deed doth *Nilus* fpring, which
lyeth in twelue degrees towardes the *Pole Antarctike*, &
is compaffed about like a vault, with exceeding high
mountains

mountaines, the greateſt whereof are called *Caſates* vp-
on the *Eaſt*, and the hilles of *Sal-Nitrum*, and the hilles The ſecond
Lake.
of *Siluer* on another ſide, and laſtly with diuers other
Mountaines on the thirde part. This Riuer *Nilus* run-
neth for the ſpace of 400. miles directly towardes
the *North*, and then entreth into another verye great
Lake which the inhabitantes doo call a *Sea*. It is much
bigger then the firſt, for it contayneth in breadth two
hundred and twentie miles, and lyeth vnder the line
Equinoctiall. Of this ſeconde *Lake* the *Anzichi*, who
are neere neighbours to *Congo*, doo giue very certaine
and perfect information, for they trafficke into thoſe
partes. And they report that in this *Lake* there is a peo- The people
that dwelleth
about the
ſecond Lake.
ple, that ſayleth in great ſhippes, and can write, and
vſeth number, and weight and meaſure, which they
haue not in the partes of *Congo*; that they builde their
houſes with ſtone and lime, and that for their faſhions
and qualities they may bee compared with the *Portin-*
galles. VVherevpon it may bee well gathered, that
the Empire of *Prete-Gianni* cannot bee farre from
thence.

From this ſecond *Lake* the riuer *Nilus* runneth for- The Iſland of
Meroe.
wardes to the *Iſlande* of *Meroe*, for the ſpace of ſeauen
hundred miles, and receyueth into it ſundry other ri-
uers. The principall of them all is the riuer *Coluez*, ſo The R. Coluez
called, becauſe it iſſueth out of a *Lake* of the ſame name,
and ſituate in the borders of *Melinde*. After that *Nilus*
is come to *Meroe*, it deuideth it ſelfe into two braun-
ches, and ſo compaſſeth about a good high Territory,
which is called *Meroe*: Vpon the right hand whereof
towardes the *Eaſt*, there runneth a Riuer named *Abag-*
ni, that ſpringeth out of the *Lake Bracina*, and croſſeth The R. Abagni

ouer

ouer the Empire of *Prete Gianni* till you come to
the said *Islande*: and on the other side *Westwarde* there
are diuers other Riuers, among which *Saraboe* is one.
When *Nilus* hath thus receiued these riuers into it, &
hath compassed the *Islande* with both his armes, hee
waxeth greater then he was before, and meeteth againe
in one channell, and by *Æthiopia* (which is called *Æ-
thiopia* aboue *Ægypt*) runneth to the *Falles* (as they call
them) which lie in a very lowe valley, that is very narrowe and straite, and shutteth the riuer within a very
little channell, so that it falleth from aloft downewards
with a most horrible noyse, neere to the *Isle of Syene*.
And from thence watring all *Ægypt*, it disgorgeth his
streames into the *Mediterranean* sea, (which lyeth directly ouer against the *Islande* of *Cyprus*) by two of his
principall braunches, the one called at this day, the
Mouth of Damiata on the *East*, and the other, the *Mouth
of Rossetto* on the *West*.

And forasmuch as wee are nowe come to the very
ende of this discourse concerning *Nilus*, it will be very
conuenient, that wee touch in briefe the occasion of
his encrease. As we haue tolde you before, the principall cause of the encrease of *Nilus*, is the great quantity of waters, that raine from heauen at such time as
the spring beginneth here in these countries, but there
with them in winter, which may be (to speake generally) about the beginning of *April*. This water falleth
not, as the water falleth in these Regions of *Europe*, but
it falleth most aboundantly, and commeth downe not
in smal drops like our raine, but is powred down (as it
were with pailes and buckets.) So that because it falleth
with so great violence and in so great a quantity, the
earth

The R. *Saraboe*.
The *Isle of Syene*.
The two braunches of *Nilus* falling into the *Mediterranean* sea.
The cause of the encrease of *Nilus*.

earth cannot fucke it vp,nor drink it in: for the ground being ragged, and fomewhat bending downward, the water fcowreth away with an exceeding furie, and running into the riuers caufeth them to fwell and to rife in a maruellous manner,and fo ouerflowe the countrey : You muft herewithall confider efpecially, that they haue thefe continuall raines for the fpace of fiue whole Moones together, that is to fay in *Aprill, May, Iune, Iuly,* and *Auguft,* but principally in *May, Iune* and *Iuly:* for then are the waters in their greateft pride. And herevpon it commeth to paffe, that the Countrey being full of mountaines and very high hilles (as hath beene told you) and confequently replenifhed with diuers brookes, and rillets, and *Lakes,* they all ioyning and meeting together in the channelles of the greater Riuers, doo make them fo great and fo large, that they containe and carry more water, then all the Riuers of the vniuerfall worlde: and the *Lakes* growe to fuch an exceffiue compaffe and widenes, that it is a wonder: as may be feene in the difcourfe touching the *Cape* of *Good-Hope,* and all thefe kingdomes of *Congo,* and the Countreyes there adioyning, where there are *Lakes* of fo extraordinarie a bigneffe, that in the languages of thofe Regions, they are not called *Lakes,* but *Seas.*

And thus you fee how the Riuer *Nilus,* in the times and feafons before mentioned, on the one fide doeth runne moft furioufly from thofe Countries, into the North to water *Ægypt,* and the Riuer *Zaire,* and the Riuer *Nigir* on the other fide *Weftwarde* and *Eaftwarde:* and towardes the *South,* other huge and monftrous Riuers, which at certaine determined and limited times doo neuer faile to encreafe as *Nilus* doeth. And this

The feuerall courfes of fundrie great Riuers.

E e 2 is

is the effect of them, which is ordinarily feene euery
yeare, especially in *Cairo*, and ouer all *Ægypt*, where
Nilus beginneth to ryfe about the ende of *Iune*, and
continueth his rising till the twentith of *September*, as I
haue feene my felfe. But the occafion and caufe of this
encreafe hath beene vntill this prefent time very fecret
and obfcure: and although the ancient writers, beginning euen at *Homere*, haue after a forte and in generall
tearmes leaft in writing, that *Nilus* doeth increafe by
raine, yet haue they not fo diftinctly and plainely dif-
courfed thereof, as *Signor Odoardo* hath done, and te-
ftified the fame by his owne view and knowledge. For
fome there were, that haue affigned the caufe of this
ouerflowing, to bee the raine that commeth from the
Mountaines of the *Moone* : Others haue attributed it
to the fnowes that are melted in thofe Mountaines, &
yet *Nilus* doth not fwell or ryfe any thing neere to the
Mountaines of the *Moone*, but a great way from them
towards the *North*: and befides that the feafon of winter doeth rather breed Snow, then yeeld any heate to
melt it.

And now that I haue with good diligence enqui-
red of *Signor Odoardo* thefe matters aboue written, vpon fuch pointes as I had before plotted to my felfe, and
hee alfo propounding the reft vnto mee of his owne
meere motion, like a man of high conceite (as in truth
he is) and fatiffying me with fuch aunfweres, as are fet
downe in this difcourfe: yet I doo affure my felfe, that
euery man will not reft fully contented and fatiffyed
herewith, efpecially fuch as are curious, and practifed
in matters of the worlde, and skilfull in the Sciences.
The *Geographer* woulde peraduenture defire to vnderstand

ſtand more, and the *Phiſician*, and the maiſter of *Mine-ralles*, and the *Hiſtoriographer*, and the *Marchaunt*, and the *Marriner*, and the *Preacher*, and ſome others that are different from theſe in reſpect of their profeſſion. But *Signor Odoardo* hath promiſed with as much ſpeed as poſſible he may to returne to *Rome* from *Congo*,whe-ther he ſayled, preſently after he had finiſhed this trea-tiſe, which was in *May* 1589. with very ample infor-mations and further inſtructions, for the ſupplying of that which here wanteth touching *Nilus*, and his origi-nall, and ſuch other matter. In the meane time,that little which is contayned in theſe few leaues,is not ve-ry little. But yet if perhaps there be any thing found therein, that may be eyther profitable, or ſtraunge, or delightfull, or fit to paſſe away the time, and to driue away Melancholie, let it bee wholly aſcribed to the right noble and Reuerend Father, my *Lorde Antonio Migliore* , *Biſhop of San Marco* , and *Commenda-dor* of *Santo Spirito*,who was the authour of this worke to be publiſhed for the common benefit.

FINIS.

A

A TABLE OF
THE CHAPTERS CON-
tayned in the firſt Booke of

The Report of the Kingdome of
Congo.

He iourney by Sea *from* Lisbone *to the*
Kingdome *of* Congo. *Chap. I. fol. 1.*
Of the temperature of the ayre of the king-
dome of Congo, *and whether it bee*
very colde or hot : whether the men bee
white or blacke: Whether are more or
leſſe blacke, they that dwell in the hilles, or thoſe that
dwell in the plaines : Of the winds and the raines, and
the ſnowes in thoſe quarters, and of what ſtature and
ſemblaunce the men of that Countrey are. Chapter II.
fol. 13.

Whether the children which are begotten by Portingalles
being of a white skinne, and borne in thoſe Countries
by the women of Congo, *be blacke or white, or tawney*
like a wilde Oliue, *whom the* Portingalles *call* Mulati. *Chap. III,* *fol 18.*

Of the circuite of the kingdome of Congo, *and of the borders*
and confines thereof. And firſt of the Weſterne Coaſt.
Chap. IIII. *fol. 2c.*

Of the North coaſt of the Kingdome of Congo, *and the con-*
fines thereof. Chap. V. *fol. 30.*

Of the Eaſt coaſt of the Kingdome of Congo, *and the Con-*
fines thereof. Chap. VI. *fol. 38*

Of the Confines of the Kingdome of Congo *towardes the*
South. Chap. VII. *fol. 43.*

Of

The Table.

Of the circuite of the Kingdome of Congo *poſſeſſed by the King that now is, according to the foure borders aboue deſcribed. Chap. VIII.* fol. 58.

The ſixe Prouinces of the Kingdome of Congo, *and firſt of the Prouince of* Bamba. *Chap. IX.* fol. 60.

Of the Prouince of Sogno, *which is the Countrey of the Riuer* Zaire, *and* Loango. *Chap. X.* fol. 94.

Of the third Prouince called Sundi, *Chap. XI.* fol. 96.

Of the fourth Prouince called Pango. *Chap. XII.* fol. 99.

Of the fifth Prouince called Batta. *Chap. XIII.* fol. 100

Of the ſixt and laſt Prouince called Pemba. *Chap. XIIII.* fol. 104

A Table of the Chapters contayned
in the ſeconde Booke.

OF *the ſituation of the Royall Cittie of the Kingdome of* Congo. *Chap. I.* fol. 107

Of the Originall beginning of Chriſtendome in the Kingdome of Congo, *and how the Portingalles obtayned this trafficke. Chap. II.* fol. 118.

Don Iohn, *the firſt Chriſtian King being dead,* Don Alfonſo *his ſonne ſucceeded. Of his warres againſt his brother. Of certaine miracles that were wrought, and of the conuerſion of thoſe people. Chap. III.* fol. 133.

The death of King Don Alfonſo, *and the ſucceſſion of* Don Piedro. *How the Iſland of* S. Thomas *was firſt inhabi-*

E e 4 *ted*

The Table.

ted, & of the Biſhop that was ſent thether. Other great accidentes that happened by occaſion of Religion. The death
of two Kinges by the conſpiracie of the Portingalles, and
the Lords of Congo. How the Kings lineage was quite
extinguiſhed. The baniſhment of the Portingals. Chap. IIII.
                                                    fol. 150.

The incurſions of the people challed Giachas, in the Kingdome of Congo.   Their conditions and weapons. And
the taking of the Royall Cittie. Chap. V.   fol. 159.

The King of Portingall ſendeth ayde, and an Embaſſadour
to the King of Congo.   The knowledge of the Mettall
Mines, which abound in Congo is denyed the King of
Portingall.   At the ſame time the King of Congo di-
ſpatcheth Embaſſadours to the King of Spaine, to requeſt
Prieſtes of him, and what befell vnto them.   He ſendeth
diuers proofes of the mettalles.   The vowe of Odoardo
Lopes. Chap. VI.   fol. 163

Of the Court of the King of Congo.   Of the apparell of that
people before they became Chriſtians and after.   Of the
Kinges Table, and manner of his Court.   Chap. VII.
                                                    fol. 177

Of the Countries that are beyond the Kingdome of Congo towardes the Cape of Good Hope: and of the Riuer
Nilus. Chap. VIII.   fol. 186

Of the Kingdome of Sofala. Chap. 19.   fol. 192

The reſt of the Coaſt of the Ocean the redde ſea. Of the Empire of Prete Gianni, and the Confines thereof.   Of the
famous Riuer Nilus, and the originall ſpring thereof.
Chap. X.   fol. 215.

FINIS.